APPLIED ICT FOR
G C S E
(DOUBLE AWARD)

P.M. HEATHCOTE AND C. HIGHMORE

Published by

PAYNE-GALLWAY
P U B L I S H E R S L T D

26-28 Northgate Street, Ipswich IP1 3DB
Tel: 01473 251097 • Fax: 01473 232758

www.payne-gallway.co.uk

Acknowledgements

We would like to thank Elaine Topping for reading the manuscript and making numerous comments and suggestions for improvement which have been incorporated into the book.

We are grateful to the following organisations for granting us permission to reproduce articles, screenshots and photographs:

BEBC

Careers Management

Computer Weekly

Computing magazine

Disabled People's Electronic Village Hall

ECDL

The Guardian

Information Commissioner's Office

Interactive Education

Internet Content Register

Lastminute.com

MJP Geopacks

Open University

Principia Products Ltd

QCA

Sage (UK) Ltd

SETI@home project

Sight and Sound Technology

Sophos Anti-virus

Texas Heart Institute

United Devices Cancer Research Project

Web User magazine

Cover picture © "Spring Rush" reproduced with kind permission from Neil Canning

Cover photography © by Mike Kwasniak, 160 Sidegate Lane, Ipswich

Design and typesetting by Direction Advertising and Design Ltd www.direction-advertising.com

Gingerjohn website designed by Ellie Harrison www.ellieharrison.com

First edition 2002. Reprinted 2003.

10 9 8 7 6 5 4 3 2

A catalogue entry for this book is available from the British Library.

ISBN 1 903112 75 3

Printed in Great Britain by W.M. Print, Walsall, West Midlands

Table of Contents

Table of Contents

Table of Contents

Table of Contents

Table of Contents

Preface

Aim

The aim of this book is to provide a clear and concise text for the Applied GCSE in ICT (Double Award).

The book consists of forty chapters covering the three units of the entire qualification, namely **Unit 1: ICT tools and Applications, Unit 2: ICT in Organisations** and **Unit 3: ICT and Society**. Within each chapter there is sufficient material for at least one or two lessons, with practical work, discussion points, exercises suitable for homework and guidance for independent study.

The Units

Unit 1 is a very practical unit and students are shown how to use all the features of the various software packages that they need to be familiar with. It is assumed that they will have had some prior experience of using Word, Excel, Access and PowerPoint, such as could have been gained from Payne-Gallway's Basic ICT Skills series. The exercises and projects in this unit show the student how to do all the tasks described in the specification and will enable students to progress at their own pace.

Unit 2 shows how ICT is used in the different departments of an organisation. It gives advice on putting together a portfolio and on completing all the stages of a practical project.

In **Unit 3**, each chapter covers a different aspect of the use of ICT and this will provide an invaluable resource for portfolio work, as well as giving students ideas and guidance for additional research. Students are encouraged to carry out independent study using the Internet, and are advised of a number of suitable websites from which to gather further materials.

Assessment grids at the end of the book for the Edexcel qualification of Applied GCSE in ICT will be a useful reference for both teachers and students.

Answers to the questions in the text are available in a separate teacher's supplement on the publisher's website www.payne-gallway.co.uk.

ICT Tools and Applications

In this unit you will learn about the ICT tools and applications available and how these are used by different organisations. You will investigate how local businesses use ICT tools and applications, or use a variety of case studies, or a mixture.

You will learn to use a range of applications, including:

- Word processing
- Publications and presentation software
- Spreadsheets
- Databases
- Multimedia
- Web browsers and e-mail

You will also learn how to use ICT tools and applications to:

- Develop documents for different purposes
- Find, store and manipulate data

Chapter 1: The World Wide Web

Introduction

Some of the exercises in this book are based around a fictitious company called **Ginger John's**. This is a chain of fast food outlets which specialises in selling snacks and meals using freshly prepared, low fat ingredients and fresh fruit and vegetables. As people become more and more aware of the benefits of healthy eating, the chain is becoming more and more popular.

The company's web site can be found at **www.payne-gallway.co.uk/gingerjohn**. In this chapter you will log on to the site and find out more about the company.

The Internet

The Internet is a huge number of computers all over the world, connected together. Just as a few computers can be connected to form a network, so the Internet is an **inter**national **net**work of networks.

The program you use to look at the Internet is called a **browser** and one of the most popular browsers is **Microsoft Internet Explorer**. To load it:

 Double-click the icon for Internet Explorer. (In Windows 98 and later versions, this is by the **Start** button.)

 Or, click **Start** at bottom left of the screen, then click **Programs**, then click

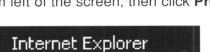

 You may see a dialogue box asking you if you wish to connect. If so, click **Connect**. An Internet page will appear on your screen – probably one that either your school or the manufacturer has set as a **default**.

You can go to a different page by typing a new **address**.

 Click in the Address box at the top of the window – the text will be highlighted.

Figure 1.1: The Address box

 Type in **www.payne-gallway.co.uk/gingerjohn** and click on **Go**.

Your screen should look like the one shown in Figure 1.2.

Figure1.2: The GingerJohn Home Page

The World Wide Web

The part of the Internet you are looking at here is the World Wide Web and this is a Web page on a Web site. Most large companies and organisations have a Web site and so do many individuals. There are hundreds of millions of Web pages stored on computers all over the world which you can access from your computer.

Moving about the web

Web pages often have **hot links** (also called **hypertext links**). When you move the mouse pointer over a hot link, the cursor changes shape from an arrow to a hand.

 Try this now.

When you click on a hot area, the browser jumps to a new page.

Click on the **Feedback** link. Fill in the feedback form. Unfortunately as this is not a real site, you won't get a reply when you click **Submit**!

Figure 1.3: Feedback form

To go back to a previous page, either on this site or another site that you may have visited, you can use the **Back** button.

 Click the **Back** button to return to Ginger John's Home page. ——————

You can use the **Forward** button to go forward again to where you just came from. ——

Adding a page to the Favorites list

To keep a note of the page so that you can return to it another time without having to remember and type the whole address, you can add it to a list of your favourite Web sites. This is called **bookmarking** a site.

 Make sure you are on Ginger John's Home page.

 From the menu bar choose **Favorites**, **Add to Favorites** and click **OK**.

Entering an address

Every Web page has a unique address. A typical Web site address is:

http://www.pretamanger.co.uk

 Type the address **www.pretamanger.co.uk** in the Address box. Press **Go.**

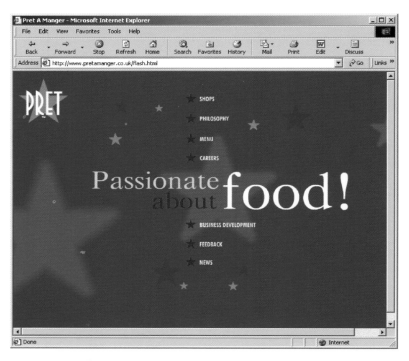

Figure 1.4: The Pret a Manger site

Almost all Web addresses start with **http://**. You don't have to type this in – it will be added automatically for you when you press the **Go** button.

When you click on a hot link, you go to a different page. Every single Web page has its own unique address, so the new address will have some extra bits at the end:

http://www.pretamanger.co.uk/careers/

> **www** means world wide web
>
> **pretamanger** is the domain name, showing the organisation that owns the site
>
> **.co.uk** shows that this company is in the UK. International companies have domain names ending in **.com**.
>
> Some other codes are **gov** for government, **org** for organisation, **ac** (**edu** in USA) for a college or university, or **sch** for a school.
>
> Web sites belonging to a different country end in a two-letter country code – **uk** for the UK, **fr** for France, **de** for Germany, **es** for Spain and so on.

Now click the **Favorites** button on the toolbar to return to the **GingerJohn** site.

The Links bar

Instead of adding a site to **Favorites** you can have it in view on the Links bar, under the Address bar. To do this, choose **Links** in the **Add to Favorites** window. Click **OK**.

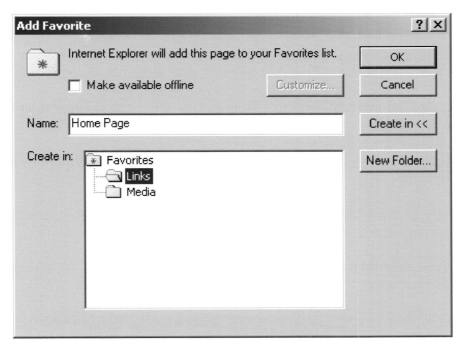

Figure 1.5: Adding a favourite site to the Links bar

Alternatively, you can drag a site's icon from the Address box onto the Links bar.

Figure 1.6: The Links bar

You can then go quickly to a favourite site by clicking on the named **Link** button.

Moving around the Internet

You have learned four ways to move around the Internet:

1. Type in the address
2. Click on a link
4. Use the **Back** and **Forward** buttons
5. Go to a favourite site by clicking the **Favorites** button or clicking on a link you have set up.

Ending an Internet session

When you have finished your Internet session, you should disconnect so that you are no longer using a phone line. There are several ways of doing this.

Note that closing Internet Explorer does not automatically disconnect you – you have to instruct the computer to disconnect.

While you are connected, this **Dial-up** icon appears in the bar at the bottom right of your screen.

 Right-click the **Dial-up** icon and select **Disconnect**. This disconnects the phone line, but does not close **Internet Explorer**.

 Close **Internet Explorer** by clicking the **Close** icon (X) at the top right of your screen, or by selecting **File**, **Close** from the menu bar.

An alternative way to finish an Internet session is to close **Internet Explorer** first, and then disconnect.

Click here

 Close **Internet Explorer** by clicking the **Close** icon (X) at the top right of your screen, or by selecting **File**, **Close** from the menu bar.

You will see a message on your screen:

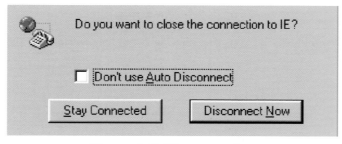

Figure 1.7: Disconnecting

 Click **Disconnect Now** to disconnect.

Exercises

Use the Internet to search for information about a company called BurgersAway! This exercise is based on one of the sample tasks set by Edexcel.

- Access the Edexcel Web site and find the BurgersAway! home page. You may want to bookmark this Web site.

- Find out more about the company by browsing through the site.

- Locate the registration page and enter your details.

- Make a note of where to find company and product information. You will need some of this information to complete later tasks.

Chapter 2: Browsing

As you can see, it's easy to spend hours browsing the web, jumping from page to page. To look up a particular topic you can use a **search engine**. There are several search engines such as google.com, yahoo.com, askjeeves.com and altavista.com.

Suppose you wanted to find out information about a healthy diet.

▶ Load **Internet Explorer** by double-clicking the icon.

▶ Click in the Address box to select the current address.

▶ Type **www.google.com** and press **Go**.

▶ In the **Search** box, type **healthy diet** and click **Google Search**.

Figure 2.1: The Google home page

You will be taken to a page which shows you the first 10 references to web sites relevant to healthy diets. There are over a million! One reason that there are so many is that the search engine will find all the references to pages containing the word **healthy**, and all the pages containing the word **diet**.

Figure 2.2: Using a search engine

Refining a search

You can refine the search by making sure that all the pages displayed contain the whole phrase.

 Type *"healthy diet"*, including the quote marks, into the **Search** box. This time you will get far fewer hits.

You can also refine your search by clicking the **Advanced Search** link. This brings up the following page:

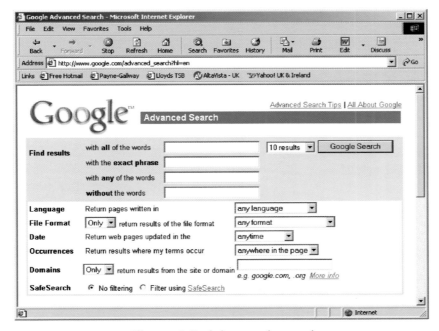

Figure 2.3: Advanced searches

See if you can use the search engine to find:

- The ideal weight range for your height

- The number of fruits and vegetables you should eat every day

- A recipe for a healthy but appetising dessert

About Google

Google was founded in 1998 by two friends from Stanford University. By the start of 2002, 150 million queries were being entered into the Google search box every day. Many people think it is the best search engine on the Web.

A search engine creates an index as it "crawls" over the web. Some web crawlers index the pages by counting the number of times particular words appear in the code. For example, if a user enters the word "minidisc" in the search box, a page containing the word "minidisc" 10 times would appear above one containing the word 5 times. However, this makes it easy for unscrupulous web page editors to fool the search engine into giving them high rankings. They repeat the same word many times, either on the page or hidden in the code.

Google works differently. It also looks at the contents of a page but it tries to see it from a user's point of view. For example, if a word appears in bold type on the page, it ranks that word as being particularly important for that page. If a word does not display on the page, it ignores it. Google also counts the number of links from other sites to that page, and how popular those other sites are.

These techniques help it to find the sites that are most likely to be useful to the user.

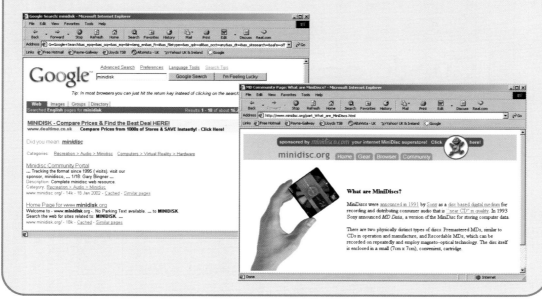

Copying text and graphics

You can copy text and graphics from a Web page to a Word document. You should only use these for reference – don't copy pages straight into your own reports!
To copy text:

 Highlight the text you want to copy. Then from the **Edit** menu, select **Copy**.

 Open a document in Word where you want to copy the text. Then click the **Paste** button.

This will copy text. If you want to copy graphics from a Web page:

 Right-click the graphic and select **Copy**.

 Paste it into your Word document.

Downloading files

You can download and save pictures, video clips, sounds and software from the Internet. You'll need to keep them in separate folders where they can easily be found again when you need them. If you don't know how to make a new folder, here's how.

Creating a new folder

 In Windows Explorer select the **My Documents** folder.

 Choose **File**, **New**, **Folder**.

A new folder appears in the right-hand pane.

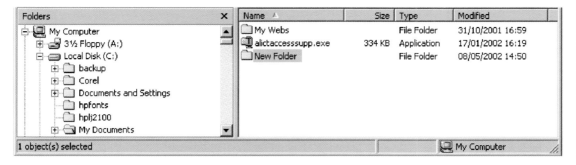

Figure 2.4: Naming a new folder

 Type **WebPictures** to rename it, then click away from it.

Tip:
To open **Windows Explorer** click **Start**, **Programs**, **Windows Explorer.** Or, right-click the **Start** button and choose **Explore**.

Looking for pictures

The Internet has lots of pictures you can download. Some are copyright but many are free. Suppose you want to find a picture of a minidisc.

 Open Internet Explorer and connect to the Internet.

 Enter **Google.com** as the address.

Click on the **Images** tab and type *minidisc* in the Search box.

Choose a suitable image and click on it.

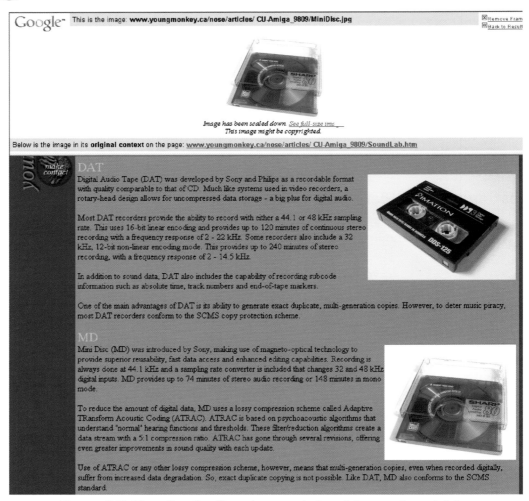

Figure 2.5: Results of a Google search for pictures of a minidisc

 To download the image, right-click it and choose **Save Picture As**.

The downloaded picture can be incorporated in a Word document.

Exercises

These exercises are based on the specimen tasks set by Edexcel.

1. Use the Internet to find information on the process of manufacturing burgers using Computer-Aided Manufacture (CAM).

   - Write down THREE ways of searching for this information using a browser.

   - Search for **manufacturing** – write down how many web-sites you find.

   - Write down a search string that will narrow this search down to find the required information.

   - Obtain information from one or more websites on the use of CAM in the process of producing burgers ready for consumption.

   - Produce a summary of your research on one A4 sheet, using size 12 font.

2. Use the Internet to find information on the use of Computer-Aided Design (CAD) software to design takeaway packaging for burger products.

   - Obtain information from one or more websites on this topic.

   - Produce a summary of your research on one A4 sheet, using size 12 font.

3. You need to search the Internet for information on the use of environmental controls in the process of producing burgers ready for consumption.

   - Obtain information from one or more websites on this topic.

   - Produce a summary of your research on one A4 sheet, using size 12 font.

Chapter 3: E-mail

E-mail or electronic mail can be sent over the Internet to anybody who has an **e-mail address**. It arrives almost instantaneously anywhere in the world.

To use e-mail, you need both an e-mail address and a program to handle it. Both are available free.

E-mail addresses

E-mail addresses are quite like Web site addresses and made up in much the same way. The format is always:

> # username@domain_name

Here, **username** is you and **domain_name** is either the **Internet Service Provider (ISP)** who gives access to the Internet, or a Web site address.

Sam Brown's personal address might look like any of these:

> sam_brown@compuserve.com
>
> sam_brown@aol.com
>
> sam@brownfamily.demon.co.uk

A school address would be something like:

> student@hill_school.bristol.sch.uk

An e-mail address has no spaces and is usually all in small letters. It MUST be entered correctly or the message will come back undelivered. Every e-mail address is unique.

Using Outlook Express

The program most often used to handle e-mail is Microsoft Outlook Express which comes with Internet Explorer.

  Click the Outlook Express icon near the **Start** button, or select **Start, Programs, Outlook Express**.

Some ISPs you may have heard of are AOL, Demon, Virgin, CompuServe, HotMail, FreeServe, BTInternet, TescoNet, ... and more are popping up all the time.

Tip:

Pronounce this as "sam underscore brown at AOL dot com".

The Outlook Express window allows you to:

● compose messages

● send and receive messages

● reply to messages

● forward messages

● print messages

● keep contact names in an Address book

● file old messages in a folder

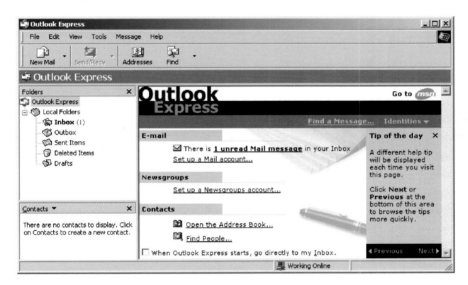

Figure 3.1: Preparing to send or receive e-mail using Outlook Express

Composing an e-mail

To start a new message to someone, you obviously need to know their
e-mail address.

 Click on the **New Mail** button on the toolbar. ———————————

 The **New Message** window opens.

 Type the address in the **To:** box.

 Leave the **Cc:** box blank. This is used if you want to send a copy of the
message to someone else.

 Type something in the **Subject:** box to say what the message is about.

Type the letter in the main window (the message box).

Figure 3.2: Writing a message

Click the **Send** button on the toolbar.

If prompted to **Connect**, click **Cancel**.

The Outbox

The **New Message** window closes and your message is now in the **Outbox**. It has not actually been sent yet – you are still offline. You can write messages to several people and store them in the **Outbox**. When you are ready, you can send them all at once – this uses only a few seconds of online time and saves on the phone bill!

You can look at the contents of the Outbox and edit a message before you send it. You can also delete a message if you change your mind about sending it.

To edit a message in the **Outbox**:

Click **Outbox** in the **Folders** pane to select it.

Double-click the message header in the **Message List** pane.

Click here to send your message

Enter the recipient's e-mail address

What the message is about - always fill this in

The message box

Tip:

Clicking **Send** is like putting a letter in an envelope ready for the post – it's not on its way yet!

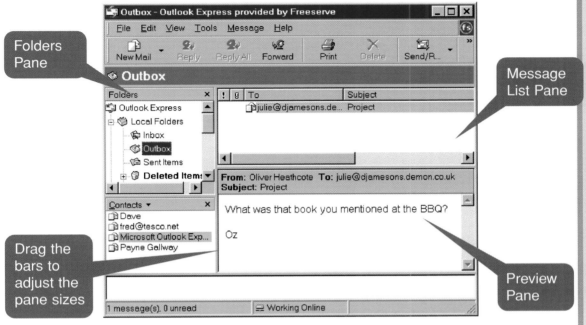

Folders Pane

Message List Pane

Drag the bars to adjust the pane sizes

Preview Pane

Having an **Outbox** means you can write any other messages and send them all at once.

*Figure 3.3: Editing a message in the **Outbox***

An **Edit** window appears and you can edit the message.

▶ Click **Send** to put it back in the **Outbox**.

▶ If prompted to **Connect**, click **Cancel**.

Sending a message from the Outbox

▶ Click the **Send/Recv** button on the toolbar. ──────

If you are offline, you will be prompted to go online. In this case click **Yes**, then **Connect** at the next prompt.

If the **Hang Up When Finished** box is checked, the **Send and Receive All** option disconnects you automatically as soon as all messages have been sent and any messages for you have been received.

Alternatively, you can send a message as soon as you have written it.

▶ Click the **Send** button.

▶ Click **Connect** when prompted.

The message will be sent straight away.

Be sure you have disconnected after sending your messages, unless you have other work to do on the Internet. If the **Dial-up** icon is visible at the bottom right of your screen, right-click it and choose **Disconnect**.

The Address Book

The **Address Book** is used to save the addresses of people you regularly send messages to, so that you don't have to type in their address each time you send a message.

Addresses

Click on the **Addresses** button (see Figure 3.1).

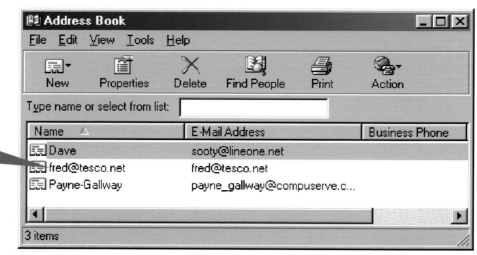

Existing addresses

Figure 3.4: The **Address Book**

Entering a new address

The **Address Book** window lists any contacts who are already entered. To enter a new contact:

 Click on the **New** button on the toolbar and choose **New Contact** from the dropdown menu.

The **Properties** window stores the e-mail, home, and other details of each contact.

 On the **Name** tab, enter the **First:** and **Last:** names and **Title:**, with **Middle:** and **Nickname:** as well if you like.

 Click the arrow on the **Display:** box and choose how you want the name displayed.

Enter an e-mail address.

Enter the name,

how you want it shown in the Contacts list,

and e-mail address

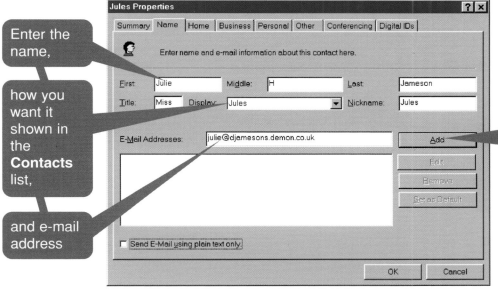

There's no need to click Add unless the person has more than one e-mail address

Figure 3.5: The **Properties** window

 Click **OK** to enter the address.

The name is now listed in the **Address Book** window.

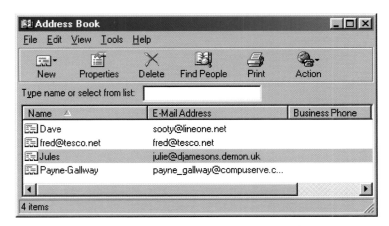

Figure 3.6: Entries in the **Address Book**

If you need to change it, say to add the home address:

 Select the name in the list and click the **Properties** button. —

Properties

 On the **Home** tab, enter the details and click **OK**.

 Now enter two more addresses and close the address book.

Using the Address Book

You can enter addresses straight from the address book when you send messages.

 In the **Outlook Express** main window, click **New Mail**.

 In the **New Message** window, click on the icon to the left of **To:** (instead of in the box).

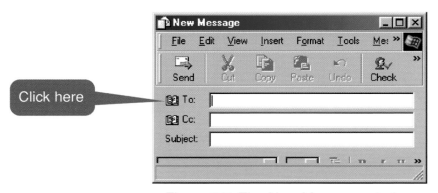

Figure 3.7: The New Message window

The **Select Recipients** window opens.

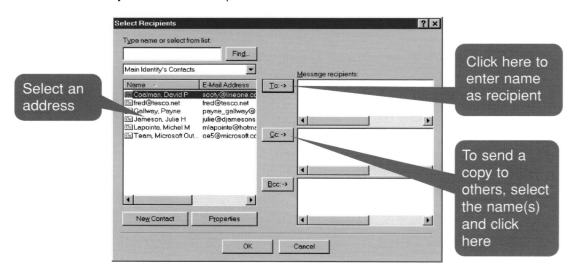

Figure 3.8: Selecting an address

 Select an entry in the **Name** list and click on **To: ->** to transfer it to the **Message Recipients** list.

In the same way you can send a copy of your message to someone else just to keep them posted.

 Select another entry in the **Name** list and click on **Cc: ->** to copy it over.

Note: Cc stands for **Carbon copy**. When the recipients read a message, they can all see who else got it too. To send someone a copy without the other recipients knowing, enter their name in the **Bcc: ->** box. (This stands for **Blind carbon copy**).

 Click on **OK** to return to the **New Message** window.

The recipients are all selected now.

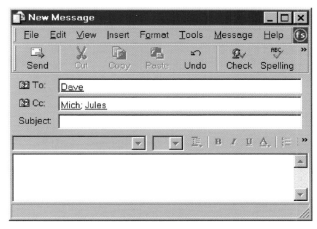

Figure 3.9: Ready to type the message

 Type in a subject line and a message.

Receiving messages

 Click on **Inbox** to show any messages received.

The number in blue shows how many new (unread) messages you have

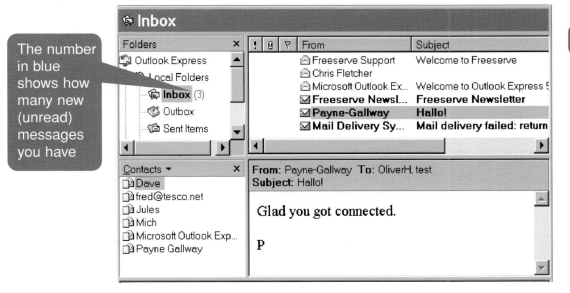

Figure 3.10: Receiving messages

Unread

Read

If you select the message title, the content is shown in the pane below.

Messages are shown on the right with icons indicating **Read** or **Unread**. The message is shown in the **Preview** pane below but it is easier to view it in a separate window.

 Double-click on the message name in the **Message List** pane.

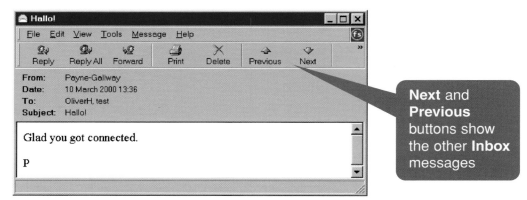

Figure 3.11: Viewing a message in its own window

Next and **Previous** buttons show the other **Inbox** messages

In the **Message View** window you can:

- read and print out the message
- write a reply
- forward it to someone else
- print a message by clicking the **Print** button

Replying to a message

Reply

 Click on the **Reply** button on the toolbar.

Tip:
If you right-click on the name in this window, or on the message in the message list, you can add the sender to the Address Book.

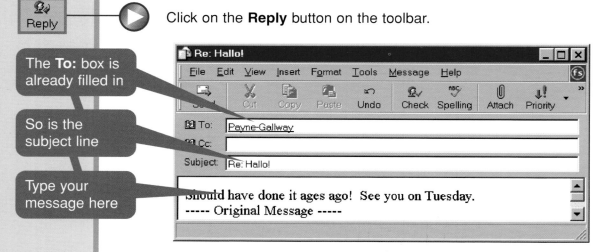

The **To:** box is already filled in

So is the subject line

Type your message here

Figure 3.12: Replying to a message

 Type your message and click **Send**.

If you are online it will be sent, otherwise it is put in the Outbox.

Forwarding a message

A message sent to you might be of interest to someone else too. Try forwarding a message.

 Double-click on the message name in the **Inbox** to show the message view window.

 Click on the **Forward** button. ————————————————————————

The forwarding window is all set up, with a subject line of **Fw: [your message title]**. The cursor is in the message area with the forwarding message below.

 Click **To:** to add the recipient's name.

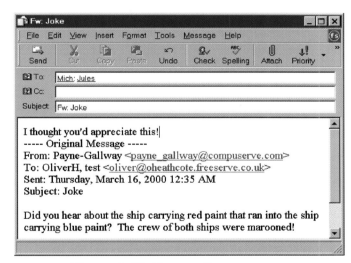

Figure 3.13: Forwarding a message

 Add your own message if you like and click **Send**.

Sending an attachment

As well as text you can also **attach** a file to the message. For example, you might want to send a scanned photograph of yourself or your family on holiday. Or, you might want to do some work on your computer at home and then e-mail it to yourself at school so that you can work on it during class.

To attach a file in the **New Message** window:

 Click on the **Attach** button on the toolbar.

 In the **Insert Attachment** window, navigate to the file and click **Attach**. ————

Instead of creating a new message and pasting it in, just **forward** it to the new address.

Forward

This could be a word-processed document, spreadsheet, graphics file, sound file, game file, etc.

Attach

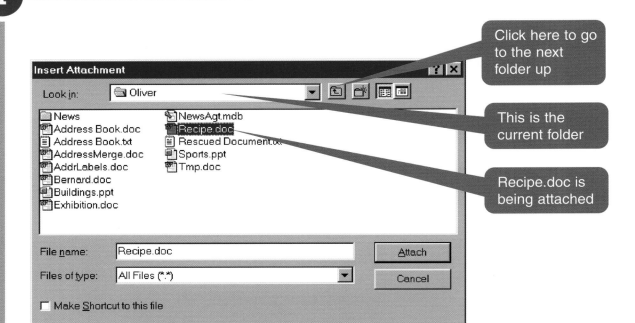

Click here to go to the next folder up

This is the current folder

Recipe.doc is being attached

Figure 3.14: Attaching a file to a message

When you send the message, the attached files go too.

Receiving an attachment

If you receive a file with an attachment, the message header has a paper clip icon beside it.

VIRUS ALERT! Make sure you have an up-to-date virus checker installed.

Shows there's an attachment

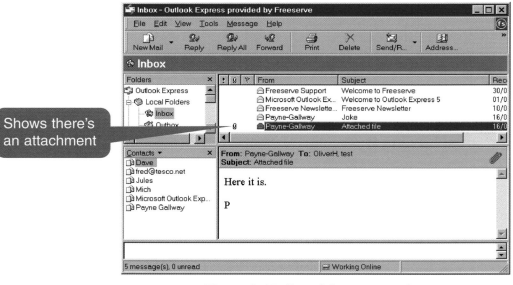

Figure 3.15: Receiving an attachment

 Double-click the attached file's icon to open it.

Saving an attachment

You might want to save an attached file to your hard disk if you want to keep it permanently. Otherwise, when you delete the message you will delete the attachment too.

 From the menu choose **File**, **Save Attachments**.

New	▶
Open	Ctrl+O
Save As...	
Save Attachments...	
Save as Stationery...	

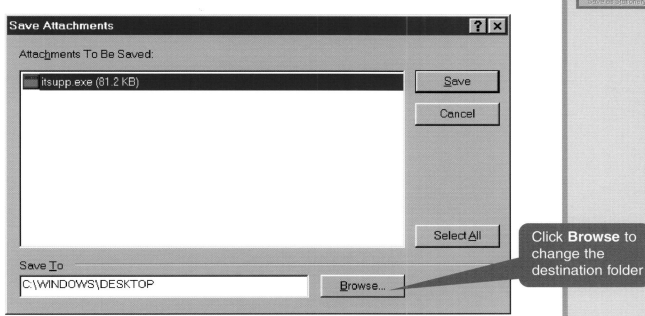

Save Attachments   ? ✕

Attachments To Be Saved:

itsupp.exe (81.2 KB)

Save
Cancel

Select All

Click **Browse** to change the destination folder

Save To
C:\WINDOWS\DESKTOP   Browse...

Figure 3.16: Saving an attachment

The default folder for saving attachments is **Windows\Desktop** but you can change this with the **Browse** button.

 Click **Save**.

Exercises

1. Write down THREE advantages of e-mail over ordinary posted mail.

2. Write down THREE things you can do using e-mail other than simply sending a message to another person.

3. A graphics artist in Bournemouth has designed a new advertisement for Ginger John's. He wants to show it to the Marketing Manager in the London office. Describe the steps he would take to do this electronically. How would the Marketing Manager be able to view the advertisement?

Chapter 4: Business Documents

There are certain standard documents that almost all businesses use from time to time. These include:

- Letters
- Faxes
- Memos
- Agendas for meetings
- Minutes of meetings

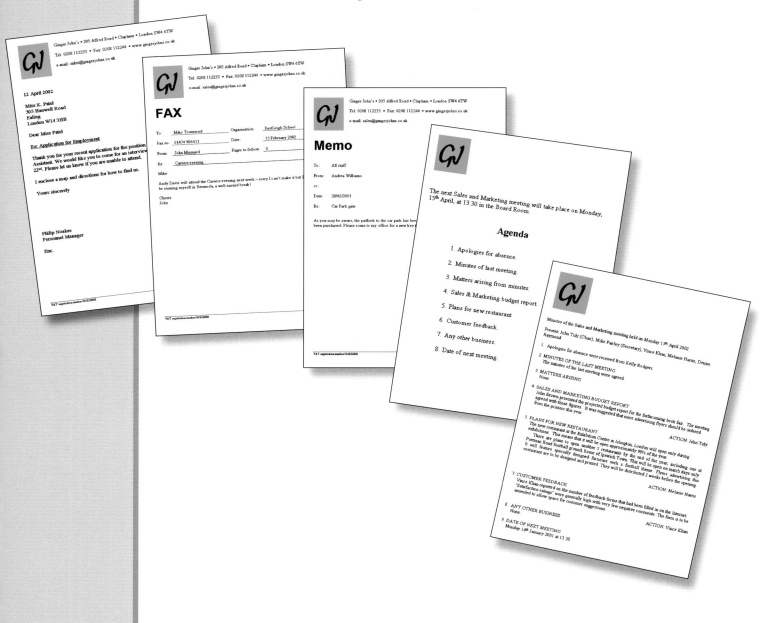

In addition, a business may need to produce:

- An invoice
- A publicity flyer
- A newsletter
- A form (e.g. an application form or an Expenses form)
- A formal report
- Business cards

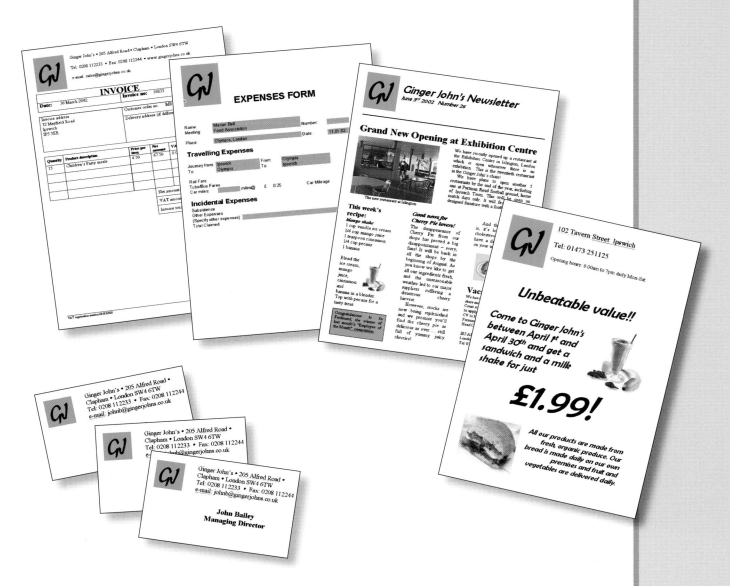

Writing style

Different types of documents must be carefully planned and the following factors considered:

- Purpose of the document
- Target audience
- Writing style and tone
- Presentation style (e.g. use of colour and images)
- Layout
- Accuracy and clarity
- Consistency (e.g. house style)

You should look at a range of documents used by companies. Look at some of the 'junk mail' and flyers that come through the letterbox. Find some newsletters, invoices, business cards, questionnaires and other documents. What presentation techniques are used? These might include column layout, bullets, text boxes, different styles and colours of text and use of graphics.

Look at the writing style of different documents. Is it formal or informal? Who is it aimed at? What is the purpose of each document? Is it to inform, to entertain, to educate, to persuade, or to collect information?

Maintaining a house style

A business usually has its own logo, which may include a graphic image and a slogan or the name of the company written in a particular font. This helps to create a strong brand image that people recognise easily. Think of the logos of companies such as McDonald's, Ford and Nike. If you saw a McDonald's restaurant with a completely different sign outside, you would probably wonder if it was run by a different company.

Tip:
The logo may vary in size, depending on where it is used, but its proportions and colour should always be the same.

The company logo will be used not only outside shops and on company products but also on stationery used to produce many different types of document. If you ever start your own business, one of the first things you will need to do is design some stationery for sending letters, faxes and invoices.

Designing a logo

You can use the drawing tools in Word to create a logo and templates for stationery.

We will design a simple logo for Ginger John's chain of snack bars.

▶ Open a new document in Word.

▶ Make sure the Drawing toolbar is visible. It may be at the bottom of your screen. If it is not, from the **View** menu select **Toolbars**. Check **Drawing**.

Figure 4.1: The Drawing toolbar

▶ Select the **Textbox** tool and draw out a box about 2cm wide by 3cm tall. ———

▶ Select a font. In the picture below, the font is **Mistral**. Select font size **72**.

▶ In the text box type the letters *GJ*.

▶ Select the **Fill** tool and fill the box with an orange colour. ———

▶ Select the **Line** tool and specify **No line**. ———

Your logo should look something like the one below.

▶ Right-click the border of the logo and choose **Copy** from the pop-up menu. You will need it in a minute.

▶ Save the document with the logo, as you will need to copy it onto various documents. Name the file *GJ Logo.doc.*

Creating a letter template

Ginger John's will need some headed stationery for its business letters. This needs to display the logo, the name and address of the company, the telephone and fax numbers. It will also specify the web site address and an e-mail address. In addition, as it has a turnover of well over £50,000 p.a., it will have to be registered for VAT and its VAT registration number should appear on the stationery.

We will create a letter template similar to the one below.

Tip:

A **template** is a document in a particular format that you can add your own text to – you can use it instead of opening a new, blank document to write a letter, fax or other document and then printing it on company stationery.

MS Word has several built-in templates. Experiment by selecting **File**, **New** and then selecting **General Templates**.
Try out, for example, **Elegant fax**. If you saved your document, the template would remain unchanged for you to use another time. This time, close without saving.

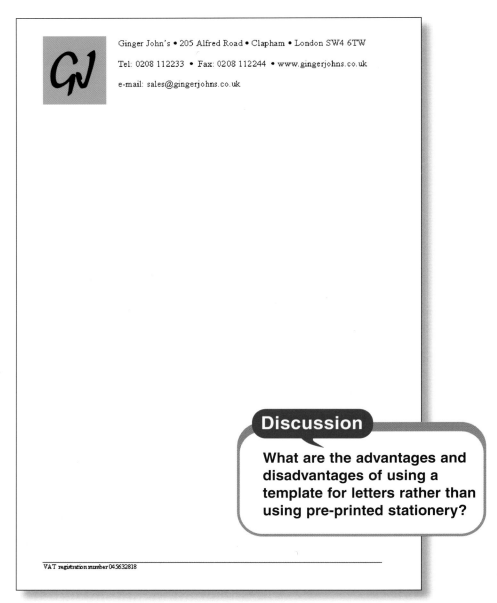

Ginger John's • 205 Alfred Road • Clapham • London SW4 6TW

Tel: 0208 112233 • Fax: 0208 112244 • www.gingerjohns.co.uk

e-mail: sales@gingerjohns.co.uk

VAT registration number 045632818

Discussion

What are the advantages and disadvantages of using a template for letters rather than using pre-printed stationery?

Figure 4.2: A letter template

Header and footer

Open a new document in Word.

We will put the logo and company information into a header and footer. This keeps it separate from the contents of the letter.

From the **View** menu select **Header and Footer**.

Paste the logo into the top left-hand corner of the header. (You'll need to drag it into position.)

Double-click to the right of the logo to create an insertion point. Type the first line of the address in **Times Roman**, size **12**:

Ginger John's 205 Alfred Road Clapham London SW4 6TW

To separate the name and the parts of the address we will insert little bullet symbols. Position the cursor between **Ginger John's** and **205 Alfred Road** and from the **Insert** menu select **Symbol**.

Select the **Wingdings** font and find a suitable bullet character.

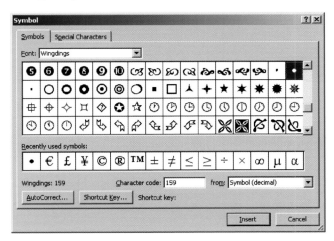

Figure 4.3: Inserting a symbol

Click **Insert**. Then insert the same character between the other parts of the address:

Ginger John's • 205 Alfred Road • Clapham • London SW4 6TW

Type the next two lines:

Tel: 0208 112233 • Fax: 0208 112244 • www.gingerjohns.co.uk
e-mail: sales@gingerjohns.co.uk

Your header should now look like Figure 4.4:

Header

Ginger John's • 205 Alfred Road • Clapham • London SW4 6TW

Tel: 0208 112233 • Fax: 0208 112244 • www.gingerjohns.co.uk

e-mail: sales@gingerjohns.co.uk

Figure 4.4: The logo and address information in a header

▶ In the Header and Footer toolbar, click the **Switch between Header** and **Footer** button.

▶ Type the VAT registration number in the footer, using size 8 Times Roman font.

▶ Click the **Outside Border** button on the Formatting toolbar and select **Top Border**.

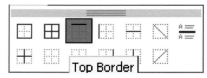

Top Border

▶ This will put a line above the VAT number to separate it from the letter contents.

VAT registration number 045632818

▶ Press the **Close** button on the Header and Footer toolbar.

▶ Your letter template is ready! Save it as *GJ Letter Template.doc*.

Writing a business letter

You should know the correct way to set out a business letter.

A business letter should show:
- The date
- The recipient's address
- A reference by which the letter can be referred to
- The recipient's letter reference if replying to a letter
- A greeting
- The topic of the letter
- The signature, name and title of the sender
- The abbreviation **Enc** if there are any enclosures

A Word template has an extension **.dot**, but you may not be able to save a **.dot** file on a school network, so we will save it as an ordinary document.

Below is a letter from the Personnel Manager at Ginger John's to a prospective employee, inviting them for an interview.

Ginger John's • 205 Alfred Road • Clapham • London SW4 6TW

Tel: 0208 112233 • Fax: 0208 112244 • www.gingerjohns.co.uk

e-mail: sales@gingerjohns.co.uk

12 April 2002

Miss K Patel
305 Hanwell Road
Ealing
London W14 3HB

Dear Miss Patel

Re: Application for Employment

Thank you for your recent application for the position of Administrative Assistant. We would like you to come for an interview on Monday April 22nd at 10am. Please let us know if you are unable to attend.

I enclose a map and directions for how to find us.

Yours sincerely

Philip Noakes
Personnel Manager

Enc

VAT registration number 045 032818

Figure 4.5: A business letter

To use your template for a letter, you will need to open **GJ Letter Template.doc** if it is not already open. Then from the **File** menu choose **Save As** and select a new name for the letter.

Note that all the text in the letter is left-justified, and there is a blank line between paragraphs.

A fax template

A fax machine is very useful for sending documents of all kinds, including maps and hand-written text. Whatever is being sent, the first sheet should show certain basic information such as who the fax is from, who it is going to, the date and the number of pages to follow.

Your next task is to create a fax header sheet like the one shown in Figure 4.6.

Ginger John's • 205 Alfred Road • Clapham • London SW4 6TW

Tel: 0208 112233 • Fax: 0208 112244 • www.gingerjohns.co.uk

e-mail: sales@gingerjohns.co.uk

FAX

To: _____   Organisation: _____

Fax no: _____   Date: _____

From: _____   Pages to follow: _____

Re: _____

Figure 4.6: A Fax header sheet

▶ Open **GJ Letter Template.doc.**

▶ From the **File** menu choose **Save As** and name the new document **GJ Fax Template.doc.**

▶ Underneath the header, press **Enter** to leave a blank line and then change the font to **Arial**, **Bold**, size **36**. Type the word **FAX**.

▶ Change the font to **Times New Roman**, size **12**, not bold. It should be left justified.

Inserting a table

We are going to insert a table to hold the headings and to leave space for the writer to enter the information.

 Click the **Insert Table** button on the Standard toolbar and drag across 4 columns and 4 rows. When you release the mouse button, a table of 4 rows and 4 columns will be inserted.

Ginger John's • 205 Alfred Road • Clapham • London SW4 6TW

Tel: 0208 112233 • Fax: 0208 112244 • www.gingerjohns.co.uk

e-mail sales@gingerjohns.co.uk

FAX

Figure 4.7: Inserting a table into a document

> **Tip:**
> A **table** is a grid of rows and columns. Tables are very useful whenever you want information displayed neatly lined up, or in rows and columns like a school or railway timetable.

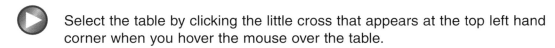 Enter headings as follows:

To:		Organisation:	
Fax no:		Date:	
From:		Pages to follow:	
Re:			

We don't want the gridlines showing.

 Select the table by clicking the little cross that appears at the top left hand corner when you hover the mouse over the table.

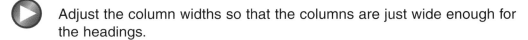 Click the **Border** button and choose **No Border**.

Adjust the column widths so that the columns are just wide enough for the headings.

Formatting and merging cells

The rows are too narrow for someone to write in by hand. They need to be made deeper.

 Select the table and from the **Table** menu select **Table Properties...**

 Click the **Row** tab and specify a height of 1cm. Click **OK**.

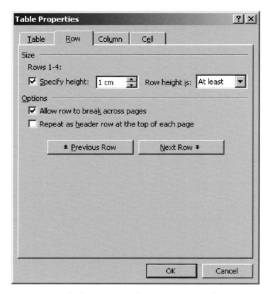

Figure 4.8: Changing the row height

 Save your template.

 Click the **Print Preview** button to see what it will look like when printed.

It could be improved by putting lines where the user writes information. You can do this by putting lower borders in the appropriate cells.

You will then see that you need to move the text down in each cell so that it lines up with the line.

 Do this by selecting the table, clicking on **Table, Table Properties**, selecting the **Cell** tab and choosing **Bottom**.

The last row does not need to be divided into 4 cells. You can merge the three blank cells to make one large cell.

 Select the three blank cells in the bottom row.

 From the **Table** menu select **Merge cells**.

It should look like Figure 4.6! Save it again.

Memos

A memo is used for informal communication within an organisation. It should specify who it is from, who it is to, anyone who is to receive a copy, the date and the topic of the memo. An example is shown below.

Ginger John's • 205 Alfred Road • Clapham • London SW4 6TW

Tel: 0208 112233 • Fax: 0208 112244 • www.gingerjohns.co.uk

e-mail: sales@gingerjohns.co.uk

Memo

To: Andrea

From: John

cc:

Date: 13th April

Re: New Employee

Karla Patel will be joining the Admin staff the first week in May. I'm sure you'll make her feel welcome.

Could you order a new desk from Webster's for her, and make room in the office for her!

Figure 4.9: A memo

> Note that a memo is not signed - it is for internal use and the name of the sender appears above the message, "From:"

Exercises

These exercises are based on the sample tasks published by Edexcel.

During busy periods, BurgersAway! employs many extra staff who do not always know about company standards and procedures. Mr Tariq feels that setting common standards will improve communication and customer service. He would also like a new logo on all the company's paper-based and electronic documents.

You need to produce five documents using relevant company information.

(n.b. Some of these documents are described in the next two chapters.)

1. Design a new company logo. Include it on all your documents.

2. The company needs a standard fax header template.

    - Create this template using suitable software.

    - Print a copy of your template on one A4 sheet.

3. The company needs a new letterhead.

    - Create a letterhead.

    - Use this letterhead to write a business letter on behalf of the Managing Director. The letter will inform the competition winner of their prize.

    - Print the letter.

Advertising flyers

Flyers are used to tell people about products or services that are being offered – for example, pizza deliveries, tree surgery or window cleaning. They can also be used to announce the opening of a new business such as a restaurant, night-club or DIY store.

The flyers are often pushed through the letterbox or delivered with a local newspaper. They can be glossy, full-page advertisements or, where cost is an issue, A5 black and white sheets. The main thing is that they should be eye-catching and have the information clearly set out.

A flyer for Ginger John's

We will produce a flyer offering a special deal on a sandwich and a milk shake from Ginger John's. The flyer should show the Ginger John's logo, the address of the store and the details of the special offer. Some graphics will be added to make the offer more appealing.

The flyer will look something like Figure 5.1:

102 Tavern Street Ipswich

Tel: 01473 251125

Opening hours: 8.00am to 7pm daily Mon-Sat

Unbeatable value!!

Come to Ginger John's between April 1ˢᵗ and April 30ᵗʰ and get a sandwich and a milk shake for just

£1.99!

All our products are made from fresh, organic produce. Our bread is made daily on our own premises and fruit and vegetables are delivered daily.

Figure 5.1: A flyer

Page setup

The flyer is to be A5 size.

▶ Open a new Word document.

▶ On the **File** menu click **Page Setup**.

▶ Click the **Paper** tab and select paper size **A5**.

▶ Click the **Margin** tab and set the margins to **2.0 cm** all round. Make sure the orientation is set to **Portrait**, not **Landscape**.

▶ Click **OK**.

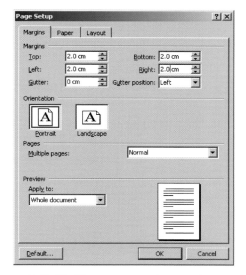

Figure 5.2: Setting paper size and margins

Inserting the logo and address

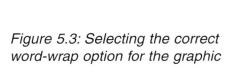 Open the document **GJ Letter Template.doc** which contains the Ginger John logo.

Double-click the logo in this document to open the header. Right-click the edge of the logo and select **Copy** from the pop-up menu.

Click the icon for the new flyer document, which should be showing in the Task bar at the bottom of the screen. This will open the flyer.

Paste the logo into this document and position it at the top left of the document.

Right-click the edge of the logo and from the pop-up menu select **Format Text Box**.

Click the **Layout** tab, select **Tight**, **Left** and click **OK**. This will position the graphic against the left-hand margin and you can type to the right of it.

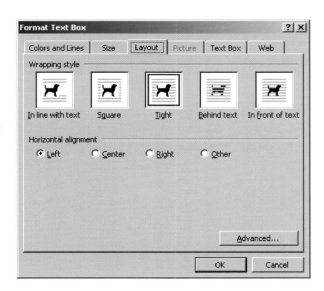

Figure 5.3: Selecting the correct word-wrap option for the graphic

Type the address and opening hours information. The font for **Address** is **Times Roman** size **14**, and the **Opening hours** information is size **10**.

102 Tavern Street Ipswich

Tel: 01473 251125

Opening hours: 8.00am to 7pm daily Mon-Sat

Formatting text

You can format text either before or after you type it.

 Type the heading *Unbeatable value!!* Make it italic and **Berlin sans FB** font, size **28**. (You can choose a different font if you like.)

  Click the **Center** button on the Formatting toolbar to centre the heading.

 Press **Enter** twice to leave a blank line and change the font size to **20**.

 Still in italics, type the text

Come to Ginger John's between April 1st and April 30th and get a sandwich and a milk shake for just
£1.99!
All our products are made from fresh, organic produce. Our bread is made daily on our own premises and fruit and vegetables are delivered daily.

 Make sure you have pressed **Enter** before and after **£1.99**. Make this line size **72**, centred.

  Click the **Align Right** button on the Formatting toolbar to right-justify the final paragraph.

Inserting graphics

The page needs brightening up with some suitable graphics. You can either find some pictures on the Internet or you can insert some clip art pictures. The graphics shown in Figure 5.1 were found using the Google Image search.

 Find a suitable image of a milk shake and copy it. Paste it anywhere on your flyer.

 Right-click the image and select **Format Picture**.

Click the **Layout** tab and select **Tight**, **Right** and click **OK**. This will position the graphic against the right-hand margin. Move it so that it is beside the first paragraph.

 Now find a picture of a sandwich and position it to the left of the final paragraph.

You should have a flyer looking like Figure 5.1!

Creating a newsletter

Newsletters are produced by all sorts of organisations such as local political parties, churches and County Councils. Businesses often produce newsletters for their own employees, to keep everyone up-to-date with the latest company news.

The newsletter we will produce will look like Figure 5.4.

Ginger John's Newsletter
June 3rd 2002 Number 26

Grand New Opening at Exhibition Centre

The new restaurant at Islington

We have recently opened up a restaurant at the Exhibition Centre in Islington, London which is open whenever there is an exhibition. This is the twentieth restaurant in the Ginger John's chain!

We have plans to open another 5 restaurants by the end of the year, including one at Portman Road football ground, home of Ipswich Town. This will be open on match days only. It will feature specially designed furniture with a football theme.

This week's recipe:
Mango shake
1 cup vanilla ice cream
1/4 cup mango juice
1 teaspoon cinnamon
1/4 cup pecans
1 banana

Blend the ice cream, mango juice, cinnamon and banana in a blender. Top with pecans for a tasty treat.

Congratulations to Jo Ferdinand, the winner of last month's "Employee of the Month" competition.

Good news for Cherry Pie lovers!

The disappearance of Cherry Pie from our shops has proved a big disappointment – sorry, fans! It will be back in all the shops by the beginning of August. As you know we like to get all our ingredients fresh, and the unseasonable weather led to our major suppliers suffering a disastrous cherry harvest.

However, stocks are now being replenished and we promise you'll find the cherry pie as delicious as ever … still full of yummy juicy cherries!

And the good news is, it's low in fat and cholesterol and won't have a disastrous effect on your waistline.

Vacancies
We have a vacancy for a store manager at the Earl's Court store. If you would like to apply, send a letter and a CV to Mary Hammond, Personnel Department at Head Office:

205 Alfred Road, Clapham, London SW4 6TW
Tel: 0208 112233

Figure 5.4: A newsletter

Importing text into a newsletter

You can create a newsletter using Word, which has many features of a desktop publishing system, or you can use a package such as MS Publisher, which has special templates for newsletters. In this chapter we will use Word. All the text that you need is held in a document called **Text for Newsletter.doc**, downloadable from **www.payne-gallway.co.uk/aict**. It is reproduced below for reference.

Grand New Opening at Exhibition Centre

We have recently opened up a restaurant at the Exhibition Centre in Islington, London which is open whenever there is an exhibition. This is the twentieth restaurant in the Ginger John's chain!

We have plans to open another 5 restaurants by the end of the year, including one at Portman Road football ground, home of Ipswich Town. This will be open on match days only. It will feature specially designed furniture with a football theme.

This week's recipe:

Mango shake

1 cup vanilla ice cream	$\frac{1}{4}$ cup mango juice
1 teaspoon cinnamon	$\frac{1}{4}$ cup pecans
1 banana	

Blend the ice cream, mango juice, cinnamon and banana in a blender. Top with pecans for a tasty treat.

Vacancies

We have a vacancy for a store manager at the Earl's Court store. If you would like to apply, send a letter and a CV to Mary Hammond, Personnel Department at Head Office:

205 Alfred Road, Clapham, London SW4 6TW
Tel: 0208 112233

Good news for Cherry Pie lovers!

The disappearance of Cherry Pie from our shops has proved a big disappointment – sorry, fans! It will be back in all the shops by the beginning of August. As you know we like to get all our ingredients fresh, and the unseasonable weather led to our major suppliers suffering a disastrous cherry harvest. However, stocks are now being replenished and we promise you'll find the cherry pie as delicious as ever … still full of yummy juicy cherries! And the good news is, it's low in fat and cholesterol and won't have a distrous effect on your waistline.

Congratulations to Jo Ferdinand, the winner of last month's "Employee of the Month" competition.

The graphics for the newsletter are called **milkshake.gif**, **cherry pie.jpg** and **snackbar.jpg**, also downloadable from the same web page. You need to save all these files in a folder of your own.

Tip:

Articles for a newsletter are often word-processed at different times by different people. These articles are saved as files and need to be brought together into the newsletter document. This is called **importing files**.

Starting the newsletter

▶ Open a new document in Word and copy the logo into it as you did for the flyer. Type the heading **Ginger John's Newsletter** and the subheading shown in Figure 5.4. Choose a suitable font and format the headings. Press **Enter** a few times to position the cursor ready for the first article.

▶ Use the **Line** tool to draw a line underneath the logo, as in Figure 5.4. Keep your finger on the **Shift** key while you draw the line to make sure it is horizontal. With the line selected, click the **Line Style** box to make the line thicker.

▶ Copy all the text from **Text for Newsletter.doc.** Position the cursor underneath the line in the newsletter and paste it in.

Now all you have to do is arrange the text and add some graphics!

Formatting the newsletter

▶ Make the first heading size **24**. Press **Enter** after the heading.

▶ From the Insert menu select **Picture**, **From File**. Insert the picture **snackbar.jpg**.

▶ Highlight the picture and the text about the new snackbar, and then click and hold the **Columns** button on the Standard toolbar. Drag across 2 columns and release.

▶ The text will be placed beside the picture. You may need to adjust the size of the picture.

▶ You need to make a little space between the heading of the article "Grand New Opening …" and the story. Right-click in the heading and select **Paragraph** from the pop-up menu. Make **Space After** equal to **12** and click **OK**.

▶ Underneath the picture in size 10 font, italic, type the caption *The new restaurant at Islington*. Select the text and centre it by clicking the **Center** button.

▶ Now highlight all the rest of the text in the newsletter and use the **Columns** button to put it into 3 columns.

The piece of text about the employee of the month needs to go in the first column, and the text about the vacancies needs to go at the end of the third column

 Cut and paste till they are in the right place.

Now your newsletter should look like this:

Figure 5.5: The newsletter in columns

You can probably finish it on your own! You need to insert the other two pictures, put a shaded box around the "Employee of the Month" story, justify the text, spell check (and there IS a spelling mistake in there!) and adjust font sizes so everything fits.

You should indent the first word of each new paragraph in a story. For example, press **Enter** just before **However to** create a new paragraph. To indent this word, first click in the ruler line to create a tab stop. Then press the **Tab** key to indent the word.

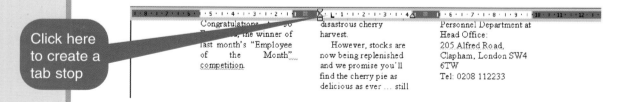

Click here to create a tab stop

Figure 5.6: Creating a tab stop

Checklist

If you have to create a newsletter for your portfolio work or in an exam, the examiners will probably use a checklist to mark your work. They will be looking out for the following features:

- Text cut and pasted or imported from a text file
- Heading typed in a font that stands out clearly
- Appropriate pictures inserted in sensible positions
- Newsletter laid out in columns
- At least one heading centred across 2 or more columns
- Subheadings in a suitable font
- All information fitting exactly on the page
- Appropriate margins or borders
- Text fully justified
- Paragraphs indented or separated by a line space
- Features which clearly divide sections – e.g. borders, dividing lines, speech bubbles
- Use of a spellchecker

Exercises

These exercises are based on the sample tasks published by Edexcel.

1. Burgers Away! Needs a promotional flyer for the opening of a new branch. The flyer must be A5 size so that two flyers can be printed on one side of A4. The flyer must include the advertising slogan.

    - Create this flyer using suitable software

    - Print two copies of your flyer on one sheet of A4 paper

2. Design a newsletter for Burgers Away! You can copy and paste suitable text and graphics from selected Internet sites rather than entering your own. Be sure you have covered all the points in the checklist.

Chapter 6: Invoices and Business Cards

Introduction to invoicing

When a company sells goods or services to an individual or to another business, an invoice is sent either with any goods that are to be dispatched or separately in the case of services. The invoice tells the customer how much they have to pay, and where to send their payment.

You need to include:

- the firm's name and address
- the date
- the invoice number
- the customer's order number
- account number and address
- a delivery address (if this is different from the invoicing address)
- details of the goods or services being invoiced
- Net amount
- VAT at 17.5%
- Carriage if applicable
- Total amount payable (Invoice total).

A possible layout is shown opposite.

Tip:
If the organisation is registered for VAT, their VAT Registration Number should appear on the invoice.

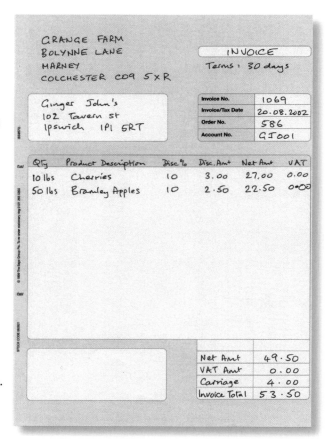

Figure 6.1: A typical invoice

Creating an invoice

We will create a blank invoice which could be used as a template by Ginger John's when they need to send out an invoice. Ginger John's will not send out many invoices as most of the time they are selling food over the counter and receiving cash, but occasionally they may provide a service such as catering for a function or party. The row for **Carriage** is not required on this invoice.

The invoice will look like Figure 6.2.

Ginger John's • 205 Alfred Road • Clapham • London SW4 6TW

Tel: 0208 112233 • Fax: 0208 112244 • www.gingerjohns.co.uk

e-mail: sales@gingerjohns.co.uk

INVOICE					
Date:		Invoice no:			

Invoice address	Customer order no.
	Delivery address (if different)

Quantity	Product description	Price per item	Net amount	VAT rate	VAT amount

		Net amount	
		VAT amount	
		Invoice total	

Figure 6.2: The Ginger John invoice template

Tip:
The VAT Registration number appears at the bottom of the invoice, which is not shown here.

▶ Start Word and open the document **GJ Letter template.doc**. This has the logo and the company name and address.

▶ Save the document as **GJ Invoice Template.doc**.

Inserting a table and adjusting row height

There are two ways of inserting a table. One is to click the **Insert Table** icon and drag out the number of rows and columns that you want.

The second way is to choose **Table**, **Insert**, **Table**. This is easier if you need more than about 6 rows.

 Select **Table**, **Insert**, **Table** and specify a table of 6 columns and 12 rows, column width **Auto**.

 With the cursor somewhere in the table, from the **Table** menu click **Select**, **Table**.

 Select **Table Properties** from the **Table** menu.

 In the dialogue box, click the **Row** tab and set the row height to **Exactly 24pt** as shown in Figure 6.3.

Tip:

If you have inserted the table on the very top line of your document, and you later decide you would like to insert a blank line above the table, you can do this by placing the cursor in the first cell and selecting **Table**, **Split Table**.

Tip:

Font sizes are measured in points (pts). One point is equal to 1/72 of an inch. Note that you can also set the cell height in centimetres if you want to. Setting the cell to an exact measurement locks the cell size, which means that the cell will not expand if the user types more text than will fit in the cell, which could cause your form to spill over the page.

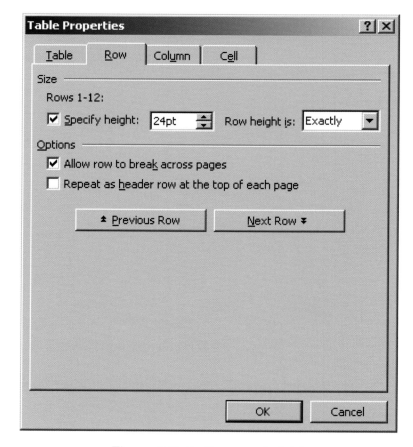

Figure 6.3: Setting row height

Merging cells and splitting the table

The invoice that we are creating from a single table contains cells of different sizes. Also, the main body of the invoice is separated from the top half containing headings and addresses etc.

▶ With the cursor in the top row click on **Table**, **Select**, **Row**.

▶ Select **Table**, **Merge Cells** to turn the whole top row into just one cell.

▶ With the cursor in the top row select the **Centre text** button, **Times New Roman 24pt Bold** and type the word *INVOICE*.

▶ In the second row, type the word *Date*: in the first cell. Set the style to **Times New Roman 14pt Bold**.

▶ Select the second and third cells and select **Table**, **Merge Cells**.

▶ Type the words *Invoice No.* in the next cell. Set the style to **Times New Roman 14pt Bold**.

▶ Merge the fifth and sixth cells in that row.

▶ With the cursor in the third row, select **Table**, **Split Table**.

You can widen the cell containing the words **Invoice no**. by dragging its right hand boundary. Similarly, you can adjust the width of the cell containing the word **Date**. At this point, your invoice should look like Figure 6.4.

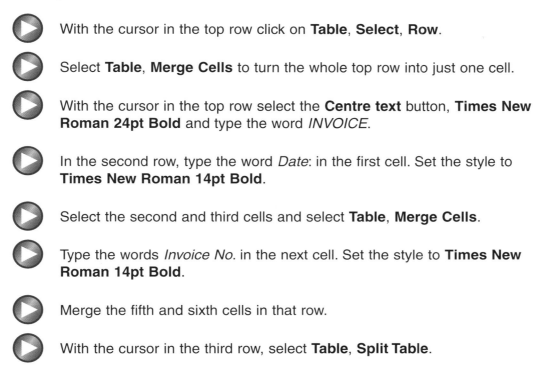

Figure 6.4: The invoice taking shape

Borders

You can customise the borders around cells or throughout the entire table. We need to remove the borders to the right of **Date** and **Invoice No.**

 Place the cursor in the cell containing **Date**, and select **Format**, **Borders and Shading**.

 In the dialogue box click on the right hand border in the diagram to remove it. Select **Cell** in the **Apply to** list box at the bottom of the window. Click **OK**.

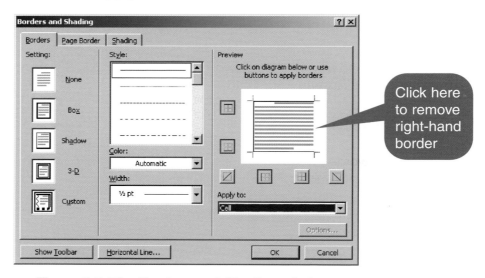

Figure 6.5: The Borders and Shading window

 Place the cursor in the cell containing the words **Invoice No.** and select **Edit**, **Repeat Borders and Shading**.

Now that you know the basics of merging cells, splitting the table, changing column widths and borders, edit your table until it looks like Figure 6.6.

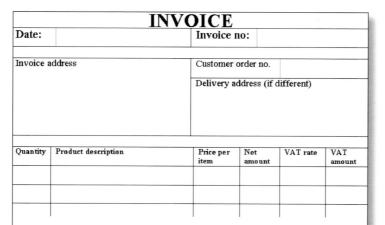

Figure 6.6

54

We're going to need a few more rows, as the bottom part of the invoice will occupy 3 rows.

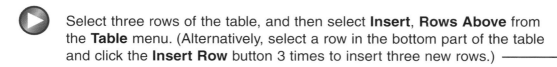 Select three rows of the table, and then select **Insert**, **Rows Above** from the **Table** menu. (Alternatively, select a row in the bottom part of the table and click the **Insert Row** button 3 times to insert three new rows.)

Changing cell text alignment

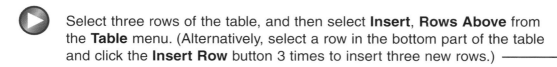 Type the text *Net Amount*, *VAT Amount*, *Carriage* and *Invoice Total* as shown in Figure 6.7.

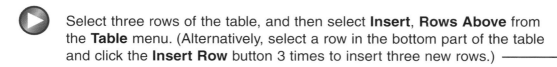 Merge the other cells in the last 3 rows and remove the borders from the left hand corner cell.

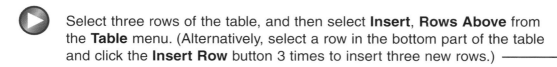 The text in the cells would look better if it was vertically centered in the cells. To do this, first select the 8 cells in the bottom right corner by dragging across them.

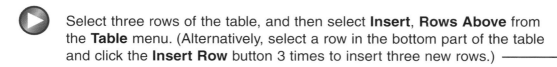 Click the right mouse button and a menu appears as shown in Figure 6.7.

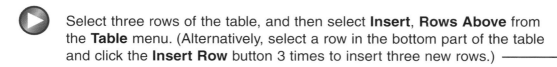 Select **Cell Alignment**, **Centre Vertically**.

Figure 6.7: Changing cell alignment

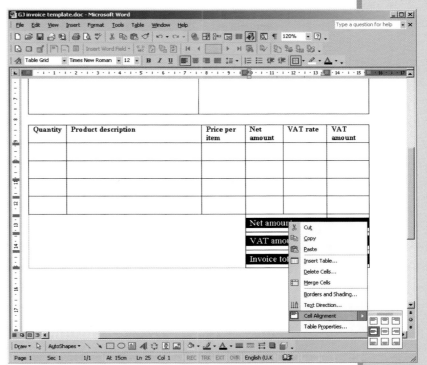

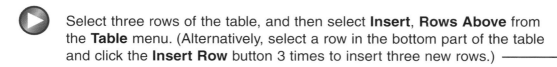 You can do the same for the rest of the table below the 'split' (i.e. starting with the row containing the headings **Quantity**, **Product Description**, etc).

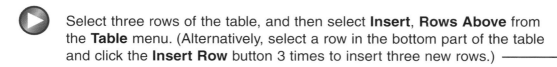 That's it – save and print your invoice!

Business cards

Many people working in organisations, especially those who come into contact with customers or people in other organisations, carry business cards. The card is printed with the company name, logo, address and so on. In addition it has the individual's name and details such as their position in the company, an e-mail address, direct telephone line and mobile phone number.

Discussion

Have you ever been given or picked up a business card? What are they used for?

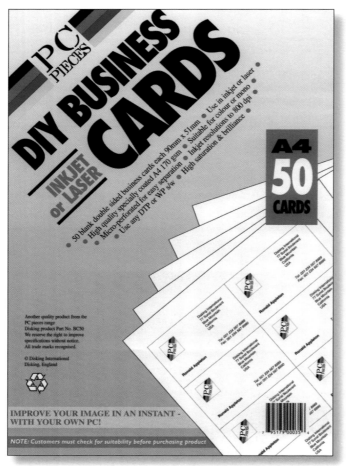

Blank perforated business stationery like that shown in Figure 6.8 is available from many outlets such as Staples. Alternatively, you can put ordinary A4 card through a laser printer and cut it carefully yourself.

In this task you'll lay out a sheet of business cards using the dimensions of the stationery shown, though of course you can vary these dimensions to suit your own needs.

Figure 6.8: Business card stationery

Open a new document and select **File**, **Page Setup**.

 Measure the margins of your chosen stationery carefully, or use the dimensions shown in Figure 6.9. Remember you cannot print right up to the edge of the page.

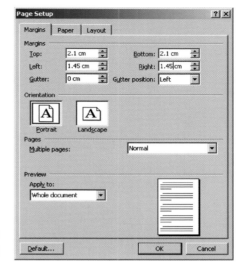

Figure 6.9: Setting margins for business cards

 Click the **Paper Size** tab and make sure that the paper size is set to A4. Click **OK**.

 Save the blank document as *BusCards.doc.*

 Measure the dimensions of the cards in your chosen stationery. In this exercise we will be getting 10 cards on the page, each 9cm by 5.1cm.

 Click **Draw** on the Drawing toolbar and select **Grid**. (If the Drawing toolbar is not displayed, select **View**, **Toolbars**, **Drawing**.)

 Set the grid to the dimensions of the business card as shown in Figure 6.10.

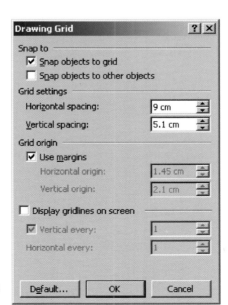

Figure 6.10: Setting the grid

▷ Make sure **Snap objects to grid** is selected and click **OK**.

▷ Use the rectangle tool to draw a box in the left hand corner of the page. It will snap to exactly the right size. This box will just be used as a guide, and will be deleted later.

▷ Select **Draw**, **Grid** again and deselect **Snap objects to Grid**. Click **OK**.

▷ Copy the company logo onto the page. Reduce the font size to about 36, and reduce the size of the text box.

▷ Right-click the text box and select **Format Text Box**. Click the **Layout** tab and choose **In front of text**. Click **OK**.

▷ Move the text box into the top left corner of the business card.

▷ Place another text box and type the address as shown in Figure 6.11.

▷ Place a third text box and type a name and position – you can type your own name instead of John Bailey's.

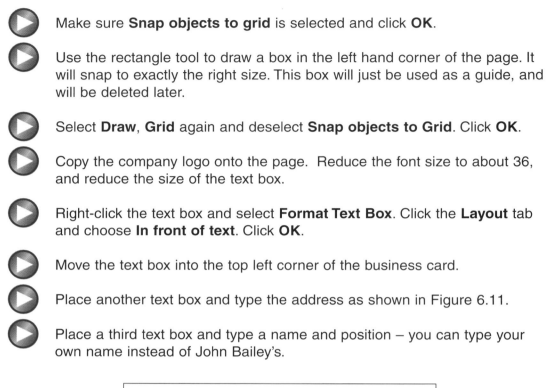

Figure 6.11: Design for a business card

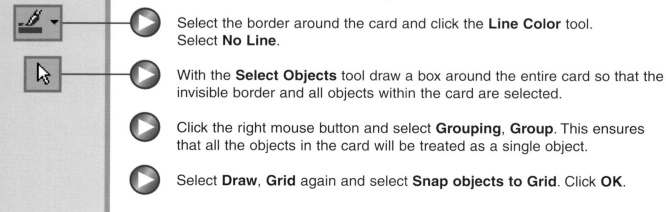

▷ Select the border around the card and click the **Line Color** tool. Select **No Line**.

▷ With the **Select Objects** tool draw a box around the entire card so that the invisible border and all objects within the card are selected.

▷ Click the right mouse button and select **Grouping**, **Group**. This ensures that all the objects in the card will be treated as a single object.

▷ Select **Draw**, **Grid** again and select **Snap objects to Grid**. Click **OK**.

Keeping the **Ctrl** key pressed and using the mouse, you can now copy the card 9 times to the rest of the page by dragging it. It will snap to the right place as soon as you are in the right area. You should end up with a sheet of 10 business cards.

 Save your document.

Set the grid back to say 0.2 before you start working on another document.

Figure 6.12: A page of business cards

Exercises

These exercises are based on the sample tasks published by Edexcel.

1. Sarah Wright is the manager of the new Westchester branch of Burgers Away!. She needs a business card.

    ● Create this business card.

    ● Print the card.

2. BurgersAway! needs a new invoice template.

    ● Create a standard customer invoice for BurgersAway!
      The company offers a discount of 5% to customers who pay their bills in full within 21 days of the invoice date. The invoice must show this information. It must also show VAT at 17.5%.

    ● Print this invoice on one A4 sheet.

Chapter 7: Relational Databases

What is a database?

A database is simply a collection of data. The data could be kept in a card index file, in a filing cabinet or on a computer. There are many software packages that allow a user to create an electronic database that holds data in a convenient way. The data can then be input, sorted, searched and reports produced.

Data in a database is held in **tables**. Some database packages such as MS Works only allow one table per database. Other packages such as MS Access allow the creation of many linked or related tables in a single database. You will soon see why this is useful.

A database for Ginger John's

In the next few chapters we will use MS Access to build a database for Ginger John's. The database is needed to hold information about each employee and the store they work in.

Using the database the management want to be able to do the following:

- Produce a report showing all the staff employed in a particular store showing their names, positions, salaries and dates of employment, and the total monthly salaries for that store, sorted by surname

- Send letters to all employees satisfying certain criteria – for example, all managers

- Produce reports from other queries, such as listing all the female employees employed before a certain date, or listing all stores in alphabetical order of town

The data that is needed is:

Employee's name, sex, date of employment, salary, position, store number and address of store.

Entities and attributes

You can probably see that if we hold all the data in one table, there is going to be a lot of data that has to be typed over and over again. If one store has 20 employees, the name and address of that store will have to be typed 20 times. It would be easy to make mistakes, and it is a waste of time typing the same data many times.

It would be better to hold the data in two separate tables, one holding the data about the employees and the other holding data about stores. The two tables can be linked using a common field.

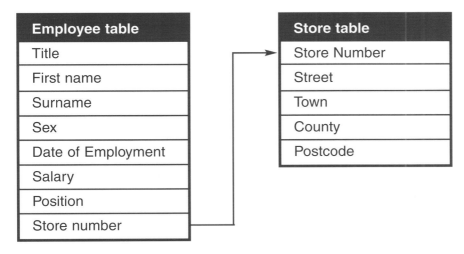

Figure 7.1: The link between employee and store

A database containing two or more tables linked together is called a **relational database**.

An **entity** is a person or thing about which data is held. Each table holds data about an entity. There are two entities in this database: **Employee** and **Store**.

An **attribute** is a piece of information about an entity. The attributes belonging to the entity **Employee** are Title, First name, Surname etc. The attributes belonging to the **Store** entity are Store Number, Street, Town etc.

Relationships

The two entities are related or linked. There are three possible types of relationship between two tables:

One-to-one   e.g. Blind person and guide dog. A blind person may have one guide dog, and the guide dog belongs to only one person.

One-to-many   e.g. Ward and patient. A ward has many patients but a patient belongs to one ward

Many-to-many   e.g. Exam and student. A student takes many exams and the same exam is taken by many students

Question

Which of these relationships applies to Store and Employee in the example above?

Chapter 7: Relational Databases

Answer

One-to-many. One store has many employees, but one employee works in just one store.

Here is the data that is to be entered into the two tables.

EMPLOYEE

Employee No	Title	First Name	Surname	Sex	Date Employed	Salary	Position	StoreID
1	Miss	Kirsty	King	F	13/04/1999	£12500	Manager	BOU01
2	Mr	Donald	Keegan	M	12/09/2001	£11000	Manager	IPS01
3	Mr	Alan	Wenlock	M	01/03/2001	£7500	Junior	IPS01
4	Mr	Tariq	Amin	M	17/06/2002	£6000	Junior	IPS01
5	Mrs	Marian	Bell	F	24/06/2000	£9500	Supervisor	IPS01
6	Miss	Janet	Oboro	F	28/10/2001	£13000	Manager	BOU02
7	Mr	David	Harris	M	28/10/2001	£6500	Junior	BOU02
8	Mr	Shane	Smith	M	20/07/2001	£8000	Supervisor	COV10
9	Miss	Brenda	Henry	F	27/02/2000	£11500	Manager	COV10
10	Miss	Helen	McGivern	F	27/03/2000	£6500	Junior	COV10
11	Mr	David	Ellery	M	20/01/2002	£9800	Supervisor	BOU02
12	Mrs	Miriam	Brown	F	20/02/2002	£6500	Junior	BOU01

STORE

StoreID	Street	Town	County	Postcode
IPS01	102 Tavern Street	Ipswich	Suffolk	IP1 5RT
BOU01	16 Cliff Rd	Bournemouth	Dorset	BH12 3YH
BOU02	15 The Square	Bournemouth	Dorset	BH1 5WP
COV10	107 Foundry Road	Coventry	W.Midlands	CV15 6DE
LON01	205 Alfred Rd	Clapham	London	SW4 6TW

Figure 7.2: The data

Primary and foreign keys

Notice that an extra field, **EmployeeNo** (standing for Employee Number), has been added to the employee table. Each table has to have one field which is unique. This field is known as the **primary key**, and it uniquely identifies a row in the table. No two rows in the EMPLOYEE table can have the same employee number.

The **primary key** of the STORE table is **StoreID**. Notice that this is the field which links the two tables, and it also appears in the EMPLOYEE table. In the EMPLOYEE table it is known as a **foreign key**.

A foreign key is defined as a field in a table which is the primary key in another table. It acts as a link between the tables.

Data types

In this chapter you will be designing and creating the tables for Ginger John's database. Before you start on this you need to understand the different data types that may be used. The table below shows the main data types used in an Access database.

Data Type	Usage	Comments
Text	Alphanumeric data, i.e. any letter, number or other symbol that you can see on the keyboard	A field can be up to 255 characters
Number	Numeric data	Can choose a whole number or a number with a decimal point. Each of these categories has several choices in Access depending on the size of the numbers you want to store – e.g. a whole number can be defined as Byte (0-255), Integer (-32,768 to 32,767) or Long Integer (for larger numbers)
Date/Time	Dates and times	You should always use a Date/Time field for a date, not a text field, because Access can calculate with dates (e.g. find how many days between 03/09/2001 and 25/12/2001) but not with text
Currency	For all monetary data	
Yes/No	True/False data	Useful when a field can take only one of two possible values such as Yes or No, True or False
AutoNumber	Often used for a key field – i.e. a field that uniquely identifies a record. No two records ever have the same key field	This is a unique value generated by Access for each record
Memo	Used for alphanumeric data	A memo field can be up to 64,000 characters

Figure 7.3: Data types

Designing the database tables

When you design your own database, you should show a design for each table which will show for each field:

Field name   This is what the field or attribute will be called. The fields have been given names *EmployeeNo*, *FirstName*, *Surname* etc. It is best not to have spaces within field names and although they can be up to 64 characters it is convenient to have fairly brief but descriptive field names.

Data type   This will be one of the types described in Figure 7.3.

Length   This will apply to text fields, and shows how many characters there are in the field. It can be shown in brackets as in Figure 7.4.

Validation rule   Validation rules are used to check that the data is allowable and sensible. Data that is not allowable or sensible should be rejected and an error message displayed. For example **Sex** can only be **M** or **F**.

Description   Fields which are not self-explanatory may be given a short description to show what data the field will store. For example **EmployeeNo** has been given the description "Number used to identify an employee".

Typical data   For each field, an example should be given of a typical value it might contain.

On the next page you will see the design for the EMPLOYEE and STORE tables.

EMPLOYEE

Field name	Data type	Validation rule	Description	Typical data
EmployeeNo*	AutoNumber	None – set by Access	Number used to identify an employee	7
Title	Text (6)	None – any value possible	Mr, Mrs, etc	Mrs
FirstName	Text (20)	None – any value possible	First name of employee	Gerri
Surname	Text (20)	None – any value possible	Surname of employee	Button
Sex	Text (1)	Must be M or F	Male or Female	F
DateEmployed	Date	Must be a valid date	Date first started work	13/05/2001
Salary	Currency	Must be between £1,000 and £50,000		£12,500
Position	Text (20)	None – any value possible		Cleaner
StoreID	Text (5)	Must be on Store table	Code used to identify store	IPS01

STORE

Field name	Data type	Validation rule	Description	Typical data
StoreID*	Text (5)	3 letters followed by 2 digits	Code used to identify a store	IPS01
Street	Text (30)	None – any value possible	Street address	16 Cliff Rd
Town	Text (20)	None – any value possible		Bournemouth
County	Text (20)	None – any value possible		Dorset
Postcode	Text (8)	None – any value possible		BH12 5WP

* = Primary key

Figure 7.4: Table design

Exercises

1. A school database is to be constructed to help the school keep track of who has been entered for each examination. Each student may be entered for several examinations.

   a) Name two entities in the database. Suggest a primary key for each entity.

   b) What is the relationship between the two entities?

2. A hospital database is to hold details of which patients and which nursing staff are assigned to each ward. Each nurse may be assigned to a single ward, but each ward may have several nurses. A patient is assigned to a single ward.

   a) What is the relationship between WARD and PATIENT?

   b) Name a third entity in this database.

   c) Suggest 3 fields for the table WARD and 5 fields for the table PATIENT. Include a foreign key in one of the tables. Which of the fields is the foreign key?

3. A Sports Competition database is created showing all the competitors and events, and who entered which event. Some of the data is shown below.

COMPETITOR

CompetitorID	Surname	Firstname	DateofBirth	Sex
1	Grand	Jane	01/04/84	F
2	Keino	Michael	14/02/85	M
3	Dowsett	Robert	12/04/84	M
4	Perez	Juanita	31/07/85	F

EVENT

EventID	EventName	Mens/Womens
1	Long Jump	M
2	Long Jump	W
3	100M	M
4	100M	W
5	100M Hurdles	M

EVENT-ENTRY

EventID	CompetitorID

Michael Keino entered Long Jump and 100M Hurdles.

Robert Dowsett entered the 100M race.

Jane Grand and Juanita Perez entered the 100M race.

Fill in the data in table EVENT-ENTRY.

Chapter 8: Creating Database Tables

A new Access database

In this chapter you will use MS Access to create the two tables EMPLOYEE and STORE designed in Chapter 7.

 Load Access by double-clicking its icon in the Desktop window or by clicking the **Start** button, clicking **Programs** and selecting **Microsoft Access**. ————————————————————————

 Select **Blank Database** to open a new database.

A window opens asking you to choose a folder and a name for your new database. Select an appropriate folder and name the database *GJ*. Access will automatically add the extension **.mdb**. Click **OK**.

The database window

Access databases are made up of **objects**. A **table** is an object, and is the only object we have talked about so far. Other objects, which you will come across in this book, include **Queries**, **Forms** and **Reports**.

Every Access Database has a Database window. This is a sort of central menu for your database, from which you can open the objects in your database. The window has buttons for each type of database object (Tables, Queries, Forms, Reports, etc.).

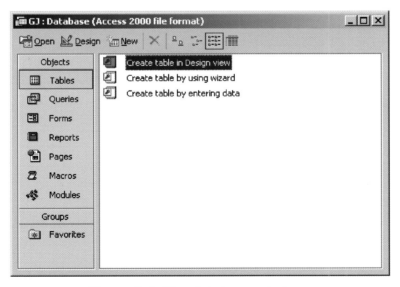

Figure 8.1: The database window

Tables is currently selected, and since at the moment there are no existing tables to Open or Design, only the Create options are active.

Creating a new table

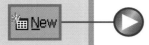

 In the Database window make sure the **Tables** tab is selected, and press **New**.

Figure 8.2: Creating a new table

 Select **Design View** and click **OK**.

Look back at the structure of the **EMPLOYEE** table in Figure 7.4. All these fields need to be entered in the new table.

 Enter the first field, **EmployeeNo**, and tab to the **Data Type** column.

 Click the down arrow and select the field type **AutoNumber**.

 Tab to the **Description** column and type *Number used to identify an employee*.

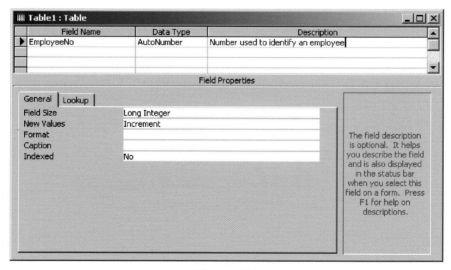

Figure 8.3

Defining the primary key

Every table in an Access database must have a primary key (also known as the key field). The field which you specify for the primary key must have a different value for each record.

 With the cursor still in the row for **EmployeeNo**, press the **Primary Key** — icon on the toolbar. The key symbol appears in the left-hand margin next to **EmployeeNo**.

Entering other fields

Now we can enter all the other fields. Don't worry if you make a few mistakes – after all the fields are entered you can move fields around, delete them or insert new fields. You can correct any mistakes at that point, and it'll be good practice.

Enter the field name **Title** in the next row. Tab to the **Data Type** column and the default is **Text**, which is fine. Enter *6* in the **Field Size** property.

Enter the field name **Firstname** in the next row, data type **Text** and field size **20**.

Enter the field name **Surname**, data type **Text** and field size **20**.

Enter the other fields, giving them all the correct data type and length.

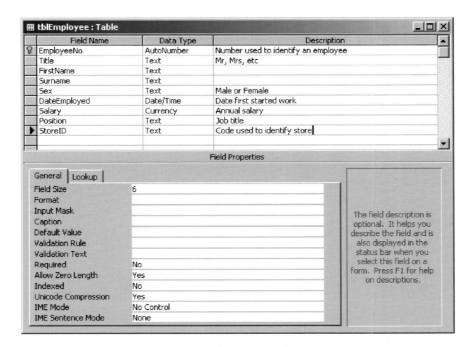

Figure 8.4: The EMPLOYEE table

Saving the table structure

 Save the table structure by pressing the **Save** button or selecting **File**, **Save** from the menu bar. Don't worry if you have made some mistakes in the table structure – they can be corrected in a minute.

> You will be asked to type a name for your table. Type the name *tblEmployee* and click **OK**.

> Click the **Close** icon (**X**) in the top right hand corner to close the window. You will be returned to the database window.

Editing a table structure

In the Database window you will see that your new table is now listed.

Select the table name, click the **Design View** button and you are returned to Design View.

Inserting a field

To insert a new row for **Initial** just above **Surname**:

> Click the row selector (the left hand margin) for **Surname**.

> Press the **Insert** key on the keyboard or click the **Insert Rows** button on the toolbar. Enter the new field name, *Initial*, data type **Text**.

Deleting a field

To delete the field you have just inserted:

> Select the field by clicking in its row selector. Press the **Delete** key on the keyboard or click the **Delete Rows** button on the toolbar.

> If you make a mistake, you can use **Edit**, **Undo Delete** to restore the field.

Moving a field

> Click the row selector to the left of the field's name to select the field.

> Click again and drag to where you want the field to be. You will see a line appear between fields as you drag over them to indicate where the field will be placed.

Changing or removing a key field

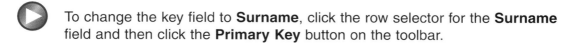 To change the key field to **Surname**, click the row selector for the **Surname** field and then click the **Primary Key** button on the toolbar.

 To remove the primary key altogether, select the row that is currently the key field and click the **Primary Key** button on the toolbar.

 Sometimes a primary key is made up of more than one field (a *composite* or *compound key*). Select the first field, hold down **Ctrl** and select the second field. Then click the **Primary Key** button. ─────────────

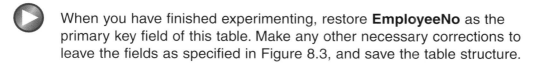 When you have finished experimenting, restore **EmployeeNo** as the primary key field of this table. Make any other necessary corrections to leave the fields as specified in Figure 8.3, and save the table structure.

Validation rules

First create the **STORE** table in the same way. Save it, naming it *tblStore* but do not close it.

Access allows you to add two types of validation. The first of these is an **Input Mask**. This specifies the format of the data – e.g. a date in a particular format or a car registration number in the format AB 123 DEF. You can get more information on Input Masks from the Access online Help system.

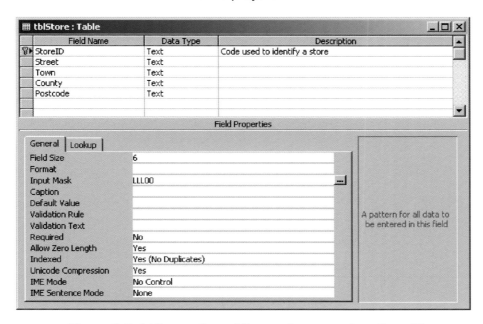

Figure 8.5: tblStore after adding an input mask to StoreID

Tip:
Where possible, it is a good idea to enter **validation rules** and/or **input masks** to your table structure. This helps to ensure that the user does not accidentally enter wrong data.

Now add an Input Mask to the **StoreID** field as shown in Figure 8.5 to make sure that the user enters a store ID of 3 letters followed by 2 numbers.

▶ Click in the row for **StoreID**. In the Field Properties box, enter *LLL00* in the *Input Mask* row.

Note: ***L*** *means that only a letter can be entered in that position.* ***0*** *(that's zero, not o) means that only a digit can be entered.*

▶ Save and close this table. We'll add some **validation rules** to fields in **tblEmployee**.

▶ In the Database window select **tblEmployee** and click **Design** to open the table in Design view.

▶ Click in the **Sex** row and in the Table Properties box, enter *M or F* in the **Validation Rule** row. Access will add quote marks automatically.

▶ Enter *Must be M or F* in the **Validation Text**.

▶ Click in the **Salary** row and enter *Between 1000 and 50000* as the validation rule. Type validation text as shown below.

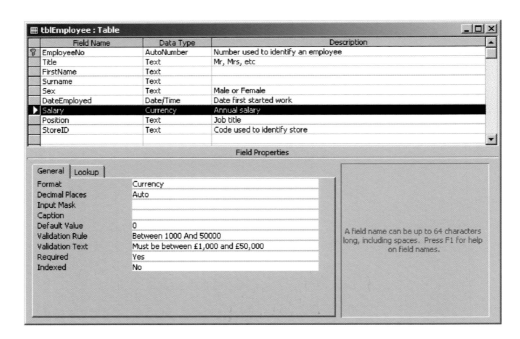

Figure 8.6: Adding validation rules to tblEmployee

▶ Save and close the table.

Creating relationships

We need to create the one-to-many relationship between **tblStore** and **tblEmployee**. We can then ensure that the store ID entered for an employee is a valid ID that already exists on **tblStore**. (This is another of the validations specified in Figure 7.4.)

 Close any tables that you have open to return to the Database window.

 Click the **Relationships** button on the toolbar or select **Tools, Relationships** from the menu.

The following window opens. Select both tables by holding down **Ctrl** while you click each in turn.

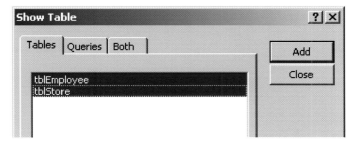

Figure 8.7

 Click **Add** and then **Close**.

The Relationships window opens as shown in Figure 8.8.

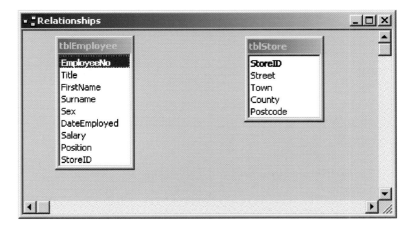

Figure 8.8: The Relationships window

Tip:
You can drag the tables around and enlarge them so that all the fields are shown on each table.

Create the relationship by dragging the primary key field **StoreID** from **tblStore** to the foreign key field **StoreID** in **tblEmployee**.

A new window opens as shown in Figure 8.9. Click the **Enforce Referential Integrity** button.

Enforcing referential integrity means that you will not be able to enter a record for a non-existent store in **tblEmployee**. The database will first check that there is a corresponding record in the correct table.

If you choose to tick **Cascade Delete Related Records**, this means that you will be able to delete a Store record and any related records in **tblEmployee** will automatically be deleted. Leave this unchecked, as we are will not want to delete Employee records just because a store closes down. Leave **Cascade Update Related Fields** unchecked too.

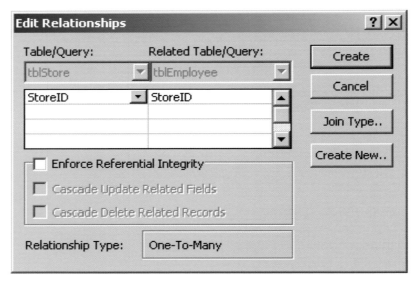

Figure 8.9: Creating a one-to-many relationship
*between **tblStore** and **tblEmployee***

 Click **Create**.

 Close the window, answering **Yes** when asked if you wish to save. Congratulations! You have laid the foundations of the Ginger John's database.

 Save and close the window and the database.

Chapter 9: Data Entry

Datasheet view

There are two ways to enter data in Access: one is to enter data into a table in Datasheet view, and the other way is to use a specially created form for data entry. We will start by looking at Datasheet view.

 Open the GJ database and in the Database window, double-click **tblStore**.

 Enter the first 4 records for this table as shown in Figure 9.1.

		StoreID	Street	Town	County	Postcode
	+	BOU01	16 Cliff Road	Bournemouth	Dorset	BH12 3YH
	+	BOU02	15 The Square	Bournemouth	Dorset	BH1 5WP
▶	+	COV10	107 Foundry Road	Coventry	W Midlands	CV15 6DE
	+	IPS01	102 Tavern Street	Ipswich	Suffolk	IP1 5RT
*						

Record: |◀ ◀ | 3 | ▶ |▶| |▶*| of 4

Figure 9.1: Entering data in Datasheet view

Note that you can look at the structure of the table and edit if necessary by pressing the **View** button on the toolbar.

 Try entering a **StoreID** of **IP0001**. You will find you cannot, because of the input mask which requires 3 letters and 2 digits. Press **Esc** to abandon the record.

 Save and close this table.

A more finished-looking user interface can be created by designing a special form for data entry. The user can then use this form to enter records, though they can still enter and edit records in Datasheet view if they prefer.

Creating a data entry form

The easiest way to create a data entry form is to use a wizard.

 In the Database window click the **Forms** tab on the left hand side of the window.

 Click the **New** button.

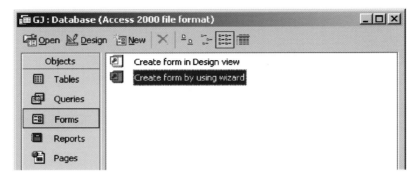

Figure 9.2: Preparing to create a form

A window appears as shown in Figure 9.3.

 Select **Autoform: Columnar**.

 In the list box at the bottom of the screen select **tblEmployee**.

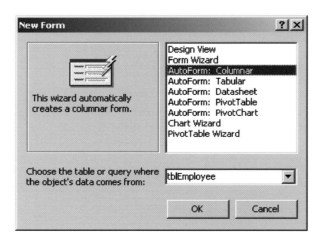

Figure 9.3: Creating a new form for tblEmployee

 Click **OK**.

A new form is automatically created, and can be used for entering data.

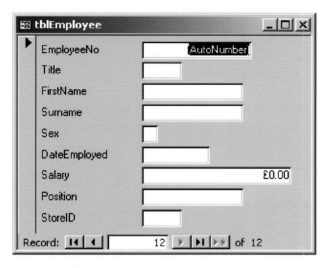

Figure 9.4: The data entry form created by the wizard

Customising the data entry form

We could improve the form by adding a heading, putting some of the fields side-by-side, and making the **Salary** field shorter. We could also edit some of the field labels.

 Click the **View** button on the toolbar to switch to Design view. ————

 Enlarge the window so that you can see the edges of the form. Drag the right-hand side of the form to make it wider.

 Drag the top edge of the Detail section down to open a space for **the Form Header** section. We will put a heading in there.

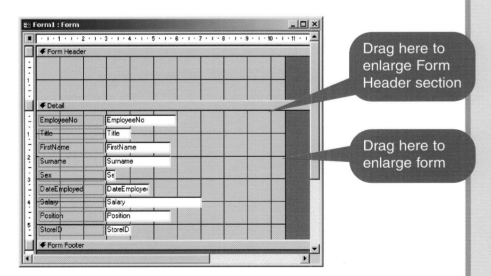

Figure 9.5: The form in Design view

Inserting a label

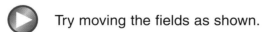

▶ Click the **Label** tool and drag out a rectangle in the Header section. Type the text *Employees* in the box.

▶ Click the edge of the box to select it. Change the font to size **24**, **Arial**, **Bold**. Centre it and make it blue or some other colour. You can make the **Fill** colour transparent or select a colour.

▶ Switch to Form view to see what it looks like, and adjust it if you are not happy.

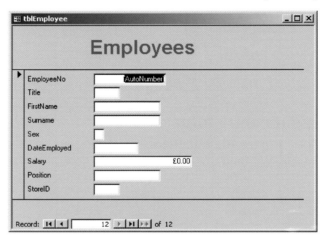

Figure 9.6: Form heading added

Moving the fields around

You can drag a field and its label to another place on the form. To drag a field, click in the field and hold down the mouse button, and the cursor will change to a hand. Drag to the new position.

▶ Try moving the fields as shown.

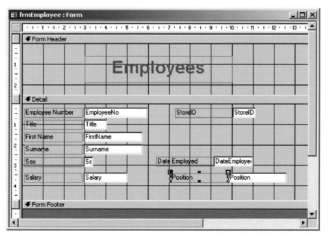

Figure 9.7: Moving fields around

Lining fields up

The form would look neater if **StoreID**, **DateEmployed** and **Position** were lined up.

 Hold down the left mouse button while you drag around the three fields. This is called "lassoing" them. You don't have to completely surround them to select them.

 From the **Format** menu select **Align**, **Left**. They should line up neatly.

Editing labels

You could add spaces to some of the labels like **DateEmployed** and **FirstName**.

 Click the label and click again where you want to insert a space. Press the **Spacebar**.

 Change the label **EmployeeNo** to **Employee Number**.

Changing form properties

The form and every field and label (called controls) on the form have numerous properties which you can change.

 To display the form property box, double-click the small square at the intersection of the ruler lines.

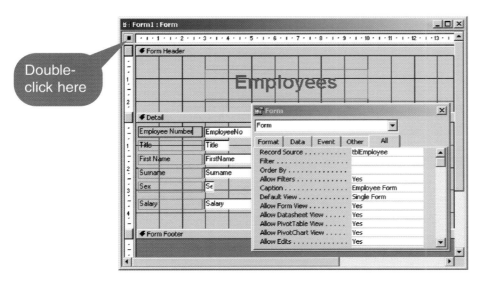

Figure 9.8: Displaying Form properties

 Change the **Caption** property to *Employee Form*. This is displayed at the top of the form in Form View.

Click the **Form View** button to check your change.

Changing the Tab order

 Try tabbing through the fields in the form. You will notice that the last field visited is **StoreID**. It would be better if this was visited second.

 From the **View** menu select **Tab Order**. This brings up a window as shown below.

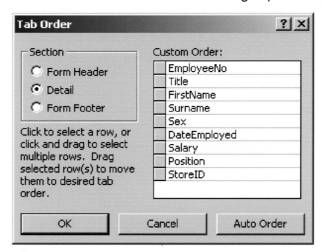

Figure 9.9: Changing the Tab order

 Select the row containing **StoreID** by clicking in the selection box to the left of the name. Then click and drag to just under **EmployeeNo.** Press **OK**.

 Now test your form again.

 Save the form when you are satisfied, naming it *frmEmployee.* You are ready to enter some data.

Using the Data Entry form

 In Form View, enter the data shown in Figure 7.2. Try entering some invalid data for the fields where you have set validations. You should see an error message displayed.

Note that you can always abandon a record by pressing **Esc**.

Exercise

Create a data entry form for **tblStore**, and name it *frmStore*. Use the form to enter the data for the Alfred Road store (LON01) shown in Figure 7.2. (Enter the other four records as well if you have not already done so.)

Making queries

Look back at the beginning of Chapter 7, where there is a list of things we would like to do with a database. They all involve finding records which satisfy certain criteria, for example all staff in a particular store, all managers, etc.

To find this information we need to **query** the database.

 Open the **GJ.mdb** database.

 In the Database window click the **Queries** tab.

Figure 10.1

 Click **New**.

 In the New Query window, click **Design View** and click **OK**.

 In the Show Table window hold down **Shift** while you select both tables.

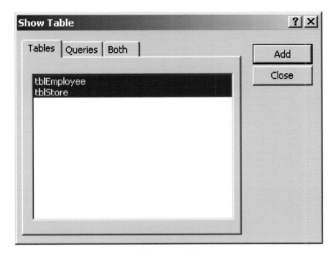

Figure 10.2

 Click **Add** and then **Close**.

The Query window opens. We will design a query that shows all the staff working in the store with StoreID **IPS01**. We will show the Employee number, title, first name, surname, position, salary, date of employment, StoreID and town.

▶ You can enlarge each of the table panes so that all the fields are visible.

▶ Double-click each of the above fields in turn to put them on the Query grid.

▶ You can adjust column widths by double-clicking between column headers.

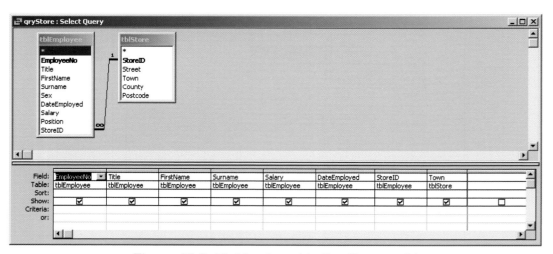

Figure 10.3: Fields placed in the Query grid

▶ In the Criteria row for StoreID, enter *IPS01*.

▶ Save the query as **qryStore**.

▶ Click the **Run Query** button to run this query.

The query results will be displayed in a table:

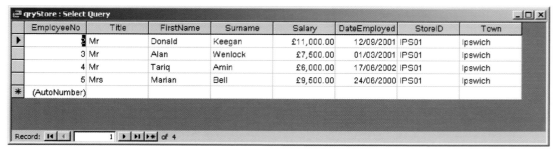

Figure 10.4: Query results

Sorting records

 To sort the records, first return to Design view by clicking the **Design View** button.

 In the **Sort** row click in the **Surname** column and select **Ascending**.

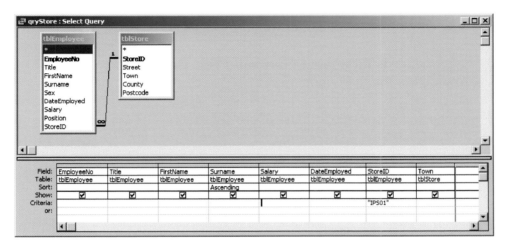

Figure 10.5

Now try running the query again. The records will be sorted in order of surname.

	EmployeeNo	Title	FirstName	Surname	Salary	DateEmployed	StoreID	Town
▶	4	Mr	Tariq	Amin	£6,000.00	17/06/2002	IPS01	Ipswich
	5	Mrs	Marian	Bell	£9,500.00	24/06/2000	IPS01	Ipswich
	2	Mr	Donald	Keegan	£11,000.00	12/09/2001	IPS01	Ipswich
	3	Mr	Alan	Wenlock	£7,500.00	01/03/2001	IPS01	Ipswich
*	(AutoNumber)							

Record: ◄◄ ◄ 1 ► ►◄ ►* of 4

Figure 10.6: Records sorted by Surname field

 Save and close the query.

Multiple criteria

In the example above we asked Access to display only people working in a particular store. In other words, we *set the criterion.* that StoreID had to be IPS01.

We can set more than one criterion. For example, we could specify that we want to find employees whose Sex is Female AND whose DateEmployed is before a given date. This is called *setting multiple criteria*.

Setting multiple criteria

Now we'll create a query to find all female employees employed before Jan 01 2001, sorted by Store ID.

▶ In the Database window click **Create Query in Design view** and click **New**. Click **OK**.

▶ Add both tables to the query window as before.

▶ Drag the fields **Firstname**, **Surname**, **Sex**, **DateEmployed**, **StoreID** and **Town** on to the query grid.

▶ Uncheck the **Show** box in the **StoreID** column. Set the criteria as shown below. Click **Sort Ascending** in the **StoreID** column.

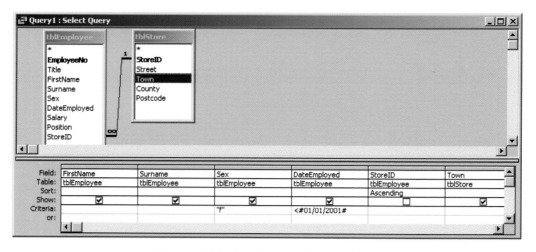

Figure 10.7: Setting multiple criteria

The query results will be displayed as shown below:

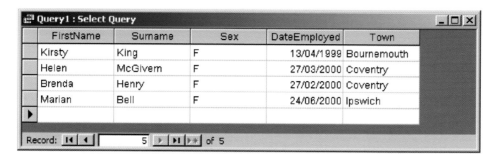

Figure 10.8: Query results

Save the Query as *qryFemales* and close it.

 Now design and save a query called **qryManager** which returns only Managers. It should show **Title**, **Firstname**, **Surname**, **Position** and **StoreID** from **tblEmployee**, and all the fields except **StoreID** from **tblStore**. You will need this query to do a mail merge.

Sorting a table

You can sort a table in Datasheet view.

 In the Database window click the **Tables** tab.

 Double-click **tblEmployee** to open it.

 Click anywhere in the **Surname** column, and click the **Sort Ascending** button.

The records will be sorted in order of surname.

Title	FirstName	Surname	Sex	DateEmployed	Salary	Position	StoreID
Mr	Tariq	Amin	M	17/06/2002	£6,000.00	Junior	IPS01
Mrs	Marian	Bell	F	24/06/2000	£9,500.00	Supervisor	IPS01
Mr	David	Ellery	M	20/01/2002	£9,800.00	Supervisor	BOU02
Mr	David	Harris	M	28/10/2001	£6,500.00	Junior	BOU02
Miss	Brenda	Henry	F	27/02/2000	£11,500.00	Manager	COV10
Mr	Donald	Keegan	M	12/09/2001	£11,000.00	Manager	IPS01
Miss	Kirsty	King	F	13/04/1999	£12,500.00	Manager	BOU01
Miss	Helen	McGivern	F	27/03/2000	£6,500.00	Junior	COV10
Miss	Janet	Oboro	F	28/10/2001	£13,000.00	Manager	BOU02
Mr	Shane	Smith	M	20/07/2001	£8,000.00	Supervisor	BOU02
Mr	Alan	Wenlock	M	01/03/2001	£7,500.00	Junior	IPS01
*					£0.00		

Record: ◄◄ ◄ | 1 | ► ►◄ ►* of 11

Figure 10.9: Sorting records in Datasheet view

 Close the file and close MS Access.

Chapter 11: Reports

When are reports used?

Reports are used when hard copy is required – a printed listing rather than just a screen display. Using a database, it is often convenient to input or look up information using an input form, but forms are not suitable for printed output. They are not the right shape, for one thing, and are often coloured. What is needed is a report.

Looking back to the beginning of Chapter 7, you will recall that we need a report of all staff in a particular store showing name, position, salary and date of employment. The total of all salaries for that store is also to be displayed.

The report that we design will be based on a query. In the last chapter we saved a query called **qryStore** which showed this information for a given store. This will be used as the source for the report.

Using the Report wizard

 Open the **GJ** database.

 Click the Reports tab and double-click **Create report by using wizard**.

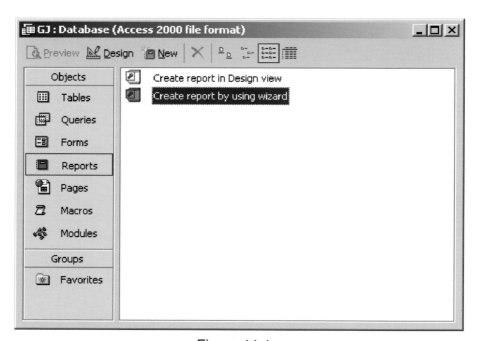

Figure 11.1

 In the next dialogue box make sure that **qryStore** is selected in the **Tables/Queries** box.

Click the double arrow between the **Available Fields** and the **Selected Fields** boxes to move all the fields over to the **Selected fields** box.

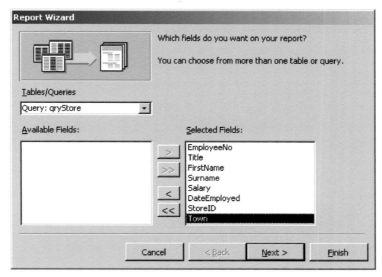

Figure 11.2: selecting the source and fields for the report

 Click **Next**.

Leave **tblEmployee** selected in the next window, and click **Next**.

In the next dialogue box, which asks if you wish to add any grouping levels, select **StoreID**, and click the arrow between the boxes. We are adding a grouping level so that the total of the salaries for that store will be calculated.

 Click **Next**.

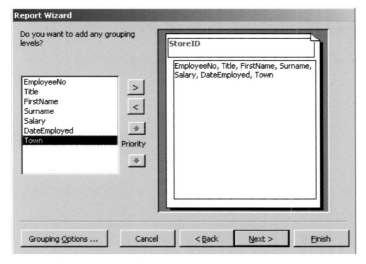

Figure 11.3: Selecting a grouping level

In the next dialogue box, select **Surname** as the first **Sort** field and click the **Summary Options** button.

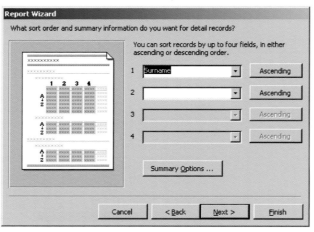

Figure 11.4

In the Summary Options dialogue box check **Sum**.

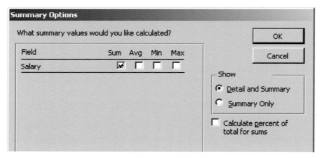

Figure 11.5

Click **OK**, and **Next** in the box shown in Figure 11.4.

Select **Landscape** in the next dialogue box. Click **Next**.

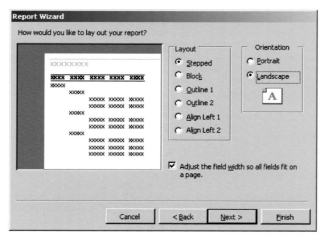

Figure 11.6

Select a style for your report. I have chosen **Soft Gray**. Click **Next**.

 Type the title *Store Salaries Report* in the next dialogue box and click **Finish**.

The report will appear as shown in Figure 11.7.

Store Salaries Report

StoreID	Surname	EmployeeNo	Title	FirstName	Salary	DateEmployed	Town
IPS01							
	Amin	4	Mr	Tariq	£6,000.00	17/06/2002	Ipswich
	Bell	5	Mrs	Marian	£9,500.00	24/06/2000	Ipswich
	Keegan	2	Mr	Donald	£11,000.00	12/09/2001	Ipswich
	Wenlock	3	Mr	Alan	£7,500.00	01/03/2001	Ipswich

Summary for 'StoreID' = IPS01 (4 detail records)
Sum £34,000.00
Grand Total **£34,000.00**

Figure 11.7: The Store report

Customising the report

You can make changes to the report in Design view. Fields and their labels can be moved or cut and pasted to another section of the report.

 Change to **Design View** by clicking the **View** button.

The report will appear as shown in Figure 11.8.

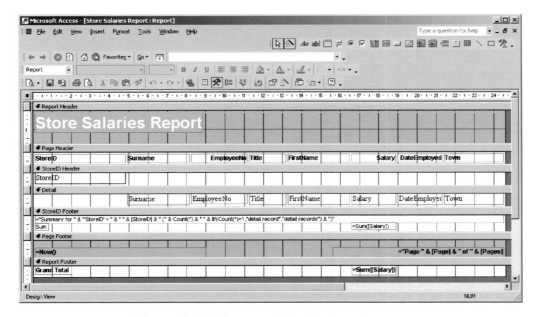

Figure 11.8: The report in Design view

You can select a field and its heading by holding down **Shift** as you select each item.

 Make the **StoreID** label and field narrower.

 Insert a space in the label **Date Employed**, but leave the field name as it is.

Check your results in **Print Preview** mode.

Exercises

1. Display in a report the results of the query which found all female employees employed before January 01 2001. The report should have a suitable heading and date.

2. Name 5 organisations that use databases to hold information. For each of the organisations you name, describe briefly

   - the information they need to hold

   - a search they might need to do to find information

   - a report they might need to print.

Chapter 12: Mail Merge

Performing a mail merge

You can merge data from an Access database into a standard letter to create personalised letters to a group of people, for example the store managers. We need to merge the information collected by the query **qryManager** into a letter which we will create in Word.

Unfortunately the process is somewhat different depending on which version of Word you are using. This chapter describes how to do a mail merge using Word 2002.

 In Word, open the document **GJ Letter Template.doc**. (If you have not got this document, open a new document.)

 Save the document as **Letter to Managers**.

 From the **Tools** menu select **Letters and Mailings**, **Mail Merge wizard**.

The Mail Merge task pane opens on the right of the screen.

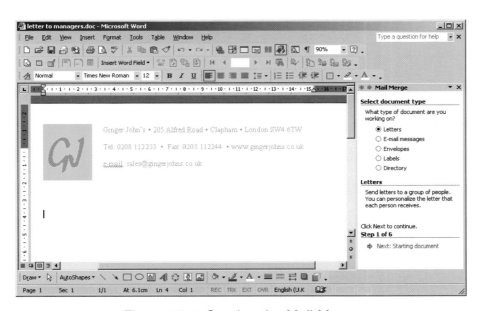

Figure 12.1: Starting the Mail Merge

 At the bottom of the Task pane click **Next: Starting document**.

 Click **Next: Select Recipients**.

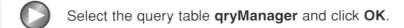 Select **Browse** and locate the database **GJ.mdb** in the folder where you saved it.

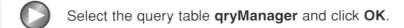 Select the query table **qryManager** and click **OK**.

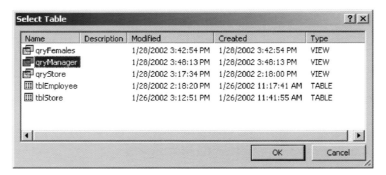

Figure 12.2: Specifying the data source

You will see the data displayed.

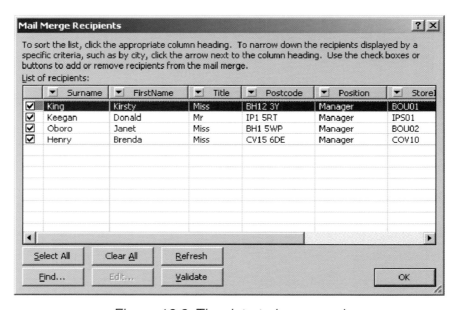

Figure 12.3: The data to be merged

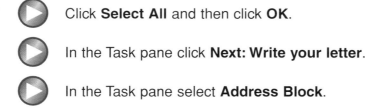 Click **Select All** and then click **OK**.

In the Task pane click **Next: Write your letter**.

In the Task pane select **Address Block**.

▶ In the Insert Address Block window, click **Match fields.**
Specify fields as shown.

Figure 12.4

▶ Click **OK**, and **OK** again. Leave a space below the address block.

▶ Now insert the **Greeting** line in a similar way.

▶ Press **Enter**, and write a short letter inviting managers to a Team
Building weekend.

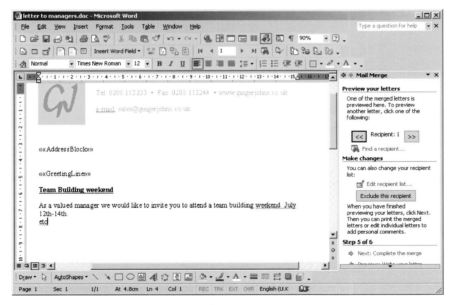

Figure 12.5

▶ In the Task pane click **Next: Preview your letters**.

You can click the **Next Record** button in the toolbar to scroll through the records.

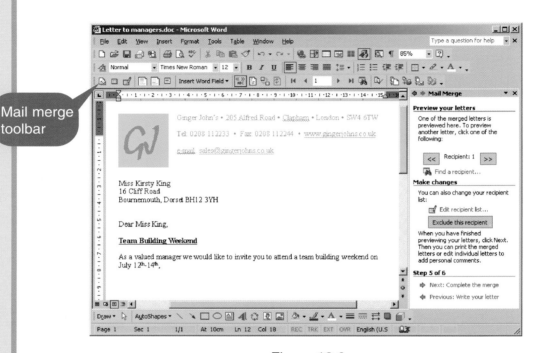

Figure 12.6

You can print out one of the sample letters. (Don't print them all out – it's a waste of paper!) To do this:

 From the **File** menu select **Print**. In the Print dialogue box specify **Current Page**.

 You can switch between the letter showing the fields, and the letter showing the actual names and addresses, by pressing the **View Merged Data** button.

 Save and close your letter.

Exercise

Write a personalised letter from the Managing Director of Ginger John's to all employees of the Ipswich store informing them that the store will be extended and refurbished at the beginning of July.

Chapter 13: Introduction to Spreadsheets

Spreadsheets are used for organising and analysing numerical information. Imagine that you are in charge of planning a ski holiday with a group of friends. You have chosen your destination, and now have to choose the method of travel, accommodation, ski lift passes/lessons etc. to fit within each person's budget. A Microsoft Excel spreadsheet model will help you to do this.

Introducing Excel

Excel is one of a number of powerful spreadsheet packages. Excel files are known as **workbooks**, with each workbook consisting of one or more **worksheets**. A worksheet is like a page from an accountant's ledger, divided into rows and columns which you can fill with text, numbers and formulae.

(The term **spreadsheet** is used rather loosely nowadays to mean either a worksheet or a workbook.)

Tip:
This chapter assumes you are familiar with MS Excel. If you have not done any work on spreadsheets before, you need to start with a book such as **Basic Excel 2000** by P.M.Heathcote, published by Payne-Gallway.

 Start Excel by clicking the Excel icon in the Office toolbar, double-clicking the Excel icon on the desktop or selecting **Start**, **Programs**, **Microsoft Excel**.

Excel will open a new workbook. By default the workbook has 3 worksheets, and the Sheet tab at the bottom of the workbook shows that **Sheet1** is currently displayed.

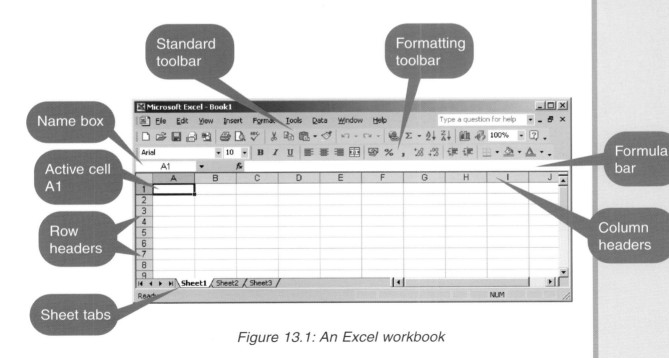

Figure 13.1: An Excel workbook

Moving round the worksheet

When you open a new workbook, **Sheet1** is displayed with cell **A1** highlighted. Cells are named according to the row and column they are in; cell C6 is thus at the intersection of Column C, Row 6. The cell with the heavy border around it is the **active cell** (A1 in Figure 13.1). If you start typing, anything you type will appear in the active cell, and also in the Formula bar.

You can move around the worksheet to make a cell active in any of these ways:

- Use the mouse to click in the cell you want.

- Use one of the arrow keys to go up, down, left or right.

- Use the **Page Up** or **Page Down** keys.

- Press **Ctrl-G** or select **Edit**, **Go To** from the menu and type in the cell reference to go to. Try going to cell **AH2000**.

- Press **Ctrl-Home** to return to A1.

As you can see, the spreadsheet is much larger than the portion of it that you can see on the screen. You can also use the scroll bars to move around the spreadsheet.

 Press **Ctrl-Right Arrow**, and then **Ctrl-Down Arrow** to get to the last cell in the spreadsheet. What is its cell reference?

Entering and copying text, numbers and formulae

To start with, you will create a spreadsheet set out like Figure 13.2.

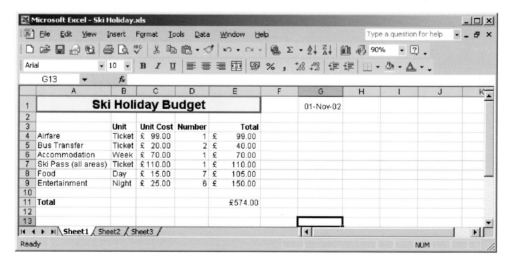

Figure 13.2: A budget spreadsheet

With the cursor in cell A1, type the heading *Ski Holiday Budget*. Press **Enter**.

Double-click between the column headers A and B to autosize column A so that the heading fits in cell A1.

Use the mouse or the arrow keys to move to cell B3.

Enter the other text and numbers as shown in Figure 13.3. Notice that text labels are automatically left-justified, while numbers are automatically right-justified.

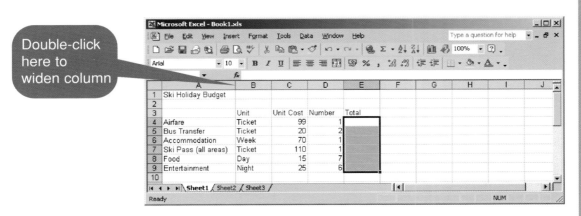

Figure 13.3: Entering budget data

Entering formulae

The real power of a spreadsheet lies in its ability to calculate the results of formulae which reference other cells in the workbook. The following mathematical symbols are used:

+	(add)
-	(subtract)
*	(multiply)
/	(divide)
()	(brackets)

 In cell E4, enter the formula =C4*D4 and press **Enter**. (You can use either uppercase or lowercase letters, but you must start the formula with the = sign to tell Excel that this is a formula and not a label.) The answer, 99, appears in the cell.

Try another way of entering a formula. In cell E5, type =, and then click in cell C5. Type * and then click in cell D5. Press **Enter**.

Tip:

This technique is called *entering a formula by pointing*. It has the great advantage that you are less likely to enter the wrong cell reference by mistake.

Copying and pasting cells

There are several ways to copy and paste cell contents in Excel. One of the quickest and easiest is to use the **Fill handle**.

 Click in cell E5.

 Drag the small handle in the bottom right hand corner down to cell E9. The formula is copied to cells E6 to E9, adjusting automatically to reference cells in the correct row.

 Click in cell E9 and take a look at the Formula bar, which shows that the formula in that cell is **C9*D9**.

 Try a different way of copying cells. We will copy the budget to cells starting in A12.

 Drag across from cell A1 to E9 to select all these cells. Either click the **Copy** button, select **Edit**, **Copy** from the menu, or right-click and select **Copy**. A moving dotted border appears around the selected cells.

 Right-click in cell A12 and select **Paste**. All the cells are copied.

Now your spreadsheet should look like this:

	A	B	C	D	E	F	G	H	I	J
	A12		Ski Holiday Budget							
1	Ski Holiday Budget									
2										
3		Unit	Unit Cost	Number	Total					
4	Airfare	Ticket	99	1	99					
5	Bus Transfer	Ticket	20	2	40					
6	Accommodation	Week	70	1	70					
7	Ski Pass (all areas)	Ticket	110	1	110					
8	Food	Day	15	7	105					
9	Entertainment	Night	25	6	150					
10										
11										
12	Ski Holiday Budget									
13										
14		Unit	Unit Cost	Number	Total					
15	Airfare	Ticket	99	1	99					
16	Bus Transfer	Ticket	20	2	40					
17	Accommodation	Week	70	1	70					
18	Ski Pass (all areas)	Ticket	110	1	110					
19	Food	Day	15	7	105					
20	Entertainment	Night	25	6	150					
21										

Sheet1 / Sheet2 / Sheet3 /

Figure 13.4: Formulae entered and range copied

Saving a workbook

You should save your workbook before you do any more work on it.

 Click the **Save** icon or select **File**, **Save** from the menu. —————————

By default the workbook will be named **Book1** and saved in the **My Documents** folder.

You need to have an appropriate folder in which to store all your work. If you have not got one, you can click the button as shown in Figure 13.5 to create one. Alternatively, you may be saving your work on a floppy disk, in which case you should select **A:** instead of **My Documents** in the list box.

 Name the workbook *Ski Holiday*. Excel gives it the extension *.xls*.

 Click **Save**.

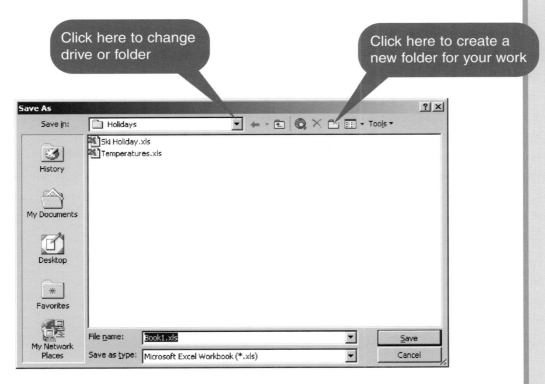

Figure 13.5: Saving your workbook

Formatting the worksheet

You should have the workbook **Ski Holiday.xls** open to continue with this exercise.

Adjusting column widths

You have already seen that by double-clicking the right-hand border of a column header, the column width is adjusted so that the text or numbers in the column fit without overflowing into the next column. You can adjust several column widths at once.

 Drag across the column headers A to E to select all those columns.

 Double-click the border between any two of the column headers. All the column widths will be adjusted so that the text exactly fits.

You can widen any of the columns by dragging the border between its column header and the next column header to the right. Widen column E to about 12.00 – a Tip appears when you position the cursor to drag the border to tell you how wide the column is.

Formatting text

First we will centre the heading **Ski Holiday Budget**, increase its font size and make it bold.

 Drag across cells A1 to E1 to select the range.

 Click the **Merge and Center** button on the Formatting toolbar. This merges the 5 cells into a single cell with the cell reference A1.

 With cell A1 still selected, change the font size to **16** by clicking the **Font Size** button.

 Make the heading bold by clicking the **Bold** button.

 Click Row Header 3 to select the whole row.

Click the **Bold** button to make all the headings bold.

The heading **Total** needs to be right-aligned so that it is over the numbers. The headings **Unit Cost** and **Number** could be right-aligned too, in case we later decide to make columns C and D wider.

 Select these three headings and press the **Align Right** button on the Formatting toolbar.

Adding borders and shading

You can add a border to a single cell or a group of cells. We will add a border and shading to cell A1.

 Click in cell A1 to select the heading.

 From the menu select **Format, Cells...**

The **Format cells** dialogue box appears. Click the **Border** tab. The dialogue box appears as shown in Figure 13.6.

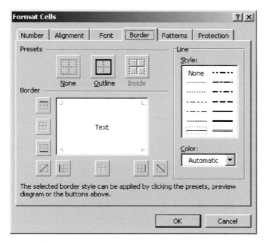

Figure 13.6: Inserting a border

 Select a line style, choose a colour and click the **Outline** button. Click **OK**. (You must choose the line style and set the colour before clicking the **Outline** button.)

 Click the **Fill Color** button on the Formatting toolbar and choose a ———— suitable colour.

Formatting numbers

Columns C and E both need to be formatted to 2 decimal places, since they contain currency amounts. You may also decide to put a £ sign in front of each number.

 Select column C by clicking its column header.

You can now select column E by keeping the **Ctrl** key pressed while you click column header E.

 From the menu select **Format, Cells...**

 In the dialogue box click the **Number** tab, and select **Currency** in the list box as shown in Figure 13.7.

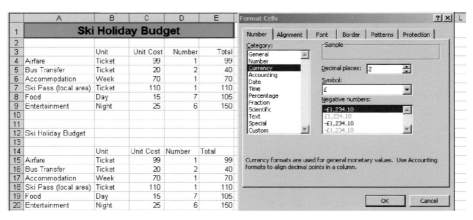

Figure 13.7: Formatting numbers as currency

 Click **OK**.

An alternative way of formatting cells as Currency is to select the cells and then click the **Currency** button on the toolbar.

 Select E4 to E9 and click the **Currency** button.

Entering and formatting dates

 In cell G1, enter the date *01/11/02* and press **Enter**.

Excel recognises this as a date, and you can format it in a selection of different ways. Instead of using the menu command **Format**, **Cells...**, you can use the shortcut menu this time.

 Right-click cell G1 and select **Format Cells...**

 In the dialogue box click the **Number** tab, and select **Date**. Select a format such as **14-March-2001**.

If the date appears as 11-Jan-00 your system is set up to display dates in American format. To change this, do the following:

 Select **Start**, **Settings**, **Control Panel**.

 Double-click **Regional Options**. Make sure the **General** tab is selected and that **English (United Kingdom)** is selected.

 Click the **Date** tab and note that the Short date format is **dd/MM/yyyy**.

Click **OK** and then **Apply** in the next window.

Inserting and deleting rows and columns

The organiser of this ski holiday has forgotten to enter the cost of ski (or snowboard) and boot rental.

 Right-click row header 8 and select **Insert**. A new row is inserted.

 Type the text *Equipment rental*, *Week*, *£70*, *1* into the cells in this row.

 Practise deleting several rows at a time. Drag across row headers 17 to 21, right-click, and select **Delete**.

 Drag across row headers 13 to 16 and delete the rest of the bottom spreadsheet.

You can insert columns in the same way. Alternatively, you can select **Rows** or **Columns** from the **Insert** menu.

What if?

Now we need to calculate the total of all expenses and make sure it is within everyone's budget.

 In A12, type *Total*. Make it bold.

 Make cell E12 the active cell, and click the **Autosum** button on the Standard toolbar. A dotted line appears around cells E4 to E11, showing that these are the cells which will be summed.

Σ

 Press **Enter**. The total of the column appears, £644.00.

Now supposing that you have told everyone that the holiday will cost no more than £600. You will have to find some way of reducing the costs. There are various options; purchase a cheaper ski pass for £90, spend less on food and accommodation, etc. Let's try out the effect of spending only £12 per day on food.

 In cell C9, type 12. The total cost reduces to £623.00.

 In cell C7, type 90. Double-click in cell A7 and change the text to *Ski Pass (local area)*. Widen the column.

 In cell C10, type 24 for **Entertainment**. There! The total is now £597.00.

Of course, you have not budgeted for emergencies, and some people may want the full lift pass. So you can keep trying out different options until you have the best deal possible.

Printing the spreadsheet

It is essential to have a look at what your document will look like when printed before actually printing it. You need to make sure that the correct range of cells will be printed, that it fits neatly onto the page, and that you have selected the correct orientation (Portrait or Landscape).

 Click the **Print Preview** button on the Standard toolbar.

A preview of the page appears. You can click the **Zoom** button to get a larger view of the page.

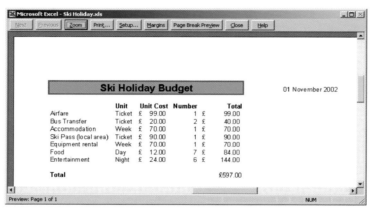

Figure 13.8: Print Preview mode

There are buttons along the top of the screen in Print Preview mode.

Click the **Setup**… button.

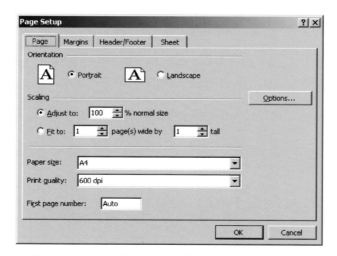

Figure 13.9: The Page Setup dialogue box

You can print the spreadsheet by pressing the **Print**… button.

Experiment with the **Margins** and **Page Break Preview** buttons. You can always get back to Normal view by selecting **View**, **Normal** from the menu.

 To return to Normal view from Print Preview, press **Escape** or the **Close** button.

Inserting a spreadsheet into a document

You may want to include the spreadsheet in a letter to one or more group members. First, you must copy the spreadsheet to the Clipboard.

 Select cells A1 to E12 and select **Edit**, **Copy** from the menu.

 Open Word, and type the text
Dear Bob
Here's the ski holiday budget.

 Press **Enter** twice.

 From the menu select **Edit**, **Paste Special**. A dialogue box appears as shown in Figure 13.10.

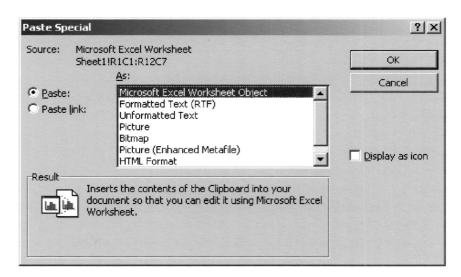

Figure 13.10: Pasting a spreadsheet

 Make sure that **Paste** and **Microsoft Excel Worksheet Object** are selected, and press **OK**.

The spreadsheet will be inserted into your document. You can move it by dragging it.

 Save the document in a suitable folder, calling it **Letter to Bob.**

Type *Hope this looks OK* underneath the spreadsheet. The letter should look like Figure 13.11.

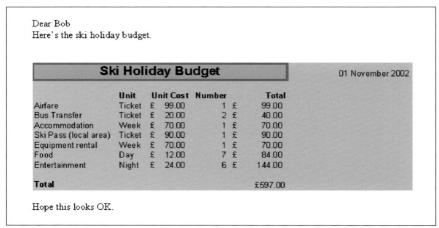

Figure 13.11: Word document with spreadsheet inserted

Double-click the spreadsheet in the Word document. It opens in Excel and you can edit it as required.

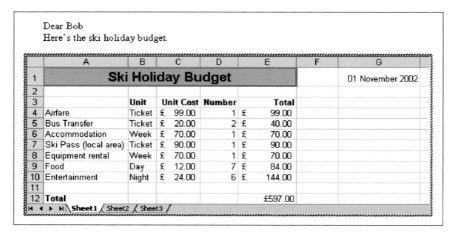

Figure 13.12: The spreadsheet ready to be edited

Change cell C9 to *£10*. The total changes to £583.00.

Click away from the spreadsheet.

Save and close the Word document.

Save and close the **Ski Holiday** spreadsheet.

Chapter 14: Functions and Charts

In this chapter you'll learn some more about Excel features, including how to draw a chart or graph. Charts are often a good way of presenting data so that it is easy to understand and take in.

You are going to create a spreadsheet and chart of monthly average maximum and minimum temperatures to insert in a holiday brochure.

▶ Load Excel and make sure you have a blank worksheet on screen.

▶ In cell A1 type the heading *Average Daily Temperatures*.

▶ In cell B3, type *Maximum*. In cell C3, type *Minimum*.

▶ In cell A4 type *January*.

Copying series

Excel has a clever feature which enables you to fill in the other months of the year very quickly.

▶ Drag the corner handle of cell A4 down to cell A15 and release it. The other eleven months of the year are automatically filled in.

▶ Fill in the figures as shown in Figure 14.1.

▶ Format the labels as shown, widening columns where necessary.

▶ Save your spreadsheet in a suitable folder, calling it **Temperatures**.

	A	B	C	D
1	Average Daily Temperatures			
2				
3		Maximum	Minimum	
4	January	5	1	
5	February	8	2	
6	March	10	3	
7	April	12	5	
8	May	14	8	
9	June	18	10	
10	July	22	13	
11	August	24	15	
12	September	19	13	
13	October	16	10	
14	November	11	5	
15	December	8	2	
16				
17	Average			
18				

Figure 14.1: The figures to be entered in the spreadsheet

Using functions

You have already used one function – the **Sum** function. This is so often required that it has its own button on the toolbar.

We will use functions to find the average maximum and minimum monthly temperatures, the highest and lowest figures in each column, and a count of the number of temperatures we have entered.

 In cell A17 type *Average* as shown in Figure 14.1.

Make cell B17 the active cell by clicking in it or moving to it, and press the **Insert Function** button on the Standard toolbar.

A dialogue box appears. In the **Select a category** list box select **Statistical**, and in the **Select a Function** box select **Average**, as shown in Figure 14.2.

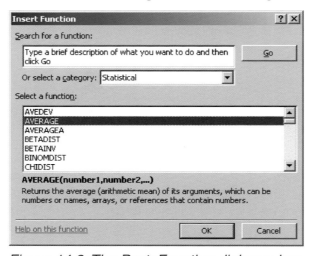

Figure 14.2: The PasteFunction dialogue box

Click **OK**. A further dialogue box appears, which you can move out of the way of the figures by dragging.

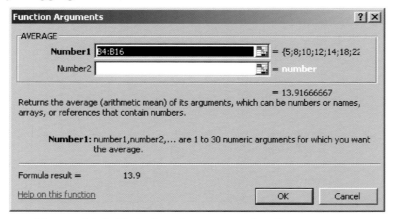

Figure 14.3: Entering the range of cells to average

Excel correctly guesses the range of cells to average. However, we are never going to have a 13th month so you can edit the range.

▶ In the **Number1** box, edit the range so that it is **B4:B15**. Click **OK**. The average maximum temperature for the year is entered.

▶ Format the average by clicking the **Decrease Decimal** button on the ———— Formatting toolbar until the number is displayed to only one decimal place.

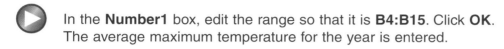

▶ Type the labels *Highest* and *Lowest* in cells A18 and A19.

▶ In cell B18, use the function **Max** to find the Maximum value in the column.

▶ In cell B19, use the function **Min** to find the Minimum value in the column.

▶ In cell A20 type the label *Number of Months*. Widen the column.

▶ In cell B20, use the function **Count** to count the number of months from Row 4 to Row 15.

▶ Copy the formulae to column C by selecting cells B17 to B20, and dragging the corner handle to the next column.

The results should appear as in Figure 14.4.

	A	B	C	D
1	**Average Daily Temperatures**			
2				
3		**Maximum**	**Minimum**	
4	January	5	1	
5	February	8	2	
6	March	10	3	
7	April	12	5	
8	May	14	8	
9	June	18	10	
10	July	22	13	
11	August	24	15	
12	September	19	13	
13	October	16	10	
14	November	11	5	
15	December	8	2	
16				
17	Average	13.9	7.3	
18	Highest	24	15	
19	Lowest	5	1	
20	Number of Months	12	12	
21				

Figure 14.4: Using functions

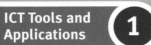

ICT Tools and Applications

Creating a chart

Next we will create a bar chart showing the monthly maximum and minimum temperatures.

 Select the range A3 to C15.

 Press the **Chart Wizard** button on the Standard toolbar.

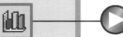

The Chart Wizard dialogue box appears as shown in Figure 14.5.

 Select **Column** as the Chart type.

Press and hold the button to view the chart. Try changing the chart type to **Line**, and pressing the button again to see what the line graph would look like.

Change back to **Column**, and click **Next**.

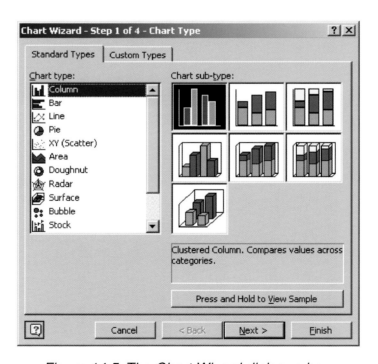

Figure 14.5: The Chart Wizard dialogue box

 Check that the correct range (A3:C15) is selected, and click **Next** in the Step 2 dialogue box.

Fill in the Step 3 dialogue box as shown in Figure 14.6, and click **Next**.

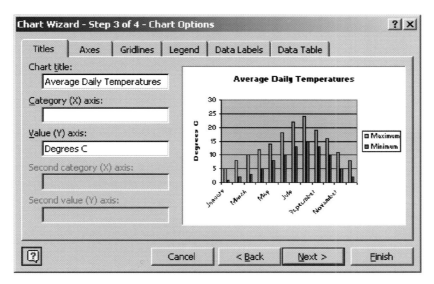

Figure 14.6: Entering chart title and axis labels

 Leave the option **As object in Sheet 1** selected, and click **Finish**.

The chart appears in the worksheet. You can drag it out of the way of the figures.

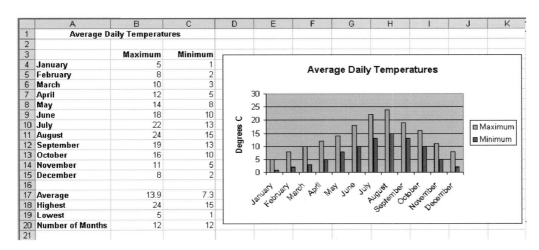

Figure 14.7: The chart inserted into the worksheet

You can make the chart bigger or smaller by dragging its corner handles. You can also change the font size of headings and labels by double-clicking, which brings up a dialogue box. Right-clicking one of the bars gives you an option to format the chart in various ways. Experiment!

Chapter 15: A PowerPoint Presentation

In this chapter you will be creating a presentation using MS PowerPoint. Using this software you can combine text, images and sound files to create slides which can be displayed on a screen. The presentation can be controlled by a speaker in a classroom or conference room, or it can be set up in, say, a Tourist Bureau or cinema complex so that people can watch it to get the information they want. Buttons can be added to take the viewer to a particular slide so that they can navigate around the presentation.

Tip:

This chapter assumes you are familiar with MS PowerPoint. If you have not used PowerPoint before, you need to start with a book such as **Basic PowerPoint 2000** by R.S.U. Heathcote, published by Payne-Gallway.

A presentation for a local swimming pool

The presentation that you will create will be displayed in the foyer of the local swimming pool, Brooks Pools. The user will be able to use it to get information on opening times, charges and party facilities.

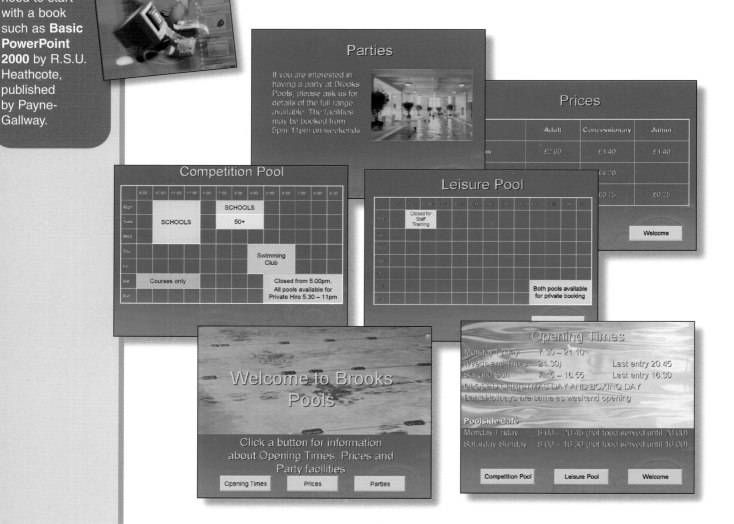

Starting a new presentation

 Open PowerPoint by clicking the PowerPoint icon in the Office toolbar, double-clicking the PowerPoint icon on the desktop or by selecting **Start**, **Programs**, **Microsoft PowerPoint**.

You will see the opening screen displayed. If you are using PowerPoint 2002 you will see the Task pane on the right hand side. If not, you will see a different opening screen, but you should be able to adapt the instructions given.

 Select **From Design Template** in the Task pane.

 Select **Ripple.pot** or another suitable template and select **Apply to all Slides** from the drop-down list.

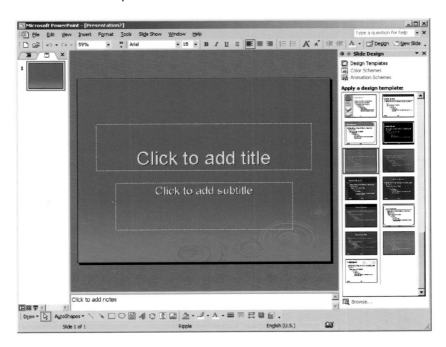

Figure 15.1: Opening screen

 Click where indicated to add a title *Welcome to Brooks Pools*.

 Add a subtitle *Click a button for information about Opening Times, Prices and Party facilities*.

 Save your presentation as *BrooksPools.ppt*.

Adding new slides

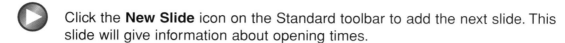

Click the **New Slide** icon on the Standard toolbar to add the next slide. This slide will give information about opening times.

The default slide layout will be **Title and Text**. Add the title and text as shown below, adjusting the text size so that there is space at the bottom of the screen for buttons which will be added later. You do not need bullets, so you can select the text and then click the **Bullets** icon to deselect it.

Figure 15.2: Slide 2

Find the **Title and Table** layout and choose **New Slide** from the drop-down list to insert the next slide. Specify a table of 4 rows and 4 columns.

Fill in text as shown in Figure 15.3. (You will need to reduce the font size.)

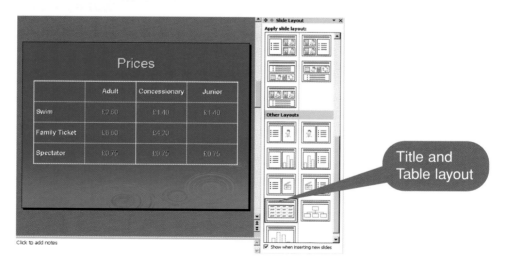

Figure 15.3: Slide 3

Working with tables

When you are entering text in a table, the **Tables and Borders** toolbar will appear on your screen. You can use tools from this toolbar to centre text vertically, merge cells and enhance the table in other ways.

Take a little time to experiment with the tools in this toolbox, and adjust the appearance of your table.

Add another slide using the same layout. This time you need a table with 14 columns and 8 rows. This slide is going to show when the Competition pool is booked for special events.

Fill in the table as shown. Use the **Merge and Centre** button on the Tables and Borders toolbar, and the **Fill** tool to colour different areas.

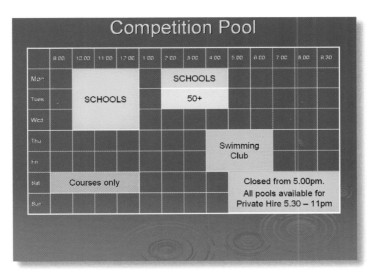

Figure 15.4: Slide 4

Add another slide using the same layout. Specify a table of 14 columns and 8 rows and fill in the table as shown in Figure 15.5.

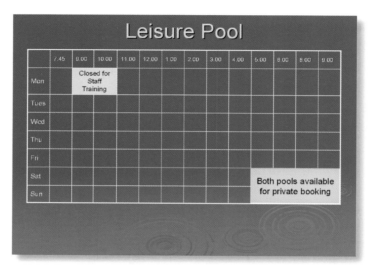

Figure 15.5: Slide 5

 Add one more slide using the **Title**, **Text and Content** layout. Add text as shown in Figure 15.6. You can find a suitable graphic to use on the Internet.

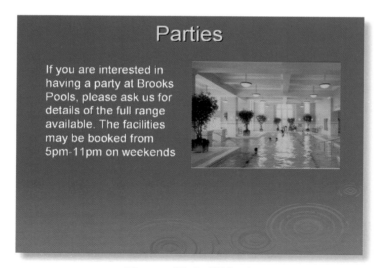

Figure 15.6: Slide 6

 You can view your slide show by selecting the first slide in the left-hand pane and clicking the **Slide Show** icon at the bottom of the pane. Each time you click the mouse the next slide will appear.

 Save your presentation.

Chapter 16: Designing Navigation Routes

Designing structure and navigation

This presentation will be running unattended in the foyer of the swimming pool complex. A customer will be able to use it to get the information they want, by clicking on buttons to take them to different screens.

You should draw the structure by hand, showing the possible routes through the presentation.

Your structure might look something like the one below.

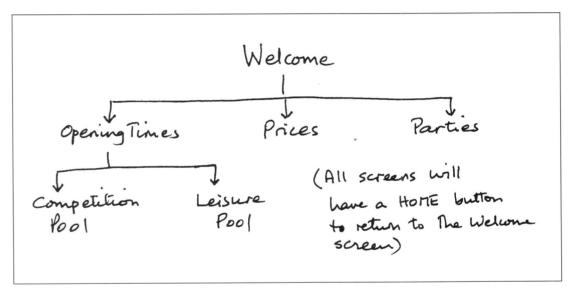

Figure 16.1: The presentation structure

Adding buttons

The next stage is to add buttons and links to each page so that the user can navigate their own route through the presentation.

Select the first slide.

Click **Slide Show**, **Action Buttons** and select the first, blank button.

Click and drag a small rectangular-shaped button on to the lower left side of the screen.

The **Action Settings** window will appear. Click **Hyperlink to**: and select **Slide**… from the list of options.

Select **Slide 2**, **Opening Times** and click **OK**.

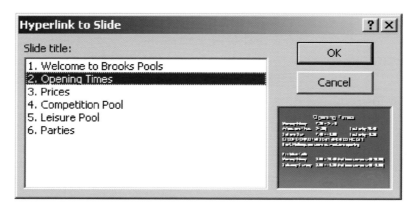

Figure 16.2: Creating a hyperlink

 Click **OK** in the **Action Settings** window.

Customising buttons

You can change the size and colour of the button and add text to it.

 Select the button and from the **Format** menu select **Autoshape**. Choose a suitable colour for your button.

 Right-click the button and select **Add Text**. Type *Opening Times*. Adjust the size, colour and font if necessary.

You need two more buttons to take you to the **Prices** and **Parties** slides. You can copy the first button and then change the hyperlinks and button text.

 Keep two fingers on **Ctrl** and **Shift** while you drag the button to the right. **Ctrl** copies, **Shift** keeps it straight.

 Right-click a new button away from the text and select **Edit Hyperlink**. Edit the link so that the second button takes you to the **Prices** slide.

 Change the text on the slide.

 Edit the third button in the same way. It should take you to the **Parties** slide.

Welcome to Brooks Pools

Click a button for information about Opening Times, Prices and Party facilities

| Opening Times | Prices | Parties |

Figure 16.3: Navigation buttons

You can copy and paste the buttons to the other slides, and edit the hyperlinks and the text. Each slide needs a button to take the user back to the **Welcome** slide.

 Test your buttons by clicking the **Slide Show** icon and trying out ─── each button in turn.

Adding slide transitions and sound

Transitions affect the way one slide changes into the next. You can add a sound effect to a transition too, though of course you need speakers to hear it play.

- Right-click the thumbnail image of slide 6 in the window on the left of the screen. Select **Slide transition**…

- From the **Apply to selected slides** box, select a transition effect. You can try out different effects at different speeds by clicking the **Play** button.

- Try adding a sound. You can add one of the standard sounds supplied, or download one of your own from the Internet.

- Close the Slide Transition window and test out your slide show.

Figure 16.4: Slide transitions

119

Adding a new background picture

You can add a picture as a background to any of your slides. You can download the picture called Pool Small from the website **www.payne-gallway.co.uk** by clicking the Student Resources link for this book, or you can find your own picture. Save the picture that you want to use in a folder.

Select the first slide. From the **Format** menu select **Background**…

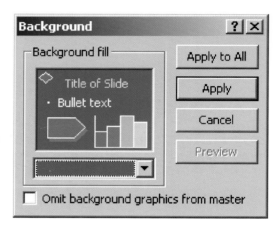

Figure 16.5

Click the arrow underneath the **Background fill** box and select **Fill Effects**…

Click the **Picture** tab and click **Select Picture**. Choose a picture that you have saved and click **Insert**.

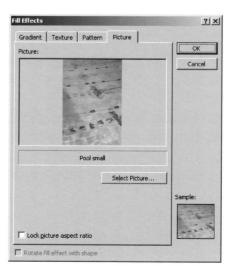

Figure 16.6: Selecting a background picture

Click **OK**, and **Apply** to apply the background only to the selected slide.

The picture will appear as a background to the slide. It may take up less than the full slide.

Figure 16.7: Using a picture as a background

Printing slides

You may need to print out your slides for documentation.

 From the **File** menu select **Print Preview**.

 You can choose how many slides to print on a page.

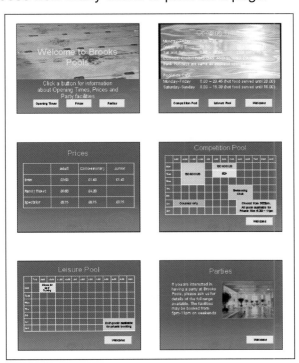

Figure 16.8: Slides printed 6 to a page

Exercises

These exercises are based on the Edexcel sample activities.

Paul Hooper, Marketing Manager of Burgers Away! has asked you to design a presentation to promote three new burgers. The presentation is to be a continuous scrolling advertisement suitable for display in the restaurant and should be produced using multimedia software.

There should be a page for each burger. The presentation should have 4-6 slides and must catch the attention of passers-by.

1. Create or find these components to go in your presentation:
   - Company logo
   - Company slogan
   - Product information
   - Suitable graphics
   - Suitable background
   - Sounds

Make a table showing the source of each component.

2. Design each of the slides, showing clearly how each component is used.

3. Design a structure and navigation routes for your presentation. The design should be on one sheet of A4 paper.

4. (a) Create the presentation.
   (b) Check the presentation runs according to your design by showing it to a group of possible customers.
   (c) Make any necessary changes.
   (d) Print out your presentation, e.g. thumbnails.

5. Write down two things that the audience liked about the presentation and two improvements you could make.

Chapter 17: Standard Ways of Working

Computers can store massive amounts of information. Large organisations such as banks, hospitals, the DVLC, the TV Licensing Authority, telephone, gas and electricity companies, examining boards and thousands of others, are completely dependent on having their customer data available at all times. Imagine what would happen if a bank suddenly lost all its customer data because a bomb or an earthquake hit their computer centre! How would they know how much everyone had in their accounts, or how much each customer owed?

Even tiny organisations and individuals can suffer awful consequences if they lose data. I've written over 100 pages of this book over the last few months – suppose my hard disk crashed and I lost it all! Excuse me for a few minutes while I just make sure I have an up-to-date backup copy…

The threats to data

There are many ways in which data can be lost.

- **Theft**. Many organisations hold sensitive data that they would not want to fall into the wrong hands. For example the names and addresses of all a company's customers may be a very valuable asset and one which they would not want a competitor to get hold of. A new design for a car, superior bottle-opener or jacket may be very carefully protected. A GCSE examiner may have a draft exam paper on a laptop computer – there could be a scandal if the laptop was stolen and the exam paper leaked the day before the exam!

● **Loss**. Data can be lost because of a hardware fault such as a hard disk crash, because a floppy disk is lost or accidentally destroyed, or because a file is accidentally deleted or overwritten.

● **Viruses**. A virus is a small program written with the intention of doing damage, which copies itself to any computer it is loaded onto. Viruses spread quickly via the Internet or from putting infected floppy disks or CDs into a computer's disk drive. They can destroy hundreds of files on a hard disk in a few seconds.

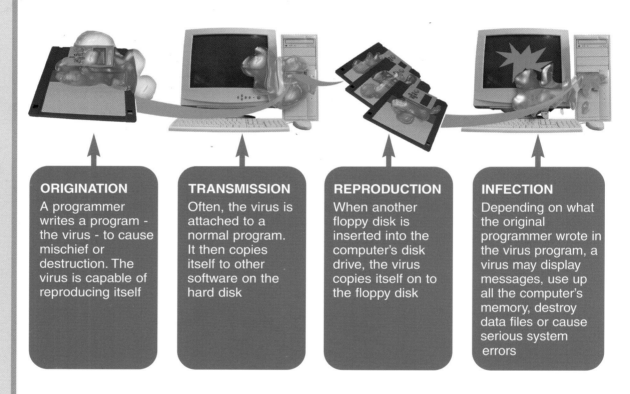

ORIGINATION
A programmer writes a program - the virus - to cause mischief or destruction. The virus is capable of reproducing itself

TRANSMISSION
Often, the virus is attached to a normal program. It then copies itself to other software on the hard disk

REPRODUCTION
When another floppy disk is inserted into the computer's disk drive, the virus copies itself on to the floppy disk

INFECTION
Depending on what the original programmer wrote in the virus program, a virus may display messages, use up all the computer's memory, destroy data files or cause serious system errors

● **Fire**. A disaster such as a fire, hurricane, earthquake or terrorist activity may destroy the building in which the computer and data is located.

Discussion

Think of some other ways in which data might be lost.

Protecting data

There are many ways of making sure that data is not lost. Organisations will have procedures to ensure that data is not lost under any circumstances, but as an individual, you can also take steps to protect your own data from loss. These include the following:

- **Use appropriate filenames and locations**. You can waste a lot of time looking for a file which was saved some time ago with a filename such as Letter1 which tells you nothing about the content or recipient. It is good practice to set up a structure of folders and subfolders with sensible, meaningful names in which to save different types of file.

- **Save work regularly**. While you are working, you should save your work regularly to make sure that in the event of a power cut or some other unexpected occurrence, you do not lose more than a few minutes' work.

- **Make backups of data**. You should make regular backups of your work, by copying it onto another disk or into another folder with a different name. If you are using a floppy disk to back up your data, you should label the floppy disk carefully and store it in a different place from the computer.

Companies who keep confidential data may use further measures to make sure the data is kept safe. They may use login names and passwords to make sure that only authorised personnel can log onto the computer system. Individual files and folders may be password-protected. Each password may have to be changed regularly to make sure it does not become known.

The most secure password is a combination of letters and numbers which is not easily guessable. Many people use the name of a friend, family member or pet and a really determined hacker may be able to run a program which tries out thousands of common names and words to find out the correct password.

Copyright laws

The Copyright Designs and Patents Act of 1988 covers a wide range of intellectual property such as music, literature and software.

It is illegal to copy software, to send copies of software over the Internet, or to use pirated software. It is also illegal to download a copyright sound track or DVD from the Internet.

You should not use someone else's work without their permission, or without acknowledging the source of the information.

The Data Protection Act

The Data Protection Act covers personal data which is stored on a computer. It protects the individual's right to privacy and gives individuals the right to see what data is stored about them and to have it corrected if it is inaccurate. All data users who store personal information about other people on their computer system must register with the Data Protection Commission.

Working safely

There are a number of health hazards associated with spending long hours at a computer. These include:

- Backache

- Eyestrain

- RSI (Repetitive Strain Injury)

The **Health and Safety at Work Act** incorporates legislation intended to protect the health of employees working at VDUs for long periods of time. For example the computer screen must tilt and swivel, and chairs should be of adjustable height, at the correct height relative to the keyboard and with a backrest. The monitor should not be positioned so that it reflects the glare from a window. Obvious hazards such as trailing cables should be avoided.

Employers have to make sure that employees take regular breaks or have changes in activity.

ICT in Organisations

2

About this unit

In this unit you will learn about:

- How and why organisations use ICT
- The main components of an ICT system
- How ICT systems are designed

Chapter 18: Organisations

Introduction

What is an organisation? We'll attempt a definition.

An organisation is a group of people who are working together for a common purpose. There are tiny organisations of two or three people, and multinational organisations like Microsoft, MacDonald's and Ford which employ hundreds of thousands of people. The school or college where you are studying is an organisation. The shops and restaurants you go to, the hairdresser's, the hospital, charities you give money to and clubs you belong to are all examples of organisations.

Discussion

As part of this unit you will need to investigate an organisation or a department within an organisation to see how it uses ICT. Think of several organisations that you have close contact with. Do any members of your family work for organisations?

Chapter 18: Organisations

Aims of an organisation

The aims of organisations vary. Many business organisations exist to provide a product or a service. One of their aims is probably to make a profit. Without making a profit, they will have no capital to invest in new ideas and new products, and nothing to keep them going through times when sales are down or their services are less popular.

Some types of organisation have different objectives.

Discussion

What are the objectives of the Royal Navy, Oxfam, the local Hospital Trust, your school, a local builder? What about some of the other organisations you have discussed?

Main functions of an organisation

Businesses exist to sell a product or a service. Although different businesses sell completely different products, from teddy bears and jigsaw puzzles to submarines or jumbo jets, they do all have certain elements in common. In fact, almost all organisations, whether they exist to sell a product or service or for some other reason, carry out four main functions:

1 **Sales** – involving the sale or distribution of the goods or services provided by the organisation

2 **Purchasing** – involving the purchasing of goods or services required by the organisation

3 **Finance** – managing the flow of money in and out of the organisation

4 **Operations** – carrying out the main business of the organisation

Discussion

Does a hairdressing salon carry out these four functions?

Discussion

Does a local Brass Band carry out these four functions?

Cottenham Brass
Photograph Robert Ellis, Norwich

Discussion

Does a hospital, a garage, an optician's, the local Scout group, carry out these four essential functions?

What about other organisations you have discussed?

Exercises

Browse the Internet to find out information about different organisations, large and small. Look at the **About Us** page for the organisations you find. Write a report about two different types of organisation and how they carry out the four essential functions discussed in this chapter. Include some downloaded photographs if possible.

Chapter 19: ICT for Communications

Uses of ICT

Most organisations in this country, except the very smallest, could not survive without computers. ICT is used to:

- communicate effectively internally and with suppliers and customers

- manage and control production processes

- manage finance, including payroll, budgeting, processing transactions and reporting

- manage stock control

- market products and services efficiently

We will look at each of these in turn.

ICT for internal communication

All organisations need to ensure that people in different departments communicate with each other. Internal communication can take many forms, both formal and informal, from a company-wide newsletter to a lunch-time chat. Here are some methods of internal communication which use ICT.

Newsletters

Many organisations produce newsletters for their employees. These can be used to give news of forthcoming developments, events such as Trade shows that the company is participating in and new policies as well as informal news such as who won the company golf tournament.

> **Discussion**
>
> How can ICT help in the production of a company newsletter? What software packages may be used?

Company intranet

An intranet is similar to the Internet but is internal to an organisation, owned and used only by people in the organisation. It allows employees to share information, fix up appointments with each other, circulate important documents internally and many other functions. Remember that in a large organisation not everybody will be working on the same site or even at the same time.

Look at the screenshot in Figure 19.1 which is of a website called Intranets.com, belonging to a company which will set up a company intranet. You could browse this site and others to find out more about intranets.

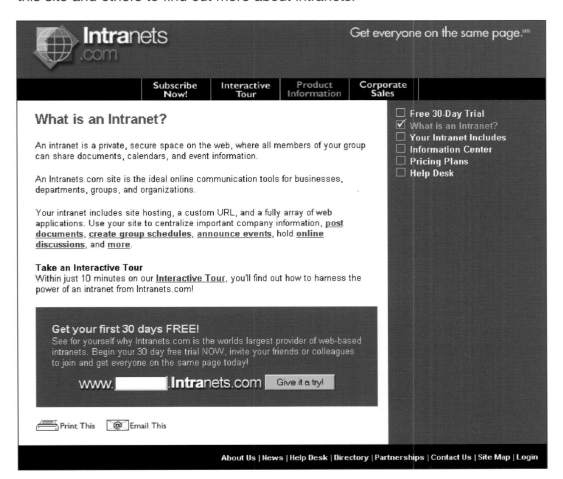

Figure 19.1: About Intranets

Using an intranet, e-mails can be sent internally without the use of an external Internet Service Provider or e-mail address.

Videoconferencing

This technique allows people to communicate face to face over long distances. At each end, participants sit in a room equipped with several video cameras, microphones and television monitors or PCs.

> ### Discussion
>
> **Alternatives to videoconferencing include travelling to a meeting or using an ordinary telephone. What are the advantages and disadvantages of videoconferencing over these other methods?**

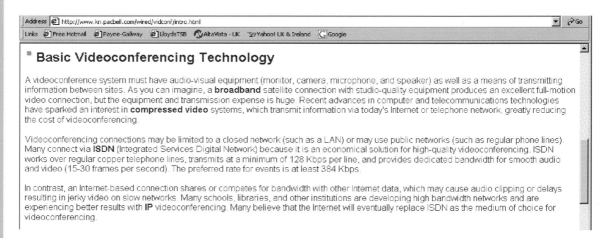

Figure 19.2: Look up 'videoconferencing' on Google

The Internet may be used for videoconferencing, both one-way and two-way. You may have watched Big Brother or other TV programs live on the Internet.

Internal memos and letters

Other forms of communication using ICT include memos and letters. In addition, word-processing software may be used to type meeting agendas and minutes.

> ### Discussion
>
> **Can you think of any other ways in which ICT is used for internal communication?**

Formal documents

Information about routine business activities also needs to be communicated between departments. Invoices, purchase orders, payroll slips, stock reports and many other documents will be produced by computer and sent from one department to another. These documents will be considered separately in later chapters.

ICT for external communication

All organisations need to communicate with people in the outside world. For example, they need to communicate with:

- customers

- suppliers

- the bank

- the Inland Revenue

Some of the communication will be routine. Consider the example of a mail-order company selling a range of clothes. A customer may use the telephone to order some goods. The Sales Department will use the computer to enter the order and produce an invoice as well as other documents. The invoice will be sent with the goods to the customer.

Voice mail

Many medium-sized and large companies use a voice-mail system. When you telephone the company, you will be connected to a voice menu and asked to press a number depending on the service or department you want. You may end up talking to a real person, or you may be asked to leave a message.

Some callers find these systems frustrating. Employees, too, may find it time-consuming having to record messages to be played, and having to listen to messages and respond appropriately to them.

Fax (Facsimile transmission)

Very few offices could manage without a fax machine. If you look at any office stationery or business card, you will normally see a telephone number, a fax number and probably an e-mail address as well. A fax is a fast and efficient way of transmitting printed or hand-drawn documents and drawings. The sending fax machine scans the document and converts the image into a series of electric pulses. These are then sent over a phone line to a recipient's fax machine, where a copy of the page is printed.

Discussion

What are some of the advantages and disadvantages of fax transmission?

E-mail

E-mail is an enormously convenient method of communication. Here are some of its advantages over regular mail:

- An e-mail message arrives almost instantaneously anywhere in the world.

- It is very quick and easy to reply to an e-mail, simply by pressing the **Reply** button and writing a message.

- The same message can be sent to several people at once.

- Long documents or photographs can be sent as attachments.

- A message can easily be forwarded to another person.

Figure 19.3: Sending and receiving e-mails

Software such as Outlook Express is needed to send and receive e-mails. The hardware needed is a computer, telephone line and a modem (see Chapter 26).

Discussion

Can you think of any disadvantages of e-mail? What are the advantages of e-mail over using the telephone to communicate with somebody?

Chapter 20: ICT in Sales and Purchasing

Functions of Sales and Purchasing

Most businesses exist to sell a product or service. Manufacturers of raw goods such as paper, cloth, plastic or steel may sell to manufacturers who use these materials to make their products. They may sell to wholesalers who buy large quantities of finished goods. The wholesalers in turn will sell goods to retailers who put the goods in their shops or advertise them on the Internet or in catalogues, and sell them to the customer.

> ### Discussion
>
> **You buy a pencil made of wood and carbon. What different businesses may have been involved in turning the original tree into pencils and selling the finished product to you?**

All business involved in selling goods or services also need to purchase goods. These may be raw materials that their products are made of, stock that they buy from wholesalers to sell on to the customer, or items like stationery and computers that they need for the smooth running of their business. Businesses also have overhead costs such as heat, light and telephones.

ICT in Sales

We will look at an example of a manufacturer of goods (for example software, clothing or stationery) selling to a retailer. The sequence of events will be something like this:

- The manufacturer receives an order from the store.

- The order may have been received electronically by **Electronic Data Interchange** (EDI) (see below). If it was received by mail, fax or phone, it will be keyed into the **Sales Order Processing** system.

- This system will produce several documents. They may be carbon copies of a single document, with some parts blacked out on certain copies. One document will be a picking note, which tells the staff in the warehouse which items to pick off the shelves and pack ready for dispatch. An invoice is printed, and this will be sent to the customer to tell them how much they need to pay. A second copy of the invoice (the dispatch note) will accompany the goods. This allows the customer to check off items in a large, mixed dispatch to ensure that he has received all the goods invoiced. A third copy will be kept by the carrier (e.g. Securicor), who will ask the customer to sign for the goods. This acts as proof that the goods were delivered in case of any query arising.

Electronic Data Interchange

EDI permits companies to communicate and process business transactions electronically. These transactions include such documents as purchase orders, invoices and enquiries.

A Standards committee ensures that everyone using a process such as EDI follows the same rules and methods, making the program universally accessible. As a result of the standard, all businesses share a common interchange language, which minimizes the need for users to reprogram their internal data processing systems.

EDI has the advantage that an order only needs to be entered into the computer once (by the purchaser), thus reducing errors, saving paper and speeding up order processing.

Customer queries

The sales staff will also use the computer to answer customer queries about availability and prices of stock items.

Discussion

What items of information do you think would be stored about each item stocked by the manufacturer?

What items of information need to go on the customer invoice?

What software is used?

A Sales Order Processing system, either manual or computerised, is essential to all businesses selling goods or services. Most businesses of any size will have a computer system that handles sales, purchasing, stock control and accounts. Sage Accounting software is an example of a package that is used by many small businesses. There are hundreds of other software packages which perform similar functions, and which are specially suited to the needs of a particular type of business or organisation.

Using software such as Sage, every time an order is received, details are entered into the computer system using a screen like the one below.

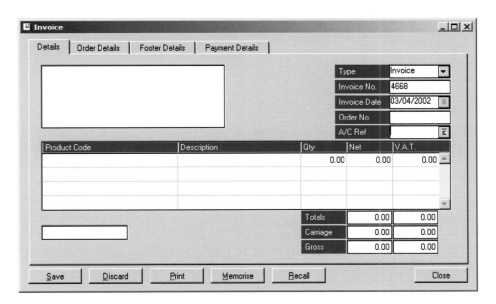

Figure 20.1: Entering an order

The system will check that there are enough of the required items in stock to fill the order. Then the invoice is printed out and the quantity in stock is automatically adjusted to show how many of each item is left.

Using a system like Sage, a small business can keep track of who its customers and suppliers are, how much customers owe, how much the company owes to its suppliers, and so on. Many users in different departments can look up information on the system and enter different types of transaction.

A **transaction** could be details of a new customer, an order from a customer, an order to a supplier, a payment from a customer, details of new stock received, etc.

Options on the Sage menu allow many different types of transaction to be entered and reports to be printed.

The screenshot below shows the menu that appears when **Customer** is selected from the main menu.

Main menu

Customer menu

Figure 20.2: Some of the menu options in an Accounting system

ICT in Stock Control

Manufacturers, wholesalers and retailers keep a stock of goods so that they have some ready when customers place orders. They do not want to hold too much stock as the money tied up in the stock would be better off earning interest in the bank. On the other hand, they do not want to be caught short. If they know that it takes about 2 weeks to replenish stock, then they need to keep about 2 or 3 weeks' supply of stock in the warehouse.

It is essential that the exact quantity of goods in stock is known. Otherwise, sales staff will not be able to answer queries about whether a certain item is in stock, and no one will know when to order more stock. The computer system is needed to keep records of how much stock is in the warehouse, how much is on order, and other information about each product.

Discussion

What other information needs to be kept about each stock item?

What stock transactions will need to be recorded?

The main functions of a stock control system are to:

- Keep track of how much of each item is in stock

- Record the reorder level for each item in stock

- Generate reports to show, for example, current stock levels, which items need to be reordered, what stock transactions have taken place within a given date range.

Each item will have its own reorder level, depending on how quickly it is used or sold and how quickly new stock can be obtained. When the quantity in stock falls below the reorder level, more stock needs to be ordered.

ICT in Purchasing

Ordering new stock may be one of the tasks of the **Purchasing Department**. The computer system will hold details of who supplies each item they need to order.

The business will need to order many other items besides raw materials or items that they themselves sell. They will need to order things needed for the smooth running of the office, such as stationery and computer equipment, and services such as insurance or hotel rooms if staff have to travel.

A clerk in the Purchasing Department will enter the details of a purchase order and send it to the supplier. They in turn will receive the goods or services and an invoice which will be passed to the Accounts or Finance Department.

In the next chapter we will look in more detail at how ICT is used in the Finance Department.

Exercise

Create a simple stock control system for a small snackbar. The manager of the snackbar will use the system to keep track of what is in stock, what has been sold each week and what needs to be ordered.

You can create the system using the Inventory Control template in MS Access. (*Inventory* is another word for stock.)

Enter the company information, and details of 4 different products. Enter some purchase orders and print one of them. Enter some stock receipts to put a quantity of each item into stock. Then enter some transactions for sales and shrinkage. (*Shrinkage* means items lost, for example spoilt or stolen.) Print a report to help the manager decide what items need reordering, and a report of all transactions.

Write a short user manual with screenshots for your system, explaining what menu options to select to enter new products, new supplier details, and sales transactions, and how to print a report to show what needs reordering.

Chapter 21: ICT in Finance

The Finance Department manages the flow of money into and out of the organisation. Their activities will include:

- Credit control

- Supplier payments

- Budgeting and forecasting

- Payroll

We will look at each of these activities in turn.

Credit control

Some organisations deal only in cash sales. A small restaurant or hairdresser, for example, will serve the customer and then expect to be paid right away. If you order something like a book or CD over the Internet, you will have to give a credit card number, so that the company knows it will be paid before it dispatches the goods.

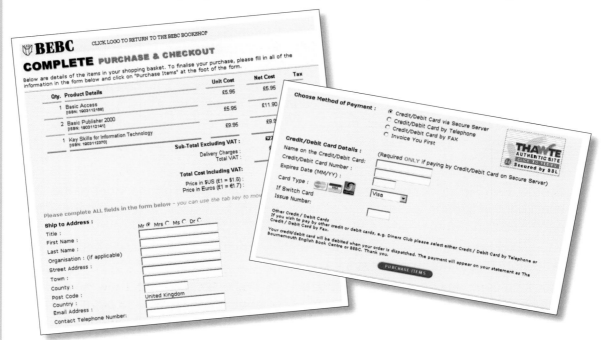

Figure 21.1: Paying by credit card for an Internet purchase

Some customers will not have to pay instantly for goods ordered from companies. For example, if a school orders a class set of books from a bookseller or a publisher, they will normally be given 30 days credit. This means they will not have to pay anything for 30 days after the date of the invoice.

If, for example, a shoe store regularly orders shoes from a particular manufacturer, placing an order say once a week, the manufacturer will not expect the customer to pay each invoice separately. A monthly **statement** will be sent, listing the amounts due on each invoice. They may be given 60, 90 or 120 days to pay, because they need to sell the shoes before they have enough cash to pay the supplier.

Unfortunately, not all customers pay within the set number of days. They may not have enough money in the bank to pay all their suppliers, or they may simply forget to pay. It is the job of the **credit controller** to chase up customers who have not paid their bills. He or she will probably spend a lot of time on the telephone reminding customers of the outstanding debt, answering queries regarding debt and sending duplicate copies of lost invoices.

Reports produced by the computer system will help the credit controller to do this job. An **Aged Debtors Analysis** will show which customers owe money, and how old the debt is.

| Date: 04/04/2002 | | | | DEMONSTRATION | | | | | Page: 1 | |
| Time: 14.19.15 | | | | **Aged Creditors Analysis (Summary)** | | | | | | |

Report Date:	04/04/1999							Supplier From:		
Include future transactions:	No							Supplier To:	ZZZZZZZZ	
Exclude Later Payments:	No									

A/C	Name	C Limit	Turnover	Balance	Future	Current	Period 1	Period 2	Period 3	Older
CON001	Concept Stationers	3,000.00	155.00	36.63	0.00	0.00	0.00	0.00	36.63	0.00
NEW001	Newtown Builders Ltd	10,000.00	4,113.01	0.00	0.00	0.00	0.00	0.01	0.00	-0.01
QUA001	Quality Motors	20,000.00	47.00	286.58	0.00	72.85	-42.63	0.00	0.00	256.36
STU001	Studio Designs	4,500.00	2,042.63	171.25	0.00	0.00	171.25	0.00	0.00	0.00
SUP001	Superior Castings Ltd	2,000.00	-25.00	33.87	0.00	0.00	-29.38	0.00	0.00	63.25
SUP002	Superclean	3,000.00	100.00	11.53	0.00	0.00	0.00	0.00	0.00	11.53
THO001	Thompsons Electricals	4,000.00	10,855.00	-185.13	0.00	0.00	-135.13	-50.00	0.00	0.00
WED001	Wedgwood Marshall & Wilson	5,600.00	1,500.00	63.00	0.00	0.00	0.00	0.00	0.00	63.00
WIS002	Wiseman Products	0.00	158.00	50.00	0.00	0.00	50.00	0.00	0.00	0.00
	Totals:		18,945.64	467.73	0.00	72.85	14.11	49.99	36.63	394.13

Figure 21.2: Aged debt report

A company may have hundreds of customers owing money. The credit controller has to know the customers' circumstances, and whether they are likely to pay. They may sometimes exceed their credit limit if they place a big order and already have an outstanding payment. The credit controller will have to decide whether to increase their credit limit, chase them for payment or refuse the order.

Discussion

The aged debt report may be very long. In Figure 21.2 it is printed in alphabetical order of customer. What other sequence might be more helpful to a credit controller?

Supplier payments

Another job of the Finance Department is to make sure that the company pays its own suppliers in time. They in turn will probably be given a month or more in which to pay their bills.

An Aged Creditors report similar to the one showing the aged debts will show the Finance Department who the company owes money to.

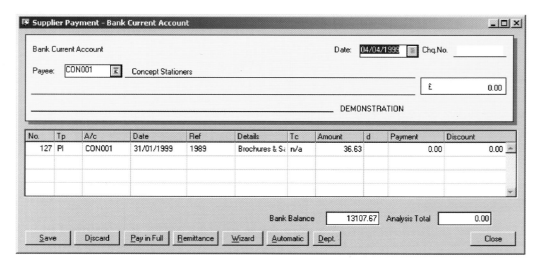

| Date: | 04/04/2002 | | | | | DEMONSTRATION | | | | | Page: | 1 |

Aged Creditors Analysis (Summary)

| | | | Time: 14:19:15 | | | | | | | | | |

Report Date:	04/04/1999								Supplier From:			
Include future transactions:	No								Supplier To:	ZZZZZZZZ		
Exclude Later Payments:	No											

A/C	Name	C Limit	Turnover	Balance	Future	Current	Period 1	Period 2	Period 3	Older
CON001	Concept Stationers	3,000.00	155.00	36.63	0.00	0.00	0.00	0.00	36.63	0.00
NEW001	Newtown Builders Ltd	10,000.00	4,113.01	0.00	0.00	0.00	0.01	0.00	-0.01
QUA001	Quality Motors	20,000.00	47.00	286.58	0.00	72.85	-42.63	0.00	0.00	256.36
STU001	Studio Designs	4,500.00	2,042.63	171.25	0.00	0.00	171.25	0.00	0.00	0.00
SUP001	Superior Castings Ltd	2,000.00	-25.00	33.87	0.00	0.00	-29.38	0.00	0.00	63.25
SUP002	Superclean	3,000.00	100.00	11.53	0.00	0.00	0.00	0.00	0.00	11.53
THO001	Thompsons Electricals	4,000.00	10,855.00	-185.13	0.00	0.00	-135.13	-50.00	0.00	0.00
WED001	Wedgwood Marshall & Wilson	5,600.00	1,500.00	63.00	0.00	0.00	0.00	0.00	0.00	63.00
WIS002	Wiseman Products	0.00	158.00	50.00	0.00	0.00	50.00	0.00	0.00	0.00
	Totals:		18,945.64	467.73	0.00	72.85	14.11	-49.99	36.63	394.13

Figure 21.3: Paying a supplier

The clerk can then select a supplier to pay, as in Figure 21.4. Clicking the **Pay in Full** button will automatically enter the correct amount in the top half of the screen. The clerk will then have to write a cheque for this amount, entering the cheque number on the top line of the screen shown above. Alternatively, he or she may arrange payment by some other means such as Direct Debit or payment via the Internet. The important thing to understand is that entering the payment into the computer system does not actually make the payment, it simply records it.

Figure 21.4: Recording a payment to a supplier

Budgeting and forecasting

Keeping a company going year after year does not happen automatically. It requires skilled and careful decision-making by senior management. Companies of all sizes from giant internationals such as Enron and Marconi to the smallest sole trader can go from being profitable for several years to near or total bankruptcy in an alarmingly short time.

Figure 21.5

Managers need to plan carefully the direction that the business will take in the years to come. Manufacturers need to decide what new products to introduce, how much to charge for them and how many to make. **Forecasting** the likely demand is a difficult job and one which will be aided by information on how similar products have sold in the past. This information will be available from the computer system.

Once a sales forecast is made, a budget can be drawn up for the new project. This will show what the costs are and how much profit the company can expect to make if they charge a particular price. A sample budget is shown in Figure 21.6.

	A	B	C	D	E
1	**Year 1**				
2	**Product:**	**Surround sound speakers**			
3	Recommended price	£120.00			
4					
5	**Sales Revenue**				
6		**Discount**	**Quantity**	**Revenue**	
7	Home sales	30%	10200	£856,800.00	
8	Export sales	55%	1200	£64,800.00	
9	**Total**			**£921,600.00**	
10					
11	Design	£ 15,300.00			
12	Prototype build	£ 3,500.00			
13	**Total**	**£ 18,800.00**			
14					
15	**Variable costs**				
16					
17	**Estimated quantity**	12,000			
18	Manufacturing costs	£ 560,000.00			
19					
20	**Margins**				
21					
22	Sales revenue		£921,600.00		
23	Fixed costs	£ 18,800.00			
24	Variable costs	£ 560,000.00			
25	Distribution	£129,600.00			
26	Marketing	£100,000.00			
27	Total	£ 808,400.00	£ 808,400.00		
28	Gross margin		£113,200.00		
29					

Figure 21.6

Discussion

What software would be useful for preparing a budget?

What features of the software would be particularly useful?

A Cash Flow forecast is another type of forecast that needs to be prepared each year. A company can be profitable but nevertheless short of cash. Therefore, they need to have a good idea of what cash will be coming in and going out each month.

Discussion

The forecast above shows that the company expects to make a profit of over £100,000. Nevertheless, they could run into financial difficulties. Why?

What outgoings will the company have apart from the costs shown in Figure 21.6?

Think of reasons why some of these companies might run into cash flow problems: a giant insurance company, a small builder, a private training organisation.

You need Cash to Survive!

Payroll

Decades ago, payroll was one of the first applications to be computerised in thousands of companies. It is ideally suited to computerisation because the same calculations have to be made hundreds or thousands of times in a company with a large number of employees. Accuracy is essential and many different types of output are required, such as payslips and end-of-year reports for the Inland Revenue.

Most companies with more than a handful of employees use a special payroll program to calculate the monthly payroll and print out payslips. Some smaller companies **outsource** the payroll. It is not economic to have a special payroll program for just 3 or 4 employees. Specialised companies exist who for a modest fee will do all the work and send the payslips to the Finance Department every month.

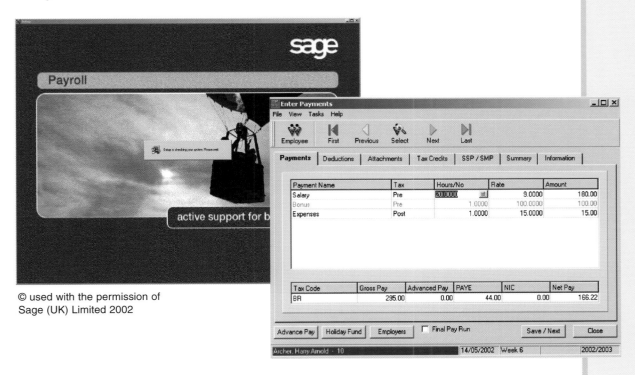

© used with the permission of
Sage (UK) Limited 2002

Figure 21.7: Sage Payroll package

Exercises

1. Search the Internet to find out how the share price of a major company, for example, Enron or Marconi, changed over the past two years. Try also to find a company whose share price has increased dramatically over the past two years. Can you explain the varying fortunes of your chosen companies?

2. Use a spreadsheet to draw up a budget for a small enterprise such as selling hamburgers or icecream from a stand for 2 months. Research costs for your chosen products and use the spreadsheet to determine what price you must charge in order to make a profit. State any assumptions you make.

Robots in industry

The word robot comes from the Czechoslovakian word 'robotnik', which means slave. Robots come in many different forms and shapes, but they all have the same basic components:

- **Sensors** which capture information from the environment

- A **microprocessor** to process the information

- **Actuators** to produce movement or alter the environment in some way, for example by turning an electronic switch on or off.

The car industry was one of the first to make widespread use of robots. The first robot was used by General Motors in the USA in 1962. There are now hundreds of thousands of robots in use worldwide.

The first generation of robots had no sensors to capture information – for example if the robot was programmed to spray-paint a door panel and the car was not there or it had run out of paint, it would go ahead and spray anyway.

Modern robots include sensors which feed back information such as exactly how or where an object is positioned, the pressure with which an object is being gripped so that it does not grip it too hard, and so on.

Computer control

Computers are used to control hundreds of processes both in industry and at home. Washing machines, cars, cameras and microwave ovens all have computer chips which control their operation. Traffic lights, rides in Disneyland, nuclear power stations and underground railways in some countries are commonly controlled by computer.

> ### Discussion
>
> **You probably use computer-controlled equipment almost every day. Think what this might be, and what functions the computer performs.**

A computer-controlled greenhouse is a good example of the basic processes involved.

- The **inputs** are provided by sensors which detect changes in temperature and humidity. Transducers convert the signals into **analogue** voltages, which vary continuously over time. An analogue-to-digital converter changes the analogue voltages into a form the computer can understand.

- The **processing** is carried out by the computer according to instructions held in its memory.

- The **outputs** are signals to various devices, which may cause the heating to be turned on or off, windows to open or close, or sprinklers to be switched on or off.

Why use robots?

- Robots can work in environments which are dangerous for humans, such as radioactive environments, deep underwater, or on the surface of Mars.

- They can tirelessly perform unpleasant or monotonous tasks, lift heavy loads and reach long distances. They are used, for example, by the US Navy to scrape and repaint ships.

- The quality of work is consistent. Robots don't lose concentration and make mistakes like humans do.

- Robots can work 24 hours a day, work faster than humans and never go on strike.

However, robots are expensive to buy and expensive to install.

Computer monitoring

Hospitals

Computers are also used to monitor conditions in thousands of different applications.

In a hospital, computers are used to monitor patients in intensive care. Measurements are taken continuously using special sensors, and if the measurement of, for example, heart rate, blood pressure or respiration rate falls above or below a set level, an alarm is set off. This equipment allows patients to be monitored constantly without having to have a nurse present at all times.

The environment

All aspects of the environment can be monitored, from car emissions, pollen counts, river levels and pollution, to climatic change which may lead to global warming.

The Thames Barrier in London was built to protect the capital from flooding until at least 2030. The water levels are continuously monitored and in the event of, say, a surge tide following severe bad weather, the barrier can be raised.

Production control

In a manufacturing environment, computers are often used to schedule production processes so that machinery is not standing idle. Production has to be carefully scheduled so that all the items or sub-assemblies required for a particular product are ready when needed.

When workers are paid by 'piece-work' – i.e. according to the amount they produce, a computer system can keep track of how much each employee has produced.

In a factory making clothing, for example, the progress of each batch of garments through the factory can be monitored. The system can also produce reports on what raw materials will be needed to fill a particular order, and report on shortages.

Discussion

**What use could these organisations make of computers
in their operations? (a) a garage (b) a bakery (c) a shop
or department developing photographs.**

Computer-aided design (CAD)

CAD systems allow designers and engineers to create designs on screen for
thousands of products ranging from the tiniest computer chip to bridges, buildings
and aeroplanes. The software allows users to create 3-dimensional 'solid' models
with physical characteristics like volume, weight and centre of gravity. The model
can be rotated and viewed from any angle, edited and stored. The computer can
perform calculations to evaluate its performance under different stresses, or crash-
test a new design of car before it is even manufactured.

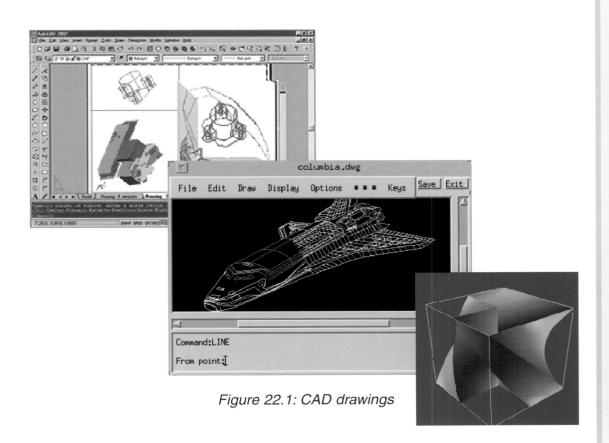

Figure 22.1: CAD drawings

Animation software can be used to enable a viewer to 'walk through' a 3-D model of say, a building, that exists only in the computer's memory.

CAD systems ('vector-based' graphics packages) store data in a different way from Paint ('bitmapped') packages. Paint packages store a picture as a two-dimensional array, with each element of the array representing one pixel (dot) on the screen. A CAD package stores drawings as a collection of objects such as lines and circles, each represented by specifying coordinates, thickness and so on. This has many advantages, including the following:

- Drawings can be scaled or resized without distortion;

- Drawings are device-independent – a drawing created using one type of VDU can be transferred to a screen of a different resolution without distortion;

- The files created tend to be smaller than for equivalent bitmapped images;

- Drawings can be made with a very high degree of accuracy by specifying coordinates.

Computer-aided Manufacturing (CAM)

Computer-aided design is often linked to *computer-aided manufacturing* (CAM). CAD/CAM systems are used in the design and manufacture of thousands of applications from aeroplane and car parts to office furnishings and sports equipment. When the design of the product is completed, the specifications are input directly into a program that controls the manufacturing of parts.

A great advantage of these systems is their flexibility: individual items can be manufactured to a customer's exact specifications.

Exercise

Search the Internet for information on robots and write a report, illustrated by screenshots, of their use in a manufacturing industry. A website such as **www.staubli.com** has some useful information about robots.

Chapter 23: ICT in Marketing

Marketing is all about promoting a product to potential and existing customers. Sometimes Sales and Marketing are lumped together, but they are really quite different functions.

Information and Communications technology is used in every aspect of marketing.

Market research

The first thing that needs to be done when a company is contemplating a new product or service is to do some **market research**. This means trying to find out whether people really want or need your product, or what particular thing about similar products they find most useful or attractive. You have probably seen market research questionnaires coming through your letterbox, or been stopped in the street and asked what brand of toothpaste, shampoo or coffee you use, along with a few dozen other questions.

Computers are used for many aspects of market research. The survey forms are probably produced by computer using a desk-top publishing package. These may be special OMR (Optical Mark Recognition) forms. Responses are made by making pencil marks in predetermined positions on the page which can be automatically read by computer.

Once read in, the computer can analyse the responses and give information which will help to make the product as successful as possible.

Figure 23.1:
An OMR form for entering Lotto

Methods of marketing

There are many different ways of marketing products. For example:

- Advertising in newspapers and magazines

- Advertising on TV, radio and in the cinema

- Advertising on posters

- Handing out flyers

- Direct mail to selected addresses

- Advertising on a website

- Exhibiting at Trade Fairs

- Having sales representatives visit stores

- Using the telephone (telesales)

Discussion

Which of these marketing methods have you seen in operation? What marketing methods do you think are most effective for selling: cars, a new type of vacuum cleaner, textbooks, trainers, holidays?

Advertising

Advertisements for magazines and newspapers are commonly produced using desk top publishing software. Posters and flyers will be produced in a similar way. Pictures may be created in a graphics package, and photos may be scanned and imported.

Creating a website

Having a company website is an excellent way of marketing a product or service. An online catalogue has several advantages over a paper one: it costs less to produce, it does not have to be mailed out and it can be kept right up-to-date. An online sales facility will encourage customers to buy there and then.

Many small companies can create their own websites or commission professional web site designers to do it for them. They will need web design software such as Dreamweaver or FrontPage, and a graphics package such as Photoshop in which to prepare their photographs and designs for the website.

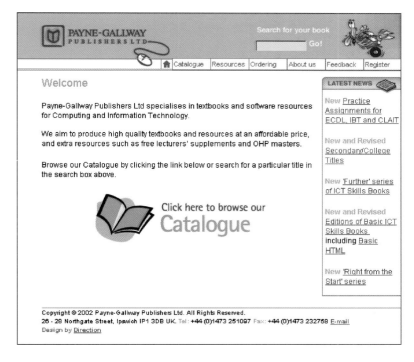

Figure 23.2: A company website

Direct mail

Sending letters, catalogues and free samples to carefully selected people can be a very effective way of marketing new products. A database of names and addresses is combined with a word-processed document in a **mail merge** operation. This creates, for example, personalised letters to each recipient.

Some companies specialise in direct mail. They keep up-to-date lists of organisations who might be interested in particular products or services. For example, a drugs company might want a list of all doctors' surgeries in a particular area. A textbook publisher might want a list of all schools and colleges. These lists can be bought for direct mail purposes, or the direct mail company will handle the entire mailing.

Where possible, companies keep a database of their customers, as they are the most likely people to buy something else. Keeping a database of customers up-to-date is a time-consuming and difficult task – over a period of time, people move or die and a large percentage of letters never reaches the addressee.

System maintenance

Finally we will take a brief look at system maintenance in an organisation.

Keeping data safe and computers running smoothly is crucial for organisations of all sizes from the smallest to the largest. Many small companies install expensive IT systems but do not have any kind of technical support. Some are casual about backing up data every day. But the cost of having no proper backup and maintenance procedures can be devastating. A recent survey concluded that a company unable to get at its data for 10 days will never fully recover, and 43% of them will go under.

Very few people would expect a car to run for years without maintenance. A regular MOT test and an occasional tune-up and oil replacement are a basic minimum to keep a car on the road. Similarly, a computer network or even a standalone PC will not run for ever without some attention.

A company has two options:

- They may have a maintenance contract with the company that supplied the system, or with another specialised company

- They may have their own in-house technical staff who can answer queries and keep the system running smoothly

Backups

Backing up data on a regular basis, usually every day, is vital if data is not to be lost when disaster strikes. Backup copies must be kept off-site in case of fire or theft.

When you study an organisation and their use of ICT, find out what maintenance and backup procedures they use.

A computer system consists of **hardware** and **software**. Hardware is the physical machinery – the components, electronic circuits and devices that make up a computer. Software consists of the computer programs (sequences of instructions) that tell the computer what to do in response to some command or event.

The components of a computer

All computers, whatever their size or function, have certain basic components. They have input devices for reading data into main memory, a central processing unit (CPU) for processing the data, output devices for printing, displaying or outputting information, and storage devices for permanent storage of programs and data.

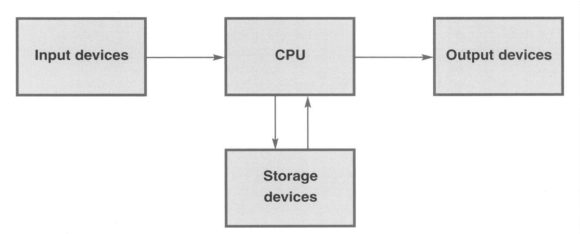

Figure 24.1: Block diagram of a computer system

Discussion

Name some input, output and storage devices.

The CPU

The CPU is the brains of the computer. This is where all the processing and calculations take place. It consists of two different parts:

● The Processor

● Memory

The Processor

The processor contains the **control unit** and the **arithmetic/logic unit (ALU)**.

The control unit coordinates and controls all the operations carried out by the computer. It operates by repeating three operations:

- **Fetch** – cause the next instruction to be fetched from main memory;

- **Decode** – translate the program instruction into commands that the computer can process;

- **Execute** – cause the instruction to be executed.

The ALU can perform two sorts of operations on data. **Arithmetic** operations include addition, subtraction, multiplication and division. **Logical** operations consist of comparing one data item with another to determine whether the first data item is smaller than, equal to or greater than the second data item.

Memory

There are basically two kinds of memory: Random Access Memory (RAM) and Read-Only Memory (ROM).

Instructions and data being processed are held in RAM. If you are writing a letter using MS Word, for example, both Word and your letter will be held in RAM while you are working on it. If you accidentally switch off the machine, or there is a power cut while you are working, you will lose the letter if you have not saved it and when you restart the computer, you will have to load Word again. When you finish your letter, save it and close Word, RAM is freed up for the next task.

RAM is divided into millions of individually-addressable storage units called **bytes**. One byte can hold one character, or it can be used to hold a code representing, for example, a tiny part of a picture, a sound, or part of a computer program instruction. The total number of bytes in main memory is referred to as the computer's memory size. Computer memory sizes are measured using the units below:

1 Kilobyte (Kb)	=	1000 bytes (or to be exact, 1024 bytes)
1 Megabyte (Mb)	=	1,000,000 bytes (more accurately 1,048,576 bytes)
1 Gigabyte (Gb)	=	1,000,000,000 (1 billion) bytes
1 Terabyte (Tb)	=	1,000,000,000,000 (1 trillion) bytes

As with processing power, the amount of memory that comes with a standard PC has increased exponentially over the past 20 years. In about 1980, BBC microcomputers with 32K of memory were bought in their thousands for home and school use.

In 1981, Bill Gates of Microsoft made his famous remark "640K ought to be enough for anybody". In 2002, a PC with 128Mb or 256Mb of memory is standard, costing around £1,000 including bundled software.

XP 1800+GT Package
- AMD Athlon XP1800+ Processor
- 256MB SDRAM
- 60GB Hard Disk
- CD Rewriter & DVD ROM Combo Drive
- 4x AGP Graphics
- 3D Wavetable sound
- 17" SVGA Colour Screen (16" Vis)
- 4 USB Ports
- Windows XP (preloaded)
  Time PCs use genuine Microsoft ® Windows ®
- Future Case
- 59K V90 Internal Modem
- PS/2 Keyboard and Mouse
- Future Look Speakers
- 1.44MB Floppy Drive
- Epson Stylus C40UX printer ⓘ
- Portable 3-in-1 Digital Camera ⓘ
- **£971.73 EXCLUDING DELIVERY (£49.99)**

Figure 24.2: An offer from Time Computers in 2002

The PC advertised above has 256Mb of RAM – that's enough to hold more than 256 million characters!

In contrast, **ROM** is not even mentioned. A PC will only have a very small amount of ROM, and you won't get a chance to use it because all the instructions held in ROM have to be burned into the memory chip before it leaves the factory. The contents of ROM are not lost when the computer is switched off, but they can never be changed. The bootstrap loader – the tiny program which starts running as soon as you switch the computer on – is held in ROM. This program tells the computer to start loading the operating system (e.g. Windows) from disk.

Discussion

By the time you read this, you will be able to find better offers than this! Look in some magazines and newspapers and find the best offer for a desktop PC.

Processor speed

The speed of the processor is one of the main factors that determines how fast the computer processes instructions. Each year processor speed increases. Twenty years ago a computer with a processor speed of a few hundred kilohertz (KHz) would have been considered very powerful. The PC advertised above has a processor speed of 1.8GHz – that is, about 10,000 times faster!

The other factor in determining the performance of a computer is the amount of memory it has. Modern software takes up a huge amount of memory. If a computer does not have enough memory to hold say, all of Word in memory at once, it will swap bits of the program in and out of memory from disk as they are required. The same happens when you have several programs running at once. They all take up memory space, and your computer may run more slowly because instructions and data are being copied from disk to memory as needed. Increasing a computer's memory will help to alleviate this problem.

You can find out how much memory a PC has by clicking **Start**, **Programs**, **Accessories**, **System Tools**, **System Information**. A screen like the one below shows information about the computer:

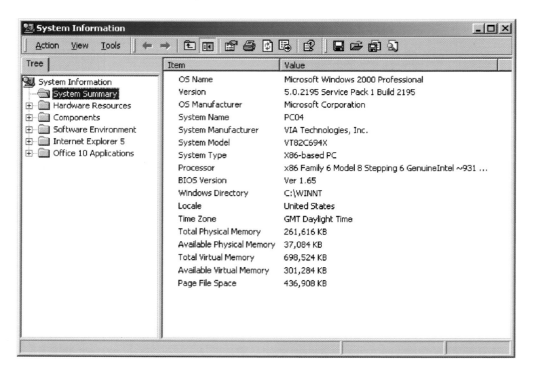

Figure 24.3: System information

Notice that the figure given for Total Virtual Memory is nearly three times the amount of the total physical memory. Virtual memory is not really extra memory; it is the 'trick' described above to enable your computer to hold more data than it really has room for in memory.

Exercises

1. Look through some computer magazines and identify the most powerful PCs that are advertised.

2. Figure 24.3 shows that the total physical memory of the computer being used is 261,618Kb. How many megabytes is this?

3. Find out the Total Physical Memory and the Total Available Memory of your computer. Close down some applications (or open new ones). What difference does this make to the Total Available Memory?

4. If you are using Office software on a PC, use the System Information to find out which Office applications are installed on your computer.

Chapter 25: Input Devices

In this chapter we will look at some of the various input and output devices that different computer systems may need.

Keyboard

All standard PCs come with a keyboard. The layout of keys on a keyboard has hardly changed since the earliest manual typewriters. The QWERTY layout was designed to stop typists typing too fast, which jammed the action of the letters striking the paper – and it seems as though we are stuck with this for ever now!

Some keyboards incorporate a wrist rest for added comfort. Others have a tracker ball which performs the same function as a mouse.

Figure 25.1: Computer keyboards

Keyboards are used in every office for routine tasks such as writing letters, using the Internet, creating spreadsheets and querying databases. But they are also used for high-volume data entry. For example, a mail-order firm may receive thousands of orders every day which have to be keyed in. People who spend all day keying in data may suffer from a number of problems such as RSI (Repetitive Strain Injury which results in severe wrist pain), eyestrain or backache. There are strict rules on the design of workstations and the number and frequency of breaks that must be taken to try to prevent these problems.

Mouse

Most PCs also come with a mouse as an input device. The mouse usually has a rubber-coated ball inside it which drives two rollers, one for right-left movement and one for up-down movement. A message is then sent to the PC to tell it that the mouse has moved a certain amount. Two or three buttons on top of the mouse also send signals to the PC each time they are pressed.

Figure 25.2: Types of mouse

Some mice work with a laser beam instead of a ball, and others are cordless.

Scanner

An optical scanner can be used to scan graphical images and photographs, and software can then be used to edit or touch up the images. Scanners can also be used to read typed or even hand-written documents and OCR (Optical Character Recognition) software can then be used to interpret the text and export it to a word processor or data file. Scanners are also used to input large volumes of data on pre-printed forms such as credit card payments, where the customer's account number and amount paid are printed at the bottom of the payment slip.

Figure 25.3: A flatbed scanner

Optical Mark Recognition (OMR)

An optical mark reader can detect marks in preset positions on a form. It is widely used for marking multiple-choice exams and market research questionnaires.

Magnetic stripe

Cards with magnetic stripes are used as credit cards, debit cards, railway tickets, phone cards and many other applications such as customer loyalty cards. The magnetic strip can be encoded with up to 220 characters of data, and there are over 2.4 billion plastic card transactions every year in Britain, with 83% of adults owning at least one card. The information provided when someone signs up for a loyalty card with Sainsbury, Tesco, Boots or W.H.Smith, for example, plus a few months of shopping records, can provide a detailed portrait of customers' habits.

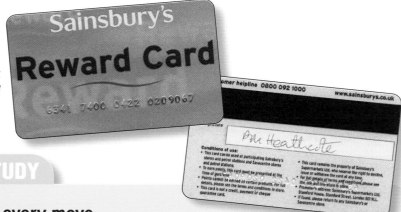

Figure 25.4: Magnetic Stripe card

CASE STUDY

Tracking your every move

With its reward scheme, Sainsbury's records every purchase made using the reward card, including the store name, the date and time and the price paid. Over a period of time this helps them to monitor trends in purchasing, which helps the store to predict the level of stockholding required in future, and ensures that they send customers information that they will be interested in. Sainsbury's will draw conclusions from your address; are you in an area classified as "rising", "prosperous and metropolitan professional", or "gentrified multi-ethnic"?

Customers are also classified by frequency of visits, average spend per visit and the type of goods they buy. For example, you might fall into the category of customer that "buys products which suggest they enjoy trying new and different ingredients in their cooking".

Under the Data Protection Act, you are entitled to see exactly what information is held about you. For a maximum charge of £10, a company from whom you request your personal information must send it to you within 40 days.

Bar code reader or scanner

Bar codes appear on almost everything we buy. The pattern of thick and thin bars represents the 13-digit number underneath the bar code.

Figure 25.5: A product bar code

Bar codes can be used in a wide range of applications that require fast and accurate data entry. These include:

Warehousing. Bar coded containers of raw materials are stored in racks of bins which are also bar coded. When goods are put into the warehouse, the computer system instructs an automatic crane to retrieve the nearest available empty bin. The filled bin is then returned to an empty location. The crane relies entirely on bar codes to move goods in and out.

Transport and distribution. All major road freight carriers now use bar codes. Individual packages are bar-coded as are depot consignments. The exact location of any package is known at any one time together with details of the type of service used. Individual customers can be billed quickly and missing parcels traced more easily.

Manufacturing. Very accurate data relating to work in progress can be obtained using bar codes as the data entry method. Management can obtain up-to-date data on the progress of unfinished goods, enabling bottlenecks and over-production to be reduced and production efficiency to improve.

Marketing. Many polling companies now use bar coded multiple-choice questionnaires to enter data quickly and accurately. Survey times can be dramatically reduced.

Libraries. Bar codes are used to record loans and provide more information on stock.

Banking, insurance and local government. Bar codes are used extensively for accurate document control and retrieval. Many cheque book covers, insurance claim files and council tax forms are bar coded.

Hand-held input devices

Portable keying devices are commonly used in such applications as reading gas or electricity meters, where the meter reader displays the next customer name, address and location of meter on a small screen, then reads the meter and keys in the reading. At the end of the day all the readings can be downloaded via a communications link to the main computer for processing.

Touch screen

A touch screen allows the user to touch an area of the screen rather than having to type the data on a keyboard. They are widely used in tourist centres, where tourists can look up various local facilities and entertainments, in fast food stores such as McDonald's for entering customer orders, in manufacturing and many other environments.

Figure 25.6: A touch screen

Sensors

Sensing hardware and software can be used to collect measurements such as temperature, light, movement or pressure in a laboratory, manufacturing plant or other environment, and convert it to computer data for analysis or for use in a control system.

Some common examples of computer-controlled systems are described below.

- Computer-controlled greenhouses use moisture sensors and temperature sensors to monitor the greenhouse environment. **Actuators** can then adjust the temperature and airflow or sprinkler system.

- Traffic lights have sensors to detect traffic. The sensor may be an infra-red movement detector mounted on top of the traffic lights, or a movement sensor under the road.

- Robots use vision, touch, heat or auditory sensors to modify their actions based on feedback from their environment.

Discussion

Think of some other examples of sensors found for example in homes, transport systems or manufacturing plants.

Exercises

1. Match up the following input devices with the most appropriate use: touchscreen, magnetic stripe reader, joystick, optical mark reader, voice input, bar code reader.

    a. Someone using a computer for games

    b. A journalist suffering from RSI

    c. Someone finding information on film times in a cinema complex

    d. A library assistant recording book loans to customers

    e. A telephone card used in a public telephone box

    f. Marking multiple choice exam papers

Chapter 26: Output Devices

Common output devices supplied with a PC include a screen (also called a Visual Display Unit or VDU) and printer. Both of these devices come in numerous different shapes, sizes and prices.

VDU

A VDU has three basic attributes: size, colour and resolution. It has its own fixed amount of RAM to store the image being displayed on the screen, and the amount of RAM that it has will determine the resolution and the maximum number of colours that can be displayed.

An image on the screen is displayed as an array of coloured **pixels**. A pixel, or picture element, is a tiny dot on the screen, and the resolution of the screen is measured in pixels. A common screen resolution is 800x600 pixels, but this can be changed by the user on the Display option of the Control Panel in MS Windows. You can also set the number of colours that can be displayed, from say, 256 colours to about 16 million colours.

More colours takes up more RAM, and so does higher resolution. The amount of RAM that is supplied with the screen will limit the resolution and number of colours that can be selected.

A screen used for graphic design will need to be large, high resolution and capable of displaying a good range of colours.

Figure 26.1: A graphic designer at work

Flat screens

Flat screens using LCD (Liquid Crystal Display) are becoming increasingly popular. They are similar to those supplied with laptop computers and although they are more expensive, have a number of advantages:

● they take up less space on the desk

● they consume much less power and emit less heat and no electromagnetic radiation

● they do not flicker since the pixels remain constantly lit, unlike conventional monitors which refresh the image 70 or 80 times each second

Figure 26.2: A flat screen

Printers

Printers can be obtained very cheaply for under £100. A printer has to be chosen carefully for its suitability to the job that it has to do. Colour-printing, noise, speed and running costs all need to be taken into account.

Dot Matrix printers

A dot matrix printer is an impact printer, producing its image by striking the paper through a ribbon. Its print head consists of a number of small pins, varying between 9 and 24 depending on the manufacturer. A 24-pin print head will produce a better quality of print than a 9-pin print head because the dots are closer together.

As the print head moves across the page, one or more pins strike the ribbon and make a dot on the paper. The figure below shows how the letter F is produced.

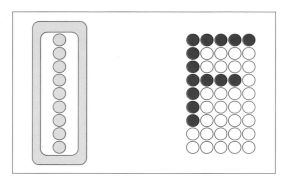

Figure 26.3: Dot matrix print head

Dot matrix printers are relatively cheap but have largely been replaced by newer technology, as the print quality does not compare with, say, laser-printed output. Also, they are noisy and are sometimes supplied with acoustic covers. They are useful for jobs (e.g. invoices) that require multi-part stationery which has holes down each side and is loaded onto sprockets on the printer. This is the cheapest method of printing multiple copies. Wide-carriage models are also available for printing on large custom stationery.

Figure 26.4: An Epson FX-1170 dot matrix printer

Ink Jet printers

These have become the most popular option for home printing as they are relatively cheap but provide reasonable quality text and graphics including colour printing. Ink jets work by forcing small dots of ink through tiny holes to form the text or graphics on the page. The ink is stored in replaceable cartridges, normally separate for colour and black ink.

This type of printer is capable of printing envelopes, labels, acetates and other specialist paper.

Figure 26.5: A colour ink jet printer

Laser Printers

Laser printers use fine black toner (powdered ink) similar to that used in photocopiers to produce high quality text and graphics.

Figure 26.6: An HP laserjet 2100 laser printer

A laser heats up a cylindrical drum and creates electrical charges on its surface which represent an image of the page to be printed. The toner sticks to the electrically-charged areas creating a 'negative image'. Paper is then rolled around the drum and the toner sticks to it creating a 'positive image'. The paper becomes heated which fuses the toner onto it.

The replaceable toner cartridges are relatively expensive, but can be refilled and recycled. Most laser printers have their own memory to store pages being processed which can make them quite expensive to purchase. However they are ideal for volume printing as they can print up to twelve pages per minute with the larger network models like the one shown in Figure 26.6 able to print 30 to 40 pages per minute or more.

Speakers

Multimedia computers need a sound card and speakers to be able to play music, spoken text or other sounds.

Some of the important things to consider in their specification are as follows:

- Power output per channel in watts RMS – usually in the range of 10-30 watts per channel.

- Frequency response – a high-quality card will reproduce the low-frequency sounds at 20Hz through to the high-frequency sounds at 20,000 Hz.

- Distortion, measured in percent. The lower the figure the better.

Figure 26.7: Powered speakers

When the volume of a sound changes, our ears can become less sensitive to higher notes. A Dynamic Bass Boost switch on speakers allows you to enhance the bass and treble sound quality to compensate for this.

Chapter 27: Storage Devices

Computer storage devices can be classified into two categories:

- **Primary storage**, i.e. random access memory (RAM). This type of storage holds data and instructions that are being worked on. When the computer is switched off, the contents of RAM are lost. This is known as **volatile** storage.

- **Secondary storage**, such as hard disks, floppy disks, CDs, DVD and magnetic tape. This type of storage is **non-volatile**.

Floppy disks

The standard 3½" floppy disk is a thin, flexible plastic disk coated in metal oxide, enclosed in a rigid plastic casing. A standard high-density disk has a storage capacity of 1.44 Megabytes.

A diskette consists of two surfaces, each of which contains typically 80 concentric circles called tracks. Each track is divided into sectors. A floppy disk has to be **formatted** before it can be used, and this process performs the following tasks:

- deletes any data already on the disk

- divides the disk into tracks and sectors – one sector holds 512 bytes of data

- sets up a root directory which lists the files on the disk and which sectors the data for each file is kept in

- finds any bad or damaged sectors on the disk that cannot be used

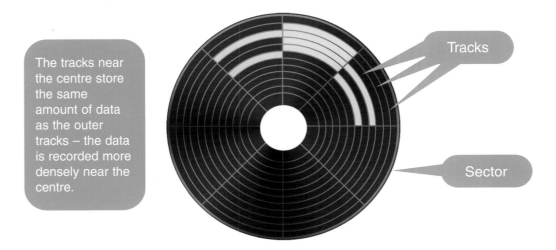

The tracks near the centre store the same amount of data as the outer tracks – the data is recorded more densely near the centre.

Figure 27.1: Tracks and sectors on a magnetic disk

Hard disks

The hard disks used with PCs consist of one or more disk platters permanently sealed inside a casing. Hard disks typically have a capacity of between 10Gb and 30Gb. (1Gb = 1,000Mb.)

Each surface has its own read-write head. The heads are mounted on a single spindle so they all move in and out together.

The hard disk inside a PC holds the operating system and all your files and programs. A typical hard disk supplied with a PC holds up to 30Gb or more.

The computer can read data much faster from a hard disk than from other types of disk.

CD-ROM drives

Compact disk read-only memory (CD-ROM) drives are now supplied with most PC systems. Up to 650Mb of data can be stored on these disks. Almost all software packages are supplied on CD-ROM. CD-ROMs use a laser beam to read the data from the rotating disk surface. The light reflected back is interpreted as data.

CD-ROMs have increased greatly in speed over the past few years but are not as fast as hard disks, nor do they store as much data. However they have the advantage of being very cheap and easily transportable.

Writeable CDs

Writeable CDs are now available in two different formats – CD-R (CD Recordable) and CD-RW (CD-Rewritable). Recordable CDs may only be written to once, though they can be read over and over. Writeable CDs can be written over many times. They are more expensive and have slower recording and playback times but they are useful as backup devices.

DVD-ROMs are used in many homes as a replacement for video tapes. DVD-ROM drives are read-only and have several advantages over CD-ROM:

- They have a much higher capacity, holding up to 17Gb of data.

- They are much faster.

- DVD-ROM drives can also play standard CD-ROMs and audio CDs.

- A DVD-ROM can hold up to 135 minutes of high-quality video and CD-quality sound. Many films are now released on DVD-ROM.

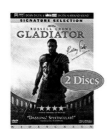

Discussion

Find out about other types of drive. For example, what is a combi-drive?

Figure 27.2: A DVD drive

Zip disks

When you study an organisation you may find they use other storage devices such as Zip, Jaz or tape drives for backup.

Zip disks are reasonably cheap (under £10 each) and more reliable than floppy disks. The older type holds 100Mb of data, while the newer disks hold 250Mb. They look more or less identical, but you cannot read a 250Mb disk in a standard 100Mb drive.
(The 250Mb drives will read both types.)

A Zip drive is often an option on a PC, together with a CD-ROM or DVD drive and a floppy drive. Alternatively, you can purchase an external disk drive for any of these. While they are faster than floppy disks, they are still much slower than hard disks.

An external Zip drive

Jaz disks

Jaz disks are bigger versions of Zip disks. They hold 1Gb of data, and like Zip disks, can be used on PCs and Macs. Because they hold so much data, they are ideal for multimedia applications, where graphics, animations, video and sound are used. They are much faster than floppy disks but still slower than hard disks.

DAT (Digital Audio Tape)

DAT is used almost exclusively for backups and for archiving old data that needs to be kept but which will probably never be used. Large amounts of data can be stored very cheaply and compactly using this medium.

Exercises

1. Fill in the table below, by writing the most appropriate storage medium to use for each application:

Application	Storage medium
Distributing commercial software	
Transporting data between two computers	
Making back-up copies of important information	
Storing software and information that you don't need to access constantly	
Copying information to give to someone else	

2. Look up the Internet (e.g. **www.howstuffworks.com**) to find out more information about storage devices. Arrange the following storage media:

    a. in order of speed, starting with the fastest

    b. in order of storage capacity, starting with the largest

DVD, floppy disk, CD-ROM, hard disk, Zip disks, Jaz disks.

For each of these storage media, give a typical storage capacity.

Interfaces

We've looked at the CPU, input, output and storage devices. Next we'll look at how the various devices are connected to the CPU.

All peripherals (input, output and storage devices) are connected to the computer through an **interface**. The use of an interface means that equipment from different manufacturers, having different speeds, voltages and so on can all be connected to a computer. There are a number of internationally accepted standard interfaces including **RS232**, **SCSI** and **Centronics**. Each peripheral is provided with an interface and is connected, usually via a cable, to the equivalent type of interface or **port** on the computer. The picture below shows the various ports on the back of a PC.

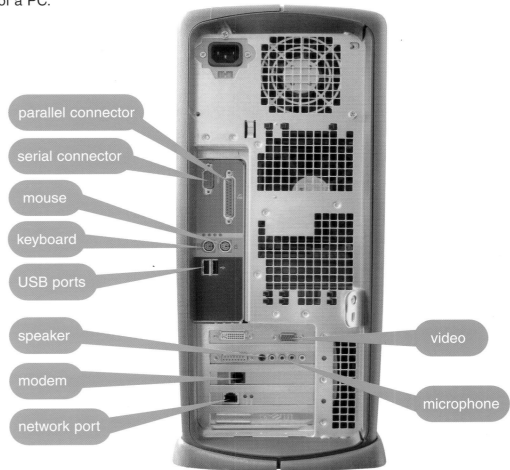

Figure 28.1: I/O connectors

Parallel interface

On most desktop PCs the parallel port is used to connect printers. Using parallel data transmission, 8 bits of data are sent down 8 parallel wires simultaneously. This is fast, but can only be done over a short distance no greater than say, two or three metres. Scanners, tape backup, and Zip drives are also designed to use the parallel port.

Serial interface

Most PCs have two serial port connectors – one 9-pin and a larger 25-pin. These ports are used by external peripherals such as modems (discussed later in this chapter) and scanners. Data transfer is much slower than through a parallel port as one bit follows another down a single wire.

Universal serial bus (USB)

USB ports have solved a major problem for PC users – the lack of sufficient serial  and parallel ports to plug all the peripherals into. Most desktop PCs now have two USB ports, into which any USB-compliant devices can be plugged. These include 'plug and play' devices such as mice, keyboards, scanners, printers, joysticks, digital cameras and audio speakers. USB ports have several advantages including:

- The snap-in connectors will support up to 127 linked peripherals (daisy-chained)

- Very fast data transfer rate, many times faster than a parallel port

- Devices can be swapped without restarting the PC

- Low-power devices such as modems and scanners can run without their own power supply

The USB standard uses **"A" and "B" connectors** to avoid confusion:

- **"A"** connectors head **"upstream"** toward the computer

- **"B"** connectors head **"downstream"** and connect to individual devices

Many USB devices come with their own built-in cable, and the cable has an "A" connection on it. If not, then the device has a socket on it that accepts a USB "B" connector.

By using different connectors on the upstream and downstream end, it is impossible to ever get confused -- if you connect any USB cable's "B" connector into a device, you know that it will work. Similarly, you can plug any "A" connector into any "A" socket and know that it will work.

Networks

A computer network is a collection of computers and peripherals connected together to enable users to communicate and share resources. These resources include hardware such as hard disks, printers and scanners, as well as software and data.

There are two different types of network:

- Local Area Network (LAN). This is a collection of computers connected together by cables, in the same building or on the same site.

- Wide Area Network (WAN). Computers anywhere in the world may be connected together by telephone or radio links.

In order to connect computers together in a LAN, each computer needs to be fitted with a **network interface card** (NIC). The network cable then plugs into a socket on the NIC.

Most organisations with more than two or three computers have them connected in a LAN. Then, each workstation can have access to the main **file server** on which all their data is stored. This means that anyone in the organisation can, for example, access and update a database or work on a document such as a letter or spreadsheet that was created at another computer.

Having all the company's data stored on a central file server also makes it much easier to back up. The file server may have a tape drive and software which automatically backs up the hard disk every night. The tape is then removed in the morning and the next day's tape inserted in the drive ready for the next night's backup.

Figure 28.2 shows one way of connecting computers in a LAN.

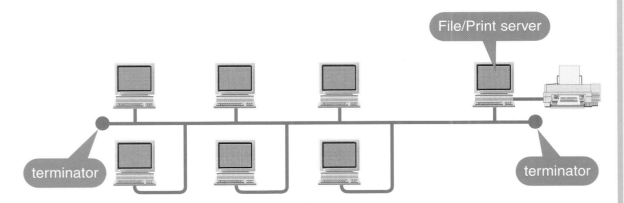

Figure 28.2

Wide area network

The best-known wide area network is the Internet. Anyone can be part of a wide area network. The hardware needed is a **modem** (**mo**dulator-**dem**odulator) and a telephone connection.

A modem is needed when connecting via a normal telephone line because these lines are designed to transmit **analogue** signals in the form of sound waves. Computer data is in digital format – a pattern of 0s and 1s. A modem at one end converts the digital signal to analogue, and a modem at the other end converts the signal from analogue to digital so that the computer can receive the data.

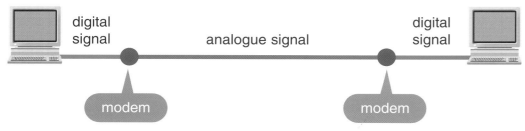

Figure 28.3: A modem

ISDN

The amount of data that can be sent over a line depends partly on the **bandwidth**, which is the range of frequencies that the line can carry. The greater the bandwidth, the greater the rate at which data can be sent, as several messages can be transmitted simultaneously. A network that is capable of sending voice, video and computer data is called an **Integrated Services Digital Network (ISDN)**, and this requires a high bandwidth.

ADSL

Asymmetric Digital Subscriber Line (ADSL) is a new technology which enables existing copper wire telephone lines to be used to transmit computer data at extremely fast rates. The subscriber needs an ADSL modem and two ADSL devices. A 'splitter' (which is a filter), one at the user end and one at the exchange end, separates the telephony signal from the ADSL signal. This means that telephone calls can be made at the same time that data is being sent or received (i.e. a customer can surf the Internet and still make telephone calls).

Network protocol

In order to allow equipment from different suppliers to be networked, a strict set of rules (**protocols**) has been devised covering standards for physical connections, cabling, speed, data format etc. Any equipment which uses the same protocol can be linked together.

Exercises

1. One common type of network is an *Ethernet* network. Look up Ethernet on **www.howstuffworks.com** and make notes on how this technology works.

2. What is the difference between a **LAN** and a **WAN**? What hardware is needed in order to connect to a WAN?

3. Give **three** advantages of connecting computers together in a local area network.

Chapter 29: System Design and Implementation

In the preceding chapters you have looked at the different departments in an organisation, how each department may use ICT, and some of the hardware that may be used. If you have had a chance to visit different organisations, you will have seen people using ICT for a variety of purposes.

For this course you will have to design and implement an ICT system. You may be able to choose your own project for a real user, or your teacher may suggest a scenario for you. You will be able to use software such as Excel or Access to implement the project.

Input-Process-Output

The first step is to find a suitable project. It needs to be an application which accepts data, processes it in some way and then produces output. It will not be sufficient to produce a word-processed or desktop-published document, or a PowerPoint presentation.

Here are some examples of what is meant by the three stages **Input**, **Process**, **Output**.

Project	Input	Process	Output
Student grades system	Teacher keys in student marks	Computer system calculates percentages	Report on student grades
Mobile Phone Tariff Selector	List of mobile phone tariffs and a user's average monthly usage	Calculate the best tariff for the user	Best network and tariff displayed on screen
Royalties systems	Monthly book sales, authors' royalty rates	Calculate royalty for each author	Report on royalty payments
Video shop system	Details of videos members, details of video loans and returns	Query to find overdue videos, most popular videos, monthly loans etc.	Reminder to members about overdue videos, reports on most popular videos monthly loans etc.
Theatre bookings system	Dates of plays, seats sold	Calculate total ticket revenue. Query to find available seats	Report on revenue. Screen display of available seats

Data Flow Diagrams (DFDs)

One way of documenting how data flows through an organisation is to use a data flow diagram. These diagrams show where the data comes from, what processing takes place, where the data is stored and who receives the output from the system.

The following four symbols are used in data flow diagrams:

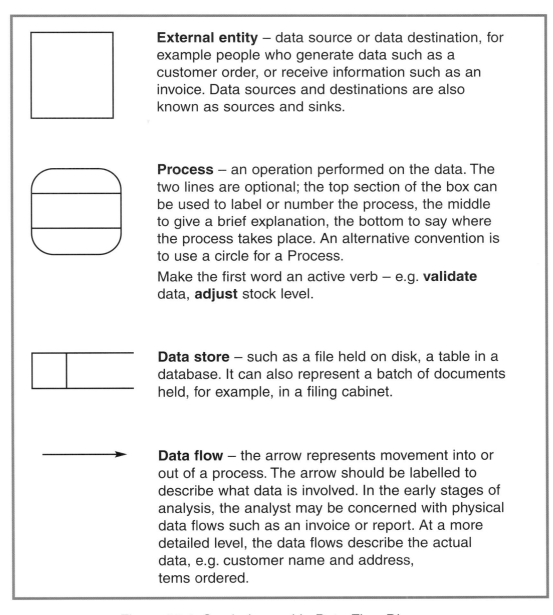

External entity – data source or data destination, for example people who generate data such as a customer order, or receive information such as an invoice. Data sources and destinations are also known as sources and sinks.

Process – an operation performed on the data. The two lines are optional; the top section of the box can be used to label or number the process, the middle to give a brief explanation, the bottom to say where the process takes place. An alternative convention is to use a circle for a Process.

Make the first word an active verb – e.g. **validate** data, **adjust** stock level.

Data store – such as a file held on disk, a table in a database. It can also represent a batch of documents held, for example, in a filing cabinet.

Data flow – the arrow represents movement into or out of a process. The arrow should be labelled to describe what data is involved. In the early stages of analysis, the analyst may be concerned with physical data flows such as an invoice or report. At a more detailed level, the data flows describe the actual data, e.g. customer name and address, tems ordered.

Figure 29.1: Symbols used in Data Flow Diagrams

We will look at some examples of data flow diagrams.

Example 1:

An Examining Board receives student marks from the examiners who mark the papers. The Board enters the marks to their computer system which calculates the grade (A-E or U) which is to be awarded, and sends the results to the students. A report on the results of all students entered from each school is sent to the school concerned.

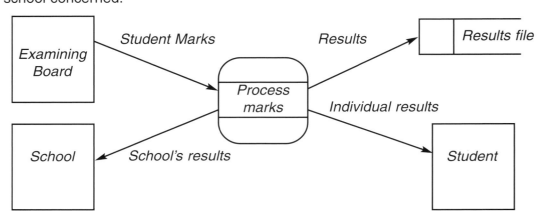

> **Note:** There are not many hard and fast rules to follow when drawing data flow diagrams. However, you should not draw a flow line from one entity to another without going through a process, as this does not involve the computer. So in the above example, the action of examiners sending the marks to the Examining Board is not shown, as it is not part of the computer system.

Example 2:

A customer orders some CDs from an online store. The order is entered into the sales order processing system. The price of the CD is looked up from a file of stock items, and an invoice is printed to be sent to the customer with the CD. Details of the sale are stored on the Sales file.

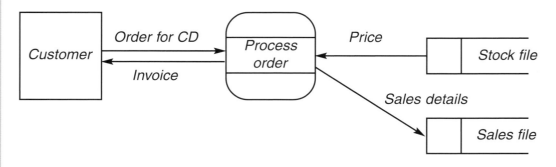

Example 3:

A customer orders some CDs from an online store. All customers are given 30 days credit. The customer is looked up on the customer file and if they are a new customer, their details are stored.

The order is entered into the sales order processing system. The price of the CD is looked up from a file of stock items, and an invoice is printed to be sent to the customer with the CD. Details of the sale are stored on the Sales file.

At the end of each month the Accounts Department prints statements to send to all customers. A report of overdue accounts is kept in the Accounts Department.

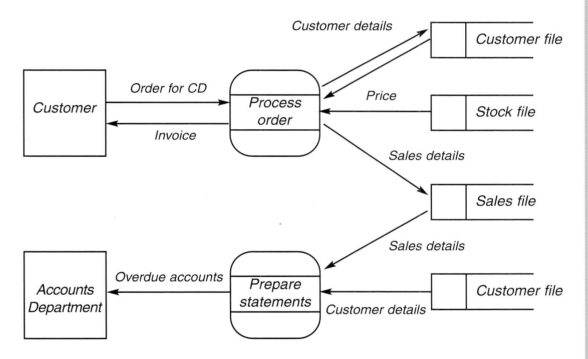

Example 4: (For you to complete)

The manager of a Video Club queries the computer to find all the customers with overdue videos and sends out reminders to those customers.

Ask: Who are the external entities? What is the process? What data is stored? What data flows are there?

Design, implementation and testing

Once you have found a suitable problem for your project work, you must go through the following stages:

- Identify the user requirements

- Analyse the existing system and the objectives of the new system

- Produce a design specification

- Implement the system

- Test the system

- Produce user documentation

- Evaluate the design and implementation

You will need help with writing up all these stages. You are strongly recommended to buy a book such as **ICT Projects for GCSE** by Robert Heathcote, published by Payne-Gallway Publishers. This shows how four different projects are taken through the various stages and documented for a GCSE project.

User documentation

The user documentation for a project may be a separate document. It should be aimed at the user of your system, telling them what the system does and how they should start it up, enter data and get the required output. Some sample user documentation for the Access project given in **ICT Projects for GCSE** may be downloaded from our website www.payne-gallway.co.uk/aict.

Chapter 30: Portfolio work

This chapter gives you some advice about each stage of project work. For the Edexcel specification you will need to do two major pieces of work for Unit 2.

Investigating an organisation

For the first task, you will have to investigate an organisation (or a department in a large organisation) and compile a portfolio that includes a report on:

(a) the different purposes for which the organisation/department uses ICT

(b) the ICT system used in the organisation/department, and how it meets the needs identified in (a).

Your first task will be to choose a suitable organisation to investigate. Do you have parents who work in an organisation, or do you have a part-time job? Have you had any work experience? Personal contacts are very useful when you want to find out information.

The organisation you choose could be a local factory, shop, hotel, theatre or restaurant, a library, doctor's surgery or even your own school. You need to approach the person in charge (the manager, Head of Department, or owner) – explain what you need to do and ask for their help. Try to fix an appointment for a time convenient for them when you can come back for more information.

Gathering information

There are several ways in which you can gather information for your portfolio. For example:

- You can ask to spend some time in the organisation or Department, being shown what tasks need to be done and how ICT is used. You should have a notebook and make a note of what you find out so that you don't forget anything.

- You can interview the person in charge and have them explain to you the way that things are done. Make notes during the interview.

- You can collect some of the documents that are used in the organisation – these might be input documents such as order forms, or output documents in the form of reports.

You should put any documents that you collect in your portfolio, together with notes of any interviews you had. You could also ask for permission to take some photographs and use these in your report to illustrate your descriptions.

> **Tip:**
> Try to contact several local organisations and arrange visits so that you can see for yourself the different ways that ICT is used.

Interviewing

Interviewing different people in the organisation is a very good way of finding out information. You must be well-prepared, however – you will probably only have one shot at each interview and you want to make sure you come away with all the facts.

Make a list of questions. Look back at what you have studied in this unit to help you. You can ask, for example:

- Do you use ICT for communicating between people in the organisation? (This would include having a company Intranet, internal e-mails, newsletters, internal memos etc.)

- Do you use ICT for communicating with customers or suppliers? (This might include e-mails, sending out catalogues, reminders or letters using a mailing list, having a voice-mail system, using a mobile phone, etc.)

- Do you have a computerised system for sales? What software is used?

- Do you have a computerised stock control system? How does this work? What reports does it produce? Would it be possible for me to have a sample report for my portfolio?

- What hardware is used in each department?

You can also ask questions about how computers are used in Finance, Production and Marketing. Does the company have a website? Be sure you have read the chapters in this Unit so that you can direct your questions carefully. Of course, you will have to tailor your questions to the particular organisation or department you are investigating. But remember, almost all organisations carry out the basic functions of

- Sales

- Purchasing

- Finance

- Operations

You need to find out how these functions are carried out (even if they are not called by these names) and what hardware and software is used.

> **Tip:**
> If you are visiting a very large organisation you should confine your investigation to a single department and make your questions relevant to the work of that department only.

> **Discussion**
>
> **Suppose you have chosen your school as the organisation to investigate. Who will you need to interview? (You may need to interview several people.) What questions will you need to ask?**

The report

You need to organise your report into sections, and it must be word-processed. Start by giving a general description of the organisation. You will probably find a lot of useful information on their website if they have one, and you should use this source, but don't just copy and paste – write things in your own words. For example, if you are investigating a school, you might start like this:

Part 1: Using ICT in Bashford School

(This heading can have a page of its own)

Bashford School

Bashford High School is a large, thriving comprehensive school in Bashford. There is a Lower School, Middle School, Sixth Form and Science & Technology Centre. The Bashford Arts Centre is located at the school. The County Music and Performing Arts Services are also based here. Bashford is lucky to have outstanding sports facilities, and the Bashford Sports Centre complex at the school is also used by the wider community.

There are currently over 1600 pupils at the school, with over 500 students in the Sixth Form and almost 100 teaching staff. Pupils are drawn mainly from the local area and owing to its high standards and excellent results, there are always more pupils applying than there are places for.

Overview of ICT at Bashford

(Now you should give an overview of the different areas where ICT is used, from the information you have gathered in your investigation. This could include school administration systems, publicity (e.g. the website), computer labs and computers in the classrooms, and other specific uses.)

Computers in the Classroom

(Describe the computer facilities. How many computer labs are there? How many computers in each? What are the computers used for? Are they used right across the curriculum?)

Computers in Administration

(Describe the tasks that need to be done, and how ICT helps.)

Continue with other headings, covering a wide range of purposes for which the school uses ICT. Look at a relevant chapter in Unit 3, e.g. Chapter 36, to get ideas of what you should be looking for.

Tip:

Don't forget to illustrate your report with scanned photographs and/or screenshots of their website.

The hardware and software

The second part of the first task involves writing a report on what software and hardware is used in the organisation, and how it meets their needs.

Part 2: The ICT system at Bashford School

(This heading can have a page of its own)

Hardware components

(Describe the hardware that is used. Is there a single network, or several networks? Is the administration system completely separate from the networked computers used in classrooms? Are there standalone computers used for special purposes? Are special devices like smart card, bar code or magnetic stripe readers used at all?

Software systems for Administration

(You will need subheadings for each separate application.) Describe the software systems that are used for different purposes within the school. Do the staff use e-mail? Do they use Word, Excel, Access, etc? Does the Sports Centre use a computerised booking system? Is pupil enrolment computerised? Does the Library use a computerised system? Is there a website?

How well do these systems meet the needs of pupils, teachers and administrative staff?

Software systems for Teaching and Learning

(You will need subheadings for each separate application.) Describe the software systems used in the classrooms. Do you use any computer-aided learning? Do teachers use PowerPoint presentations, or other technology?

How well do these systems meet the needs of pupils, teachers and administrative staff?

The complete portfolio

Your complete portfolio will need to be neatly bound in a plastic binder. You should have a header page giving your name and the title of the project. Then include a Table of Contents, followed by your report. In an Appendix, include all the source material you used. This could be questions for interview, notes you made from the interviews you conducted, sample forms and reports that you were given, and so on.

The second assessment

The second assessment is worth nearly 60% of your marks for this Unit.

Try to select a project that performs some well defined task, as described at the start of Chapter 29. You will then need to go through the stages of Identification, Analysis, Design, Implementation and Testing, Evaluation. These stages could form the five sections of your report, and this is the format followed in **ICT Projects for GCSE** by R.S.U. Heathcote. In addition, you must produce User Documentation.

Identification

In the Identification section you need to identify the user. Give a brief introduction setting the scene and saying something about the organisation. Then state what the objectives of the new system are. You should be specific in the objectives: for example, do not say 'The objective is to make the system user-friendly and efficient.' Instead, mention specific things that the system will do, such as 'The system will produce a printed report showing the number of pupil absences each day'. Consider some alternative ways of solving the problem and then justify your chosen solution.

Analysis

Here is a sample outline:

Analysis

Hardware and software

(State what software you will be using, e.g. MS Access 2000 and why. Then state what hardware will be used.)

Data collection and input

(Specify exactly what data needs to be collected and stored. E.g. Pupil/employee first name, surname, date of birth, etc. State how this information will be collected.

Data manipulation

(Specify exactly how the data will be stored, e.g. table design in an Access database. Explain how the data will be processed to produce these reports – e.g. a database may be queried, totals may be calculated etc.)

Draw a Data Flow Diagram showing data sources, processes and destinations.

Output

(Consider whether output will be on screen, printed reports, or even through speakers.)

Design

In the Design section, you must produce initial designs with enough information for the user to have an idea about suitability. Get feedback from the user to make sure you are on the right track, and then create your final designs. These should show details of input screens and output reports, and an explanation of the processing. You should break the project down into subtasks and your design documentation should be sufficiently detailed that someone else could implement your system from it. Finally, you should include a test plan that will test the whole system.

Here is a sample outline:

Design

Input

Show rough designs for any screen input forms that will be used.) A menu design can be used to show what the system will do, e.g. Add/edit customer data, Print reports, etc. Show a menu structure diagram.

Output

(Show some rough designs for output so that the user can confirm that you have correctly understood the requirements.)

User Feedback

(Show the initial designs to the user and get feedback, before you proceed to final designs.)

Final designs

(Show the initial designs to the user and get feedback, before you proceed to final designs. These should show detailed screen and report designs, and a description of processing tasks in sufficient detail that a third party could implement your design. Describe any validations that will be carried out on the data, and any security measures such as passwords that you plan to implement.)

Test plan

Your test plan could take the form of a table with the following column headings:

Test number	Purpose of Test	Test data	Expected result

You will probably need between 10 and 20 tests to thoroughly test your system.

Implementation and Testing

In this section you need to make it clear that your system fulfils all the objectives. You should describe how you implemented the system. Describe any difficulties you had and how you solved any problems. Show evidence in the form of screenshots for each test in your test plan, which should cover the whole system. Where the tests do not work as expected, include screenshots and then explain what you did to make the system work correctly. For some parts of the system, you may need to get a witness statement from a teacher or user to say that the system works as specified.

Evaluation

In this section you should evaluate how well your system meets the original objectives. If there is anything that does not work, you should say why this is so. Show the finished system to the user and get feedback from them in the form of a letter which you can insert into this section.

Then give some suggestions as to how your system could be further improved. Here is an example of how to write this section:

Evaluation

Evaluation of initial objectives

(Go through each objective and describe how the system fulfils it.)

User feedback

(Document the user's comments and include a letter if possible. You could also prepare a questionnaire to be filled in by the user or users.)

Further ideas for improvement

(Have at least two ideas for further improvement.)

User manual

The user manual is aimed at a non-technical user and should use plain English. It should include:

- A title page

- A table of contents

- An introduction, stating what the system is about and who it is for

- Examples of actual screen displays such as menus, data input screens and output screens

- Samples of printed output

- An explanation of what each item on a menu does

- Any special instructions on how to input data – for example the format of a date field, or the range of accepted values in an amount field

- A hotline help number

Taking screenshots

You will need to take screenshots of the application to put in the user manual. The easiest way to do this is to use one of the following key combinations:

- **Prt Scr** copies a picture of the whole screen into the clipboard

- **Alt-Prt Scr** copies the active window into the clipboard

You can then paste your screenshot into an open Word document (the user manual.)

Cropping a screenshot

When you have pasted the screenshot into the Word document, you may need to crop it to show only part of it.

Click the graphic, and if the Picture toolbar is not visible, right-click and select **Show Picture Toolbar**. The toolbar will appear.

Figure 30.1: The Picture toolbar

Use the **Crop** tool to crop the screenshot.

Two pages from the user manual to accompany the Access database project from **ICT Projects for GCSE** by **RSU Heathcote** are shown on the next two pages. You can download the whole user manual from the Payne-Gallway Website.

Student Mark Record System User Manual

Introduction

This system is designed to record the grades obtained by each student for all types of assessment (e.g. homework, coursework projects and exams) in a particular subject. It is for use by a teacher in a school. Reports are produced to show an individual student's grades for all assignments, all students' grades for all assignments and all students' grades for a particular assignment.

The system is written in MS Access 2002, and will run on a Pentium PC or a similar specification. It is not necessary for the user to have any knowledge of Access.

Installation

The software should have already been installed onto your computer. It is in a folder named **Access** on the hard disk.

Starting up the system

- Load MS Access.

- From the **File** menu select **Open**. Find the **GradesDatabase.mdb** file in the folder **Access** on the hard disk.

- You will be asked to enter a password:

Figure 1

- Enter the password, **Grades**.

Now you will see the Database window:

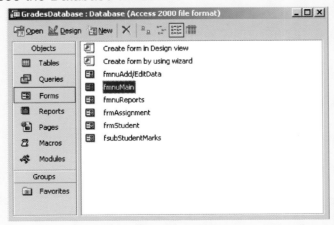

Figure 2

The Main Menu

- Make sure the Forms tab is selected, as in Figure 2.
- Double-click **fmnuMain**.

The main menu will be displayed.

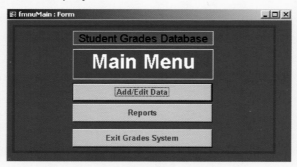

Figure 3

Add/Edit Data Menu

When you select this menu item, a submenu will appear:

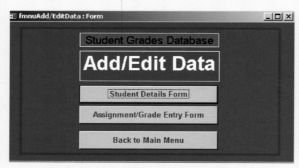

Figure 4

Tip:

You will find the rest of the user manual on the website www.payne-gallway.co.uk/aict

Adding Student information

The Student Details form is used to add new students to the database, to amend a student's details or to delete a student's details.

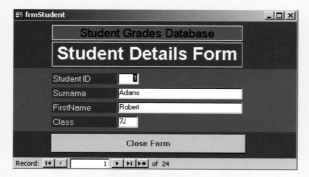

Figure 5

ICT in Society

3

About this unit

This unit will help you to understand how far ICT systems affect your everyday life. You will explore how individuals, families, clubs, people at work and community groups use ICT. Some individuals and groups do not have access to ICT, yet ICT may still affect them in their social, personal and professional lives.

New ICT products and applications are constantly being developed and the pace of development is so fast that technology that seemed extraordinary a year or two ago now seems normal or even outdated by the next arrival.

You will also explore how and why ICT can have negative as well as positive effects.

World Wide Web

The Internet is a worldwide collection of interconnected computers; the **Web** is a way of using some of these computers to share files and **Web pages**. These private and public Web pages are owned and managed by Universities, schools, government departments, companies and private individuals. Each website consists of pages of information, and billions of websites are stored on computers known as **servers** all around the world.

The Internet started life as a military research project in the United States. In the 1980s US academic institutions joined the network. Gradually companies and other institutions from all over the globe began connecting to the growing 'net' and building Web pages.

When you make a website, you save it on a server somewhere so that other people can visit your site. Every website has a unique address or **URL** (Uniform Resource Locator).

Did you know?...

Addresses on the Internet are located by the use of a URL which is typed in the address space in your browser's toolbar. Each part of the URL is separated by dots.

e.g. **http://www.payne-gallway.co.uk**

Identifies the site as using HTTP (hypertext transfer protocol)

Tells your browser that the next words will be a URL

Identifies the site as part of the World Wide Web

This is the registered *domain name*

This is the **top-level domain name**; it identifies the type of organisation e.g. commercial (.co or .com), government (.gov), or educational (.ac or.edu) and the country that the website belongs to e.g. uk (UK), fr (France), de (Germany), es (Spain)

Individuals on the net

Internet usage has expanded exponentially over the past few years. A few years ago, only a handful of schools had Internet connections to enable their students to log on. Now, students are using the Internet to download notes and tests, to e-mail their work between home and school, and to carry out research on any number of topics.

> **Discussion**
>
> **For what other reasons do individuals use the Internet?**

Task: Using the Internet

Carry out some research about the best deal for a holiday. Identify a specific need e.g. a holiday for a family of four travelling in late July to Majorca for two weeks from a specific airport and needing full-board accommodation. You may also want to specify other criteria, for example a hotel with a swimming pool. Select four or five different online travel companies and find out about each deal, especially price.

a.   Write a short introduction explaining how you carried out this task and then write a short report of your findings.

b.   Include a table showing the different prices and deals on offer for your chosen holiday.

c.   Illustrate your findings with relevant images.

E-mail

E-mail allows you to communicate electronically with friends or organisations. You may be able to use a home computer, your mobile phone or your Personal Digital Assistant (PDA) to transmit messages, graphics, sound, video files and data.

To use e-mail you must have:

- access to a device which has the ability to connect to the Internet

- Internet services provided by an Internet Service Provider (ISP)

- suitable software to send and receive e-mail. One of the most commonly-used programs is Microsoft Outlook Express, which is normally supplied with Windows. Many people use Webmail accounts such as Hotmail, Yahoo or MSN. The advantage of this type of account is that it is free, and you can access your e-mail from any computer all over the world.

More and more business is now being conducted using e-mail. The number of e-mails sent worldwide person-to-person on a daily basis is predicted to become 36 billion by 2005.

(Source: E-mail Usage Forecast and Analysis Report 2001-2005 by IDC).

Advantages of e-mail

E-mail has many advantages over ordinary mail:

- the message is usually received almost instantaneously

- it is very simple to compose, send and reply to e-mail

- large files such as video clips, audio files and documents can be attached

- e-mails can be encrypted for extra security

- it is a convenient and low-cost form of communication

- messages can be sent from your PC without having to leave your desk

Disadvantages of e-mail

E-mail also has some disadvantages:

- sometimes an important message may get lost along with other 'spam' (junk) e-mails

- an e-mail message may seem less formal and important so may only get a casual response

- constant e-mailing can be an intrusion on a worker's day

- personal working relationships do not develop as well without voice contact

- can be abused and used for unsavoury communications which may offend people

- viruses sent with attachments can infect the recipient's computer

E-mail has opened up a new way of communicating that is used by millions of people across the globe. Students hitchhiking abroad can keep in touch with their parents simply by dropping into an Internet café and e-mailing from their Hotmail address. A grandmother in Tooting can receive photographs of her grandchildren in Australia, taken the same day, and respond instantly.

At work too, many people would find it hard to imagine a day without e-mail communication. Business deals that used to take days or weeks can be completed in a few hours, thanks to the ability to e-mail draft documents, designs, manuscripts and so on which are received almost instantly.

Instant messaging

Instant Messaging is a fairly new form of communication which has increased in popularity recently.

- You can send and receive messages in an extra window on your desktop PC in real time, getting immediate feedback.

- If you have a microphone, you can actually talk to someone using the same software (e.g. MSN Messenger).

- The program informs you when your online friend is typing you a message, away from their desk or even too busy to chat.

- The software (e.g. MSN Messenger) is easily and freely available for downloading via the Internet.

- It may soon be available to mobile phone/PDA users in the form of wireless instant messaging.

Instant messaging has huge business potential. A technical support member of the team could give quick and no-nonsense answers whilst the sender is in the middle of taking another call. A secretary could let her boss know, whilst he is busy chatting to his friend, that another urgent call had come in. Messages can be sent instantly to more than one person at a time and the receiver can respond to the first reply, making response time much more efficient. Of course, the technology relies on the receiver being at their desk to take the message.

Scenario Double trouble for Internet booker

Web user Claire Manning was really proud of herself when she booked her honeymoon online with FarAway Places. She had never heard of them before but the holiday looked fantastic value. In fact she has organised the entire wedding using her computer and the Internet. She has booked the cars, the hotel for the night before the wedding for her and her friends, the wedding cake, the flowers and the band using the Internet. She has even sent the wedding invitations via e-mail!

However, it is now only a week before the big day and she has found lots of e-mails in her Inbox returned with invalid addressee information. Some of the things she has ordered for her wedding have not arrived, as the addressee details on the e-mails she sent were incorrect. Almost worse, two pairs of tickets and holiday details have arrived from FarAway Places for her planned holiday to the Maldives.

Further problems surface when Claire gets a call from her bank to say she is overdrawn by £1500. It seems that she has been charged twice for the holiday. The bank tells her that some of the cheques for items she has purchased for the wedding cannot be honoured and have been returned to the companies from whom Clare has ordered goods and services. Claire refuses to panic but when she tries to access the FarAway Places website she cannot locate the page on her browser and the phone number given in the documentation accompanying the tickets is unobtainable.

Questions:

1 What should Claire do and in what order?

2 What could Claire have done to avoid these problems happening?

3 What do you think Claire has learnt about using the Internet?

4 Draw up a list of tips for someone using the Internet for transactions.

CASE STUDY

Dr. Cooley performs open heart surgery broadcast live on Internet

Dr. Denton A. Cooley performed a quadruple coronary bypass surgery on August 19th 2001. America's Health Network (AHN) broadcast the surgery from St. Luke's Episcopal Hospital. This was the first time such an operation has been broadcast live simultaneously on the Internet and cable television.

Dr. Cooley led the surgical team, assisted by cardiovascular surgeon Dr. J. Michael Duncan. AHN's Dr. Walt Larimore provided continuous medical commentary.

"We elected to take part in the Internet broadcast because it offers us an unprecedented opportunity to teach the public the importance of heart disease prevention, and to inform them about the new technologies and treatments that have helped many patients live longer and more satisfying lives," said Dr. Cooley.

"Someone dies every 33 seconds in the United States from heart disease, but at the Texas Heart Institute we believe this is a statistic

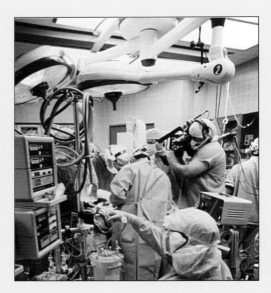

Figure 31.1: The Heart Operation (Photograph courtesy of America's Health Network)

that can be reduced through greater awareness, because a healthier heart is within everyone's reach."

The operation was performed on Rena Fluker, a 48 year-old woman from Pasadena, Texas. A wife and mother of three children, Fluker was diagnosed with multi-vessel coronary artery disease. "This is a very intelligent woman whose attitude is, 'If this will help someone else, I'm happy to do it," Dr. Cooley said.

Questions:

1   What are the moral arguments for and against this type of broadcast?

2   What types of broadcast do you think should never be shown?

3   Describe the motives of the doctors at the hospital in agreeing to this operation being broadcast across the globe.

Multimedia

Multimedia is the combination of some or all of text, graphics, animation, sound and video. You have probably already discovered how simple it is to download pictures, sounds, video and animation clips for use in your own presentations.

Music has become extremely popular on the Internet because of MP3 technology. MP3 (which stands for Mpeg 1 Audio Layer 3) is a form of compression which dramatically decreases the time that it takes to download an album. The file size is reduced to around one-tenth of the original size while the sound quality remains good.

The downside of the new file format is that it has become very easy to pirate music without the knowledge or consent of the artist or record company.

Security on the Internet

Online shopping has grown massively over the past few years. Everything from groceries, books and clothes to airline seats and tickets to a Broadway show can be purchased over the Internet. But making a purchase generally involves typing in a credit card number, and many people are reluctant to do this for fear of fraud. In order to reduce the chance of credit card numbers being intercepted and then used fraudulently, they are **encrypted** before being sent.

Encryption is the process of scrambling messages so that they cannot be read without the 'key' to the code. Of course, given sufficient time and money, almost any code can eventually be broken by a determined hacker.

There are many different types of encryption software, although most modern encryption systems use public-key encryption. This uses two keys, a public key and a private key; the public key is used for encrypting the message and the private key (different for each individual) is used for decoding the message.

Discussion

Some governments forbid the use of so-called strong encryption which is virtually impossible to break. This is so that they can keep watch on the activities of terrorists and criminals. However, this means that legitimate businesses cannot use strong encryption to prevent criminals hacking into their data. What is your view on this? Can you propose any solution?

If you or your parents have a credit card, are you or they happy to give the number over the Internet to a 'secure site' - that is, one that uses encryption? (See Case Study: 'Hacker "Curador" Escapes Jail' on page 255.)

Connecting to the Internet

There are several ways of connecting to the Internet. The most common are as follows:

Modem

A modem is a device which enables your computer to be connected via a telephone cable to another computer, usually an Internet service provider or ISP, in order to access the Internet. It converts the digital output of your computer into analogue signals, which can be understood and transmitted along analogue telephone cables. At the receiving end, another modem converts the analogue signal back to digital to be input to the recipient's computer.

A modem may be internal to your computer's hardware or external as an additional input/output device. Top speed is, theoretically, 56Kbps.

ISDN (Integrated Services Digital Network)

This is used mainly by businesses owing to the relatively high cost. It allows much faster transmission of voice, video and computer data without the need for a modem as the connections all speak 'digitally' to one another using a dedicated private line. ISDN operates at either 64Kbps or 128Kbps.

Broadband

Broadband is a relatively new technology used for accessing the Internet.

- It allows more information via your phone line, cable TV or satellite dish owing to the higher bandwidth (think of a large-diameter water pipe, which allows more water to flow than a narrow one.) When Internet access is shared between several people in a class of students or a small business, everyone gets faster access.

- Connections operate at a much faster speed.

Currently in the UK there are two main types of broadband access:

1. ADSL (Asymmetric Digital Subscriber Line)

This is a newer and cheaper technology offering broadband services. An ADSL line converts an ordinary telephone line into an extremely fast Internet connection at least 40 times faster than currently popular 56Kbps modems. What's more, the line can still be used for voice at the same time. There is no need for dial-up connections as you are constantly connected. Usage is unmetered 24 hours a day, 7 days a week.

Not all geographical locations are being upgraded by telecommunications companies so not all Internet users will be able to take advantage of this.

In the future, this technology could make video-conferencing a workable option in many situations, e.g. to help with teacher shortages or to provide health and specialist consultancy services. The technology allows people at remote locations access to one another without the inconvenience and cost of travel.

2. Cable broadband

This is a service provided by cable television companies using an existing fibre-optic cable connection, facilitating high speed access to the Internet. The setup and monthly costs are cheaper than ADSL, and usage is similarly unmetered.

Greater competition between cable providers will probably mean that this is the most cost-effective choice for broadband customers and households in the future.

Exercises

1. Cryptography allows messages to be secretly passed to another person. The code may be very simple yet, without the knowledge of how the code works, other people will be unable to understand your transmissions. One simple method (too simple to be useful!) is to substitute numbers for all vowels, i.e. A=1, E=2, I=3, O=4, U=5, and move the consonants forward two places, i.e. B=D, C=E, D=F, F=H, G=I, H=J, J=L, K=M, L=N, M=O, N=P, P=R, Q=S, R=T, S=U, T=V, V=X, W=Y, X=Z, Y=A, Z=B.
   Therefore the word "HELLO" would be "J2NN4" and "INFORMATION" would be "3PH4TO1V34P"

   a. Translate the following message:
      "3VU4PNA21UAV45PF2TUV1PFYJ2PA45MP4YVJ2U2ET2V"

   b. Develop your own encryption method and write a short message (to include your name) and see how long it takes your friends to crack your code!

2. Surf the Internet for the latest available broadband technologies and products. Try to find at least 4 providers of these services to make a proper comparison.

   a. Create a table comparing monthly costs, installation/setup fees, maximum upload speed, maximum download speed, Web space included, number of e-mail addresses and availability of technical support.

   b. Which company offers the best deal?

Chapter 32: Mobile Technologies

Mobile phones

Mobile phones are a versatile and powerful communication device for sending and receiving information from anywhere in the world. Until only a few years ago they were considered to be the stuff of science fiction movies. Today they have become a disposable consumer commodity, replaceable when new technology becomes available. Mobile phones can have huge memory capacity, capable of storing address books, calendars, reminders, data, images and files. In the future we may even use our mobile phones to ring home directly to switch on the oven or turn the lights off.

There are 24 million mobile phone users in the UK at present (2002), including an estimated 300,000 children. They can be used to send and receive voice, text, picture and animation messages. In addition, with the use of additional technology such as a Multimedia Card (MMC), they can take digital photos, play the radio, MP3 (music) files and short animation files.

SMS (Short Message Service)

The enormous popularity of this technology, better known as texting, has taken the phone companies by surprise. When it first became available on mobile phones it was not even documented in the phone manuals, as no one thought it would ever be used. The method of having to use the phone's keypad to type messages was thought to be generally impractical.

- It allows users to exchange messages of up to 160 characters between mobile phones.

- It is less intrusive than answering a mobile phone in a public place.

- Predictive Text Entry (PDE), a technology which anticipates your words as you type, has spurred on the craze.

- Some websites now offer the capability to send text messages to mobile phones.

Discussion

Texting is a brand new form of communication which did not previously exist. Its major use, according to research, is for flirting. What else is it useful for? Discuss the pros and cons of texting as a method of communication.

WAP (Wireless Application Protocol)

This technology was designed to revolutionise the mobile phone. It had considerable investment by the Internet Service Providers yet so far has not become a huge popular success.

The principles of WAP technology mean that:

- the Internet is available to you whenever and wherever you are through your mobile phone

- you can enter your postcode or location and have access to unlimited amounts of information on entertainment, restaurants, compass directions and travel information, e.g. rail timetables etc.

- you can send and receive e-mail via a browser and use the browser to connect to a limited form of the Internet, i.e. those Web pages which are WAP-enabled

WAP technology has some negative aspects:

- it relies upon you being in an area with sufficiently good reception to make the connection

- you need to be tolerant of slower access speeds than you might be used to on your PC (roughly 6 times slower than a standard 56Kbps modem)

- the text-only information is limited

CASE STUDY

Arctic explorer saved by e-mail

Trapped on a shrinking ice floe, the explorer Dave Mill had just a shovel, a camera and his mobile phone with which to attempt a daring escape.

So the 34 year-old adventurer from Kenmore, in Perthshire, cut a runway in the ice, took a digital photograph of it and e-mailed it via his mobile to a rescue team in Canada. His back-up crew had warned he faced certain death if he did not find a stable stretch of ice where a rescue plane could land.

Speaking from Resolute Bay, Canada, after the daring rescue operation Mr Mill praised his rescuers and said

"In the Arctic you cannot land an aircraft by computer and I had to prove the pilot would have a clear line of sight as he needs to

see what he is coming onto. It was amazing to see the aircraft land and I think you have to put the pilot's feat up there with Michael Schumacher."

(Source: Kirsty Scott, The Guardian 21 May 2002)

Question:

 Describe some other situations in which WAP phones could be very useful.

How safe are mobile phones?

Mobile phones are not bad for your brain after all, according to the report on the government-sponsored Stewart enquiry published in May 2000. It shows that emissions from the phones heat the brain by only one tenth of a degree, while the body's normal temperature varies by one degree every day. The government enquiry, carried out by a leading professor, said that repeated claims that mobile phones "cook the brain" with microwave radiation and cause tumours and memory loss, appeared to be unfounded.

However, experts have called for the Government to fund further research on possible "non-thermal" effects of mobiles, which some studies have suggested may pose a health risk.

The number of mobile users in Britain has mushroomed to 24 million, including an estimated 300,000 children. Scientists admit "if there is a risk, children may be at increased risk", and are asking the National Radiological Protection Board to conduct regular spot checks on the 500 base stations sited near schools. Professor Stewart, who headed the enquiry, was struck by the strength of public opposition to phone masts, and is expected to recommend changes to make it easier to block the placing of masts near schools.

(Source: Website www.awooga.com)

Questions:

1 Do you feel that this kind of research is important or that it causes more people to be afraid of new technology?

2 How do you feel about the potential risks to children of mobile phones and masts?

3 If there were risks involved with using your mobile phone, how would it affect your attitude to the use of mobile technologies?

4 What other dangers and drawbacks are there in mobile phone use?

PDAs

PDAs or **Personal Digital Assistants** are handheld computers and communication devices. The PDA began as an electronic organiser, born after the success of the Filofax in the mid-1980s. The handheld device looked very much like a calculator. Later models included spellcheckers, small games and notepad functions, and some models with larger screens now have handwriting-recognition software.

Figure 32.1: A PDA

PDAs tend to fall into two categories; keyboard- and pen-based devices. Both types of devices have similar features.

Keyboard-based PDAs

- They include agendas, address books, reminders, vibrating and silent alarms and daily calendars.

- When used as a phone device they often include a headset.

- They tend to be more focused towards word-processing and data manipulation and are designed for programs which are more keyboard-dependent.

- They include the ability to upgrade memory or add a modem via a CF (Compact Flash) socket or MMC (Multimedia Card) Slot.

- They connect to a PC easily and can be used for e-mail downloads via cable, infra-red ports or USB docking cradles.

Pen-based PDAs

- These operate through pen input on touch-sensitive screens using icons and menus for program navigation.

- They have a much larger screen and use a specialist form of software for handwriting recognition. This allows simplified pen strokes to be converted into letters and numbers on the screen.

- The larger screen on these devices allows an on-screen keyboard, but they are designed more for their organiser, WAP, game, presentation and map functions than for the word-processing of long documents.

- Some models allow digital photos and compressed video clips to be taken and stored and for telephone calls to be recorded in progress.

- They also allow memory upgrades and have USB connector ports for additional devices such as digital cameras. They can be connected to a PC via a docking cradle for automatic update of files from the host PC.

- They may have cut-down versions of Word, Excel and Internet Explorer running on a **Microsoft Windows for Pocket PC** operating system.

Notebook computers

Notebooks or 'laptops', as they are commonly known, are much more sophisticated today than ever before. They can compete with a desktop PC for convenience and functionality, and use identical systems software and applications. The relatively cheap price has made them widely accessible to business people, students and computing enthusiasts.

● They contain hard disks of up to 30Gb, giving massive storage capacity.

● They may have both CD-ROM and DVD-ROM drives.

● They may possess detachable MP3 players for music storage and playback.

● They can use a variety of other extra peripherals such as CD-Rewritable or DVD-RAM drives.

Figure 32.2: A notebook computer

Scenario Lennie Vincent

Lennie, a computer sales manager, is a long-distance commuter who takes the train each morning at 6:30am from Nottingham to London. The journey takes almost two hours and he always likes to make sure he gets a table seat so he can set up his laptop. He uses this time very constructively each morning, checking first his e-mails and then his schedule for the day. He examines and revises any presentations he has prepared for meetings later that day, and then uses a digital recorder to dictate any letters he wants his secretary Joanne to type. He also dictates instructions for his sales team, which he lets Joanne put on the network at the office. He usually sends his documents from his laptop via his mobile directly to Joanne's computer.

Lennie then uses his mobile phone to make a few calls to his colleagues in the field and sometimes makes a few personal calls as well. No one ever sits near him until the train is really crowded and then all the passengers seem to ignore him completely. He sometimes wishes they would be friendlier, as he used to find it a good way to find out about new city developments, but he is so busy now! He carries on shouting down his mobile about things happening at work and showing off his new laptop, which he's sure everyone is jealous of.

By the time Lennie reaches his office at 8:30am, he has put in almost two hours work and set up the day for his sales team. He barely needs to speak to anyone all morning as there is little extra information to pass on.

On the journey home, Lennie is really tired and just nods off - in fact when he gets home he often just goes straight to sleep in his armchair, waking briefly for a 'TV supper', and doesn't talk to his wife Lucy all evening.

Questions:

1 How have mobile technologies improved Lennie's ability to do his job?

2 How have these technologies allowed Lennie's health and lifestyle to suffer?

3 Are there any potential risks, either to himself or to the business (e.g. security risks), of Lennie's actions?

Exercise

Examine and discuss the different scenarios below. In each scenario, which of the following is the most suitable device or communication method?

How would use of this technology enhance the lives or work of the user?

Phone	Notebook	Mobile phone
Pager	WAP-phone	Digital voice recorder
Pen-based PDA	MP3 player	Keyboard-based PDA
E-mail	SMS	Snail mail (Postal Service)

a.   Bill, a student from the United States, met Claudette on holiday in France whilst he was staying on an exchange. He is very fond of Claudie and wants to keep in contact with her regularly.

b.   John wishes to keep in touch with his mum who hasn't been feeling well. It's her birthday soon and he wants to make her feel really special.

c.   Louis is a travelling software salesman and he needs to be able to keep in touch with the office all day. His assistant Craig needs to be able to let him know new customer information throughout the day.

d.   Percy is a motorway engineer and basically works from his car. He travels a lot, staying in hotels, and often needs to work on complex problems using engineering software.

e.   Caroline is a busy solicitor and has regular meetings with clients in different parts of the country, often over dinner. She needs to be able to communicate with clients and find out about train times and restaurant availability.

f.   Lucy likes to communicate regularly with her family who live quite far away. She likes to exchange gossip and advice as she is a busy mum who doesn't get a lot of time to herself.

g.   George is a professor of Genetic and Biological Sciences at a university a couple of hours from home by train from his house. He often has ideas on the train and needs to keep a record of them before he forgets them. George has never used a computer in his life.

h.   Martin, a budding music producer, likes to create tracks using music software at work during his lunch break. Sometimes he gets the track nearly right, then he wants to take it home and complete it. It also helps him if he can listen to the track on the way home.

i.   Charlie is a gas engineer and visits homes to check on supply faults. He needs a customer signature on completion of the job.

j.   Amit likes to make lecture notes using a laptop but there really isn't enough room in the lecture theatre for it. He is much faster at typing than writing.

k.   Phil is a doctor who is sometimes on call 24 hours a day. The hospital staff do not need to chat to him, only to let him know he is urgently required at the hospital as soon as possible.

The consumer's changing needs and tastes are forever driving forward the development of new technology. In this chapter we will look at some of the ways that ICT is continually enhancing our home entertainment and leisure facilities.

Digital broadcasting

Computers and **digital broadcasting** are gradually converging, with more technology becoming available so that consumers will be able to buy a single box which enables them not only to watch hundreds of TV channels but also to play along with televised game shows, order goods and access the Internet. Users can access these services through set-top boxes and digital receivers (cable or satellite).

Figure 33.1: The Tompson TiVo

In addition, users can now store digitally received programmes in a new device (Figure 33.1) designed as an updated video recorder. This device consists of a processor and hard drive of approximately 40Gb. It requires a modem to connect the telephone cable to the Internet, and a browser for viewing Web pages operating over broadband ***Digital Subscriber Lines (DSL)***.

Set-top boxes include the following features:

- they include an MP3 player for listening to and storing MP3 music

- they allow pausing and digital recording of live television programmes

- they include a keyboard for writing and receiving e-mails and faxes

- the screen can be split between TV and the Internet

- viewers will be able to watch digital TV and record to an integrated hard disk at the same time

- 3D games can be played over the Internet

- they give access to interactive services such as online shopping or banking, or online voting with instant results. Future game shows with *Ask the Audience* features may attract greater participation with potentially 15 million online viewers who do not have to get up from the sofa in order to make that phone call

- the screen can have hot-spots with more specific information you can view and access, e.g. more localised weather forecasts or more information about news reports

- movies can be downloaded to enjoy when you have free time

Storage devices

Older storage devices such as floppy disks, video tapes and audio tapes are being replaced with newer technologies such as CDs and DVDs.

Compact disks

CDs are found in most homes today, being used either on a CD player or on the family PC. There are many different types of CD:

Audio CD (Compact Disk) A disk containing music that can be played in any CD player or any CD-ROM or DVD-ROM drive as well as any standalone DVD player. It is an extremely versatile format.

CD-ROM (Compact Disk Read-Only Memory) This is optical disk storage containing data placed there by its manufacturer. The contents are permanent. It can be used in a CD drive in your PC to access games, encyclopaedias, software, music and multimedia.

CD-R (Compact Disk Recordable) A blank, recordable compact disk known as WORM (Write-Once-Read-Many), that can be written to only once. When something has been written to the disk, it cannot be erased. They are known as 'gold disks' because of the reflective layer. They can contain music to be used in CD-ROM and DVD-ROM drives, or video for use in computers or DVD players, or just data for use on a computer.

CD-RW (Compact Disk Re-Writable) A compact disk that can be written over and over again. All players can read CD-RW disks except some older models and they can hold the same kinds of information as CD-Rs, but uniquely, they are reusable.

CASE STUDY

Attack of the Clones

When Sony released the **Attack of the Clones** soundtrack album in Europe, they wanted to make sure unauthorised distribution was impossible. "Will not play on PC/Mac" warn the disk's front and back covers. The disc contains extra data that stops it from operating in a PC or Mac – this prevents it from being illegally "ripped" to the net or to a hard drive, but is disappointing for anyone who legitimately listens to CDs on their computer.

Sony, EMI and others say that their business is being decimated by commercial pirates and individuals uploading and downloading music from the Internet.

(Source: Tony Smith, Guardian Online, 6 June 2002)

DVD

DVD stands for Digital Versatile Disk. A DVD is an ultra-high-capacity disk that holds seven times more data than a CD on a single layer disk. It uses similar technology to the CD but the pits in which data is held on the disks are much smaller and there are more of them, increasing the storage capacity from 650/700Mb to 4.7Gb. There are double-sided double-layered DVDs which can handle 17Gb.

This technology is available through dedicated players, portable players, DVD drives for PCs and notebooks. They can also be used in some computer games consoles. DVDs are much faster than CDs and they were designed originally for use and delivery of home cinema.

The PC-based DVD player

DVD player drives can be obtained for a PC, and are a standard option on most new PCs. DVD movies can be played and DVD-RW and DVD-RAM disks can be used for storage or back-up.

DVD players (Home Entertainment)

DVDs have been a huge success with the home entertainment market and they allow much better picture quality than traditional VHS. They allow a resolution of 500 lines, which is around twice that of videotape.

DVD movies come with a range of viewing modes, from 4:3 (normal TV) to widescreen (16:9). They support top sound standards like Dolby Digital, Pro Logic and THX. In addition, they can carry lots of extra material like multi-lingual support, documentaries, actor biographies, cut scenes, etc.

It is a much more durable and permanent medium than tape and you can access your favourite bits instantly without having to fast forward or rewind.

Figure 33.2: A DVD player

Portable DVD

Portable DVD is a luxury item that allows you to watch DVDs on the move on a very small screen. At present the batteries designed to use with them have a very short time span of around 2-3 hours. They are, however, very light at 1kg and allow the convenience of watching DVDs on the move either with or without headphones. They can be used to play back virtually any optical disk media as well as MP3s. Most models allow widescreen playback and Dolby Digital sound.

Types of DVD

DVD-ROM (Digital Versatile Disk Read Only Memory) This technology has been available in PCs for a while and is used in a similar way to CD-ROMs, but the storage capacity is much higher.

DVD-RAM (Digital Versatile Disk Random Access Memory) This was originally designed as back-up, general data storage and high-capacity data transport. They are incompatible with DVD-ROM drives or DVD video players.

DVD-R (Digital Versatile Disk Recordable) This technology is similar to CD-R. These disks can be read in most DVD disk drives and DVD players, but are expensive and limited to the write-once format.

DVD-RW (Digital Versatile Disk Re-Writable) This is the new rewritable standard in DVD technology. These disks can be read and rewritten in most DVD drives and used in most DVD players, thereby justifying the very high price for the media.

DVD+RW (Digital Versatile Disk Re-Writable Plus) This is an even newer standard, allowing higher capabilities than DVD-RW and allowing recording on both sides of the disk. These disks can be used as widely as DVD-RW.

Regional Coding on DVDs

Movies on DVDs have regional coding. Movies are often released on DVD in the United States before the movie arrives in cinemas in Europe, and if the DVD became available in Europe, this would undermine those release dates. DVDs therefore belong to one of six world regions and disks are coded differently for these regions. This prevents a disk bought in Asia from being played on a European or US player, and vice versa. Europe is Region 2 and the US is Region 1, for example. Unfortunately US disks are usually packed with more features than European ones, are better quality, and there are thousands more of them.

Minidisk (MD)

This is a compact digital audio disk using magneto-optic technology from Sony that comes in read-only and rewritable versions. The 2.5" disk stores 140Mb compared to 650Mb on a CD and holds over an hour's worth of music. The disk and track titles can be viewed on a small display.

Minidisks can be used with USB connections to your PC to enable a quick and easy transfer of MP3 files from your PC to your Minidisk player.

The disks are relatively cheap and MD is a recordable format – you can record on an MD the same way that you can record on a cassette. They can be recorded, erased, re-recorded and edited up to a million times. Individual tracks can be erased and the remaining tracks have the unique facility of 'bunching up' to eliminate the space left behind.

Figure 33.3: A portable Minidisk Player

MP3

- This is a standard for compressing digital audio with sound quality very close to that of a CD. The compressed files require only a fraction of the storage space.

- The compression formatting actually removes certain sounds within the song which are not heard by the listener, i.e. outside the normal hearing range. This allows the track to be reduced in size to about one tenth of its original capacity.

- MP3 is slightly different in audio quality when heard through a 'state of the art' hi-fi, but is far superior to the portable tape recorders of the last decade.

- MP3s are freely and easily shared across the Internet, making all kinds of problems for music companies and adversely affecting their profits.

CASE STUDY

Napster heads back to court

Napster was back in court again recently. The peer-to-peer site has been offline for more than five months. In a copyright infringement lawsuit lodged against Napster by the American Recording Industry Association of America (RIAA), Judge Patel ruled that the file-swapping site had to remain closed until it filtered out 100% of copyright-protected music.

Napster has found it difficult to adhere to the ruling, and claimed that it needed the names of specific files, not just the artist and song title lists the RIAA had provided. Napster said many of the files in its database incorrectly identify or misspell the names of artists and songs and therefore these tracks did not count under the ruling.

But while Napster's free-for-all file-swapping days are over, a handful of other free peer-to-peer swapping sites are waiting to see how the case develops and whether they can survive on a more vigilantly guarded Internet.

(Source: Computer Weekly, 29 May 2002)

Questions:

1 Why does so-called peer-to-peer file sharing concern the RIAA so much?

2 What is likely to happen if Napster is allowed to continue to let users share music files on the Internet?

Digital Audio Players (DAPs)

- These portable MP3 players allow direct transfer of MP3 and also AAC (Advanced Audio Compression) files from your computer straight to your machine.

- They are a hybrid of the principles of CD technology (music quality) and Minidisk machines (small and portable).

- They incorporate removable data storage that is easier to carry around using tiny removable disks for these files.

- They allow up to 12 hours of playing time. A 20Gb hard-disk will allow up to 6,000 tracks, the equivalent of 400 music CDs. Newer models allow between 20 to 66Gb external storage of music.

- Some models contain 1.8 inch colour LCD screens for video and text playback.

- Users download music files or documents from their office computer, travel home listening to the music files, and finally transfer the computer files to their home PC, building up a library of removable media that can be plugged-in and played anytime.

A brief history of computer games

The first really successful computer game came out in the early 70s. "Pong" was a very simple two-player bat-and-ball game with a line each side of the screen representing a bat. It was called "Pong" for two reasons; one: "pong" was the sound the game made when the ball hit a paddle or side of the screen, and two: the name "Ping-Pong" was already copyrighted. Another very successful early computer game was called "Gunfight". Consoles available in the mid-to-late 80s used large cartridges. The variety of games was limited and most of the manufacturers were fiercely competing to get the technology perfect. This warfare is still raging now almost 30 years later.

There has always been public reaction against the violence of computer games. One of the first really violent games, "Death Race 2000", was a driving game based on a 1975 movie of the same name. Points were earned by running over stick figures. Public outcry against video-game violence gained national attention and initially these violent games were removed from the market.

Some of the most popular video games of all time, which you may not have even have heard of, include:

● "Space Invaders" – an arcade game national phenomenon. Space Invaders gave you a goal by displaying the current high score for you to beat. Space Invaders broke all known sales records in arcades. Its popularity caused coin shortages in Japan and school truancy in America.

● "Asteroids" – Atari's all-time best-seller. Asteroids introduced a new feature to arcades: high scorers could enter their three-character initials at the end of the game.

● "Battlezone" – the first three-dimensional first-person game. Rolling around in a tank on a virtual battlefield, players take out targets in a warlike scenario. The US government later commissioned an enhanced version of Battlezone for military training purposes.

● "Pac-Man" – the most popular arcade game of all time. Pac-Man became the first video game to be popular with both males and females.

● Nintendo's "Donkey Kong" – the hero, Mario, is a squat carpenter racing to save his girlfriend Pauline from a crazed monkey. The game was eventually transformed into the hugely successful "Super Mario Brothers".

Video-game entertainment in the late 80s developed considerably with the Nintendo Entertainment System (NES) from Japan and the Sega Master System (SMS) from the United States. Then hand-held games developed with the introduction of the Nintendo "Game Boy". The success of this device was due to the addictive game "Tetris" and, despite a tiny monochrome screen, it began to build a historic sales record. Consoles developed and games were stored on compact disks, which meant higher capacity and more detailed graphics were possible.
In 1991 Nintendo released the Super NES (SNES) and later the N64, and in competitive response Sega introduced "Sonic the Hedgehog" which boosted

their console sales. By 1999 Sega had announced another name and console change; this time the system became the "Dreamcast".

The release of the Sony PlayStation broke all computer console records by selling millions of units all around the world. The launch of the Playstation 2 with additional RAM and doubling as a DVD player has shown that the console can continue to progress. The games are "forward compatible" with the existing PlayStation, and it will play audio CDs and DVDs. The Dual-Shock Controllers allow more realism than ever, and the player can experience the vibrating sensations of tyres on the road or, as Lara Croft, the sensation of moving over rough terrain on a motorbike.

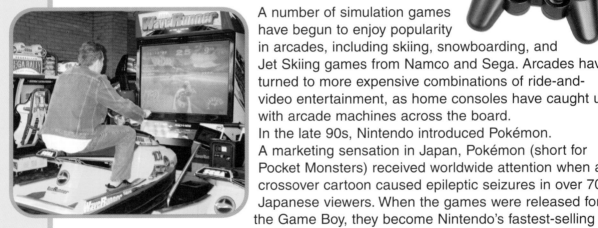

Figure 33.4: The Sony PlayStation 2

A number of simulation games have begun to enjoy popularity in arcades, including skiing, snowboarding, and Jet Skiing games from Namco and Sega. Arcades have turned to more expensive combinations of ride-and-video entertainment, as home consoles have caught up with arcade machines across the board.

In the late 90s, Nintendo introduced Pokémon. A marketing sensation in Japan, Pokémon (short for Pocket Monsters) received worldwide attention when a crossover cartoon caused epileptic seizures in over 700 Japanese viewers. When the games were released for the Game Boy, they become Nintendo's fastest-selling game ever. In 2000 Nintendo introduced the "Game Boy Advance", a 32-bit colour hand-held system, which can be combined with a cellular phone for Internet access.

In the late 90s/early 2000s Sega introduced the Dreamcast. Sega became the first company to offer broadband Internet support when it released a high-speed broadband modem for the Dreamcast. "Quake" and "Unreal Tournament" were among the first games to support the modem. PC gaming across the Internet can involve hundreds of users from all over the world simultaneously playing one game. Nintendo introduced the "GameCube" – literally a cube. Instead of using CDs or DVDs as the storage medium for GameCube games, Nintendo uses a specialised optical disk. Nintendo predicts that this medium will eventually be a standard, as its small size makes it attractive for future handhelds. The most recent console to explode onto the market has been the Microsoft "X-Box" with its super-realistic simulations.

Questions:

1 How has the technology of gaming evolved over the last three decades?

2 Do you believe that using computer games in military training is worthwhile?

3 How has competition between the Japanese and US markets led to failure of a common standard?

4 Do you think that increasing pressure for realism in computer games is an issue, with so many under-16s playing computer games?

5 What do you think is the future for console games? Which device will win the war?

6 Why do some parents restrict the amount of time that children are allowed to play computer games? Do you think this is a good thing?

Exercise

You will need to use the Internet and any computer magazines you have to research into suitable media to meet the needs of various users.

For each user identify the most appropriate type of media and describe how it could enhance their use of their computer.

● A small graphics company creating presentations for business customers.

● A business person travelling from place to place and needing to access lists of customers' details.

● A home computer user who wishes to regularly back up large files.

● Someone who wishes to give a copy of some important large files to a client.

● A surveyor who wishes to gain increased storage and backup on her computer.

● A music enthusiast who likes to listen to his CDs whilst jogging.

Chapter 34: People with Special Needs

For many people with disabilities, computer technology provides a lifeline to independence and a fulfilling career. The range of specially-designed computer equipment is vast, catering for all types of disability from visual and hearing impairment to almost total immobility.

The specially-designed devices include:

- alternative keyboards - these may be one-handed, mini, compact, ergonomic or expanded keyboards

- switches or touch-screens designed for use by people with a wide range of limited mobility and physical difficulties

- trackballs, joysticks, track pads, enlarged mouseballs, cordless mice

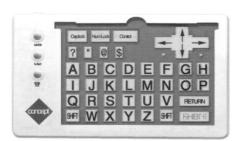

This concept keyboard has keys which are much larger and less sensitive than a normal keyboard.
It is an adapted peripheral which allows programs and games to be more accessible to those with special needs or to the very young.

Figure 34.1: A concept keyboard

People with speech or hearing difficulties may make use of the following devices:

- induction loops to allow those with limited hearing better access to spoken outputs

- voice synthesisers to speak words input by a non-speaker

- speech synthesisers to enhance spoken words in a noisy environment

In addition, communication technology such as browser software for accessing the Internet, and e-mail software for communicating with friends, colleagues or business contacts, may be used with no modification and has opened up new avenues of communication.

Discussion

In what ways are mobile phones particularly suited to people with hearing or speech difficulties?

Visually impaired users of ICT

There are two categories of visual impairment:
those who are partially blind,
and those who are totally blind.

Partially-blind people are able to make use of computer systems with screen magnification devices, using special software that displays text on an enlarged screen in extra large fonts.

For many people with a visual impairment, simply reading utility bills and bank statements and managing household accounts is very difficult.

Video magnifiers have one or sometimes two cameras, one for reading paper on the desk and one for distance viewing. The image is then magnified on the screen. This also makes it possible to read newspapers and magazines, for example.

Those who are totally blind are unable to use sight for reading and have to rely on other senses. They may use, for example, a Braille output device which converts text that is displayed on the screen into Braille characters on a 'touch-pad'. The user then 'feels' what is on the screen. Text-to-speech synthesisers and screen-reading software packages are alternatives.

The picture shows an electronic Braille display. Each cell has 6 or 8 pins which are electronically controlled to move up and down to display a Braille version of characters that appear on the computer screen.

Limited mobility devices

Computer technology has also helped those with limited mobility to achieve greater independence.

● Software modifications to toys and electric appliances have been designed so that standard household devices such as blenders, hairdryers, televisions and stereos are more accessible to those with limited mobility.

● There are environmental control systems such as adapted thermostats, adapted light and appliance switches, switches to control the movement of curtains and blinds, adapted door intercoms, adapted keys and locks.

Creating opportunities

Opportunities for employment and independent living for disabled people are better than ever, and the future outlook is excellent. Computers give people who were formerly excluded from mainstream education and a worthwhile career, a powerful tool for achieving independence in their daily lives, for learning new job skills and entering the world on a more equal footing.

A disabled person using a computer has access to vast amounts of information at their fingertips. People with disabilities can tap into practical disability-related information or converse with other disabled people.

Programs have been developed to offer training and practice for the hearing-impaired in such things as sign language, finger spelling, and even lip-reading. E-mail and chat programs are excellent for the hearing-impaired because they allow communication without speech (which a telephone requires). In addition, chat rooms allow real-time conversations through the use of a computer and an Internet connection. With the use of these applications, the user's handicap is not an issue or a problem.

Technology has much to offer MDVI (Multiply Disabled and Visually Impaired) learners. Computers, sound equipment and specialised light stimulation devices can often be controlled by the learner via switches or other input devices.

Speech output communication aids may also be used. These provide the learner with a range of sensory stimulations, encourage interaction, and allow additional control over the environment.

Case Studies

One way to learn about how computer technology has improved the lives of disabled people is to read different case studies. You can do your own research on the Internet, by reading or by talking to people to find out about some real people and their use of ICT. Here are several made-up scenarios to start you off.

Scenario 1

Norman is a blind professor at a University. He uses a portable voice synthesizer that automatically converts text in his computer into spoken words. In the past he would have had to hire a human reader or wait a week for Braille versions of

newspapers and magazines before preparing his lectures. Now he uses his computer to log on to databases of library catalogues and can listen to electronic editions of periodicals. He also uses his computer and modem to teach students on a 'distance learning' programme.

Norman uses computer technology to communicate with hearing-impaired students. They submit their assignments via e-mail, and get feedback the same way. Norman also uses computer conferencing to provide a more interactive component. The content, though, is delivered through broadcast videos and through printed texts. Computer conferencing and e-mail provides easy and rapid contact between the teacher and students and among the students. Class members who have their own computer access the school mainframe from home using a modem. Some part-time students use a computer from where they work in the same way.

Scenario 2

Jo is a student with a visual impairment. He has an assignment to follow a recent major political event, present available facts about it, write a report, and complete a presentation about the event to his classmates. A major source of information for his sighted classmates is the newspaper, but, unless someone reads it to him, Jo cannot use that source. The radio is an available option, but typically radio news coverage contains too little detail. With the available computer technologies, though, he can receive the newspaper on a computer disk and, using his personal computer equipped with synthesized speech, he can auditorily scan the newspaper, find relevant articles, and have the computer read them to him. Using the same computer, he can begin to write his paper, print it out in Braille so that he can check it and change it if necessary, and then print it in standard text to hand in to his teacher.

Scenario 3

Martin is an adolescent with severe paralysis. He is starting to show all the signs of becoming a teenager. He wants control of his own life – to decide which radio station to listen to, to decide when to turn the reading light off at night, to call his friends and have a private conversation and to stay home alone when his parents go out. Without assistive devices he would be unable to be an independent teenager, but with a single switch connected to an environmental control unit and placed on his head, he can control his personal radio, turn the lights on and off, access the telephone for calling friends, and call for emergency help when his parents are out.

Scenario 4

A toddler called Susie has severe disabilities. She attends a special educational preschool workshop. The teachers have been unable to work out her cognitive abilities (understanding) because Susie has no verbal skills (speech) and very few motor skills (movement). Now as a result of available new technologies, Susie's school program includes motor training, language and communication training, and teachers can more easily see her potential and can build upon it. The teachers are working on training her to use a special switch and battery-operated toys. Susie is learning to reach and touch a switch which turns on a battery-operated teddy bear. The language therapist is using the same switches to teach the child to make consistent "yes" and "no" responses for communication.

Questions:

1 How have the lives of the individuals involved been radically improved by their access to technology?

2 How would these individuals have communicated with others in the past?

3 Does this dependence on technology cause you any concern for their future?

4 Do you think that technology always leads to improved 'quality of life'?

Exercise

1. What technology exists or may exist in the future to help these individuals? Describe suitable solutions to their problems.

   a. Dave loves attending lectures at college but is partially hard of hearing.

   b. Amit is partially-sighted owing to an eye disease he has suffered from all his life. He needs to order groceries from his supermarket online.

   c. Sarah suffers from dyslexia; she would love to improve her reading and writing skills.

   d. Petra needs to contact her bank about her overdraft but she is partially deaf.

   e. Bob works in a noisy railway station as an engineer – he sometimes misses an important call as he doesn't hear his mobile ringing.

   f. George is paralysed following a mountaineering accident. He needs to be able to contact his nurse in emergencies when he is alone.

   g. Akram is Turkish and has been living in the UK for a few months. He is looking for work but when he writes letters to prospective employers his language skills let him down.

   h. Julie is blind but loves to go horse-riding. She would like to use the Internet to find out about horse-riding holidays.

   i. Helen has limited mobility and wishes to be independent in operating the lighting and heating controls in her home.

2. Find out more about special devices or programs for visually-impaired people, people with learning difficulties and also for people with reading difficulties, e.g. dyslexia. Try the websites:

   www.inclusive.co.uk (A special needs inclusive technology commercial site)

   www.dyslexic.com (Dyslexia home website)

   www.studentmachines.com/index-dyslexia (A commercial site specialising in providing for people with Dyslexia)

   www.rnib.org.uk (Royal National Institute for the Blind)

   www.deafblind.com (A-Z of Deafblindness)

   www.tvi-web.com (Technologies for the Visually Impaired – Commercial Site)

   www.ldresources.com (A research website on learning difficulties and specialist technology)

   www.evh1.demon.co.uk (The Disabled People's Electronic Village Hall)

   www.sightandsound.co.uk (Solutions for people who are Blind or Visually Impaired and people with Learning or Reading Difficulties)

Chapter 35: ICT in Business

The widespread use of ICT, particularly the Internet, has had a phenomenal effect on business.

The Internet offers a huge potential for trade and an opportunity for new businesses. Businesses do not have to face many of the traditional overheads and can become well-known overnight. Companies trading solely over the Internet, known as "dotcoms" (because they had Web addresses ending in .com) sprang up in their thousands in the late 90s and attracted huge investment. Although many overnight "dotcom" successes collapsed, the Internet is growing in Europe, with the "dotcom" industry gradually growing.

The development of the Internet has given increased power to consumers. Online shoppers are now only a mouse-click away from another website's products, which creates fierce competitiveness. Shoppers can compare prices from businesses all over the world via the Internet, e.g. for holidays, cars or electrical goods. Online auctions provide another opportunity for shoppers to find a bargain.

Figure 35.1: Booking a holiday online

The Christmas period each year sees a huge increase in Web traffic. A report by Jupiter Media Matrix claimed that the number of visitors to websites at that time of year swells to more than 50 million. The Internet has a Christmas holiday season much like traditional shops, with many customers waiting to search for late season discounts before making gift purchases. In addition, consumers now have increased confidence in the ability of online sites to deliver quickly.

The development of the Internet, text-based services, interactive TV, WAP phones and connectivity technologies has meant there is a huge potential for new methods of advertising and marketing that didn't exist previously. In the future, you may walk past a shop and the technology will exist to send you a discount coupon for that shop via your phone at precisely that moment.

A further benefit of modern hardware and software is that individuals feel more confident about setting up their own businesses. They can use technology to assist them in managing an enterprise efficiently.

Discussion

What software packages are likely to be useful to a small business setting up to offer a service such as building or plumbing work?

Communicating with the customer

Modern methods of communication used by businesses cater for huge volumes of enquiries and orders.

● Very sophisticated call centres where thousands of calls can be dealt with and routed appropriately all over the country are used by many organisations, especially banks.

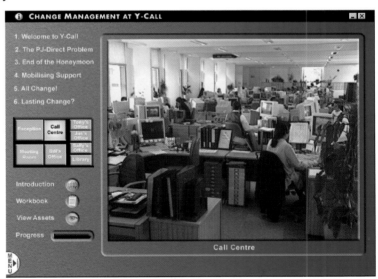

Figure 35.2: A Call Centre

● Customer Relationship Management (CRM) software can be used to plan and control all sales activities in an organisation. The software allows a customer to interact with a company by various means including the Web, telephone, fax, e-mail and snail mail and receive a consistent level of quality service.

● The progress of an order placed by a customer can be tracked on the Web – Securicor, for example, offer a tracking service to customers.

● Interactive Voice Response (IVR) is an automated telephone information system that speaks to the caller with a combination of fixed voice menus and real-time data from databases. The caller responds by pressing digits on the telephone or speaking words or short phrases. Applications include bank-by-phone, flight-scheduling information and automated order entry and tracking. These systems allow callers to get necessary information 24 hours a day.

● Companies have better communication internally and externally through the use of networks and intranets. In addition money can be saved by not travelling to meet people, relying instead upon technologies such as video-conferencing or e-mail to communicate.

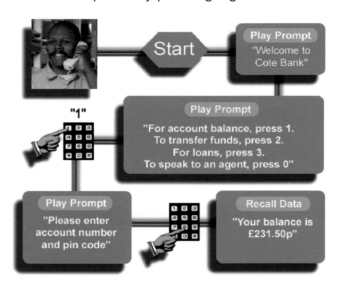

Figure 35.3: Interactive Voice Response

Click me baby one more time

Britney Spears has signed a deal with AOL Time Warner that will see subscribers gain early access to online events and concert tickets. In return, the latest version of AOL software will be included with Britney's forthcoming album. The pop star is no stranger to using the latest technology to woo her fans. In June she teamed up with search engine Yahoo to produce a website that allowed fans to follow her and boyfriend Justin Timberlake of boy band N'Sync on a shopping trip. In May she became the first artist to use so-called "immersive" DVD technology in a concert CD that allowed fans to choose the angle they viewed from. Teenage devotees will be disappointed to learn that despite the wonders of the Internet allowing them to follow her around the shops and view her from any angle, there are no plans for a website that would allow them to virtually "ask her out".

(Source: www.cw360.com
25 October 2001)

Discussion

Does this technology help to increase the popularity of pop stars such as Britney Spears? Or does it merely replace other ways of marketing pop stars?

Voice recognition

Voice recognition and activation may soon be used to access Web services and Web pages via mobile devices. It is already being used by:

- telephone information services, for times of films at cinemas, football results, information from local government offices, stock availability in department stores
- call centres for accepting orders and goods enquiries from customers and businesses.

Discussion

Have you ever used a voice recognition system to book a cinema ticket, for example?

CASE STUDY

Tesco hooks up to wireless Intranet

Tesco is planning to use wireless technology to connect in-store staff to a company intranet.

Hand-held personal digital assistants (PDAs) will give staff on-the-spot access to data via radio-frequency (RF) transmitters set up in individual stores. Pilot trials will begin in October 2002, leading to placement in stores across the entire UK chain of 678 outlets by the end of that year. The advantage of the new system is that staff will no longer need to leave the shop floor to find the answers to customer queries. The first part of the project will focus on more straightforward applications such as stock and price checking.

"The idea is to give staff more confidence by providing the information they need when the customer is actually in front of them," explained IT director Colin Cobain. "Our growth is such that, unless we make our stores more efficient, we will just have to employ more and more staff."

Cobain is not worried about the possible security issue of lost or stolen devices. A PIN code will be needed to gain access to the system, and the PDAs will not work at all outside the range of the in-store RF transmitter.

(Source: Sarah Arnott, Computing, 13 August 2001)

Questions:

1 How will this new technology speed up customer service at Tesco?

2 What are the implications of such a venture?

3 In what other ways do Tesco and other supermarkets use ICT to improve customer service?

Online groceries

Tesco has been a leader in the trend towards doing the weekly shop online. Once the customer has registered, they can order their weekly supplies from the comfort of their own home and have them delivered to the door.

Discussion

What categories of people are most likely to use this service? What effect, if any, does this type of service have on local shops, and on people who do not have Internet access?

Figure 35.4: Online shopping at Tesco

CASE STUDY

Safeway cans online shop plans

Safeway is shelving plans for its online shopping service in favour of its bricks and mortar business. Its online trial service, Collect, which was rolled out to eight stores in April, will be scrapped after the retailer decided its money will be better spent on its core business. The service allowed shoppers to buy groceries through its website and collect them at the stores.

"We decided it made sense to invest in our business and store format," said a Safeway spokeswoman, "but we are still developing the website for our customers. They can do things like pre-order Christmas food online. It's not like we have pulled the plug on it totally. We were never at the Tesco level. It was just a trial and we can still develop the system."

The disappointing news for online shoppers follows the supermarket's decision last summer to drop its online wine-shopping service, Wines Direct, after its supplier could not fulfil its orders. "We looked around for another supplier, said the spokeswoman, "but during that time we decided a lot of investment was needed from the business for online activities which could be better spent elsewhere."

(Source: Lisa Kelly, Web User Magazine, 28 November 2001)

Questions:

1. Why do you think Safeway chose not to pursue an online business?

2. Do you think Safeway will reverse this decision?

3. What will Safeway need to ensure before this happens?

Smart cards

Millions of people world-wide have become used to paying for goods either online or at a check-out, using a credit or debit card. At an EPOS (Electronic Point of Sale) terminal, a customer can hand over their debit card to be swiped. A message is sent directly to the customer's bank to check that funds are available and, if so, to deduct the correct amount. The store's bank is then credited with the amount paid.

There are plans to introduce Smart card payment systems at retail points of sale. The new cards will contain both a chip and a PIN code to enter and will require new reader equipment in retail outlets. The technology is designed to reduce card fraud by providing an alternative to swipe-based cards. Customers will have to key their PIN numbers into an EPOS terminal.

UK passport holders may be issued with a Smart identity card to improve security and reduce fraud. This card would be imprinted with biometric ID information such as iris scans, facial and voice recognition information, and fingerprints.

Discussion

Boots were the first High Street store to make use of Smart card technology for their Advantage Card. Have you used any Smart cards? Examine the back of the card.

Scenario Brave new world

Imagine a future in which, if you need to travel outside your town, you will need a biometric ID card which contains biological information about you – your fingerprints, iris scans and facial imprint. You will manage all your financial transactions by telephone, using voice recognition technology to pay bills and manage accounts. On your wrist there will be a barcode which indicates your name and address in case of an accident.

There will be no crimes committed in which there is not an immediately identifiable criminal as everyone's whereabouts will be tracked continuously using the implant chips placed in the side of each person's head at birth. Once the data is processed, a likely suspect will be identified in minutes. Terrorist threats will be virtually impossible as any travel outside of your immediate locality will be tracked and analysed for suspicious behaviour. Airport security will be watertight, thanks to biometric checks and accurate data about who is travelling where.

Questions:

1 What do you think such a scenario means for our freedom?

2 Do you believe technology could ever advance so much that it will be impossible to commit a crime and escape detection?

3 Do you think there is a limit to how much we should rely upon technology?

Online banking

Online banking is one of the largest growth areas of Internet usage. In the UK there are an estimated 5.24 million people using Internet banking each day, more than any other European country. That figure is growing.

Internet banking is generally straightforward to use, and typical features include:

● access to information about your account(s) at any time

● setting up payments and direct debits

● paying of bills and transfer of funds

● cheaper loans/overdrafts offered to online customers through reduced overheads

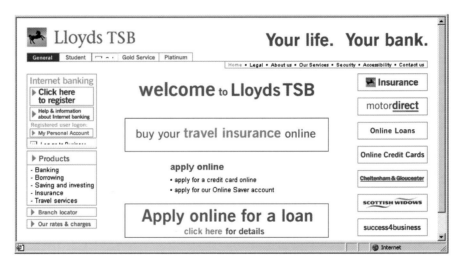

Figure 35.5: Online banking

> ### Discussion
>
> **You can do your banking at a branch, through a Call centre, using the Internet, at a kiosk or ATM, using Web TV, via mail or by telephone.**
>
> **Discuss the relevant advantages and disadvantages of each method to both the customer and the bank.**

Exercises

1. Select three or four products or services that you have bought or intend to buy, and look on the Internet to find the best deal. Write a report on how useful you find the Internet for shopping and how well it satisfies your needs. The report may form part of your portfolio work for the first assessment.

ICT in education

ICT is spreading rapidly in education from Primary schools right through to Universities. With ICT firmly on the National Curriculum, students now gain invaluable experience of ICT in the classroom before they embark on a career.

Spending on ICT facilities in educational establishments has increased dramatically over the last decade, and a majority of schools and colleges have dedicated ICT staff and management. Most schools and colleges operate their computers on a network basis so students can access their files and materials from any terminal in their institution. Some can gain access remotely, e.g. from home, which is especially useful to those who cannot attend school for whatever reason.

Figure 36.1: Most schools have at least one computer lab

ICT for research

ICT is used right across the curriculum, and no doubt you will have been asked to research many different topics by looking them up on the Internet. It seems there is almost no subject which someone has not written about!

As well as the Internet, a huge amount of material is available on CD.

Discussion

Have you used ICT to look up information recently? Do you prefer using the Internet or an appropriate CD when researching a subject? What are the advantages of each? Are CDs better than books for looking up information?

Schools fail Net test

Britain's schools are failing to offer enough pupils access to the Internet, despite a sharp increase in the number of computers available in the classroom, a 2001 survey shows. Almost every school is now online, but the limited bandwidth available means that an average of only six pupils in each school can use the Internet at any one time.

These findings from a survey of 2,000 schools by the British Educational Suppliers Association (BESA) have raised questions about the Government's plans to deliver large parts of the national curriculum online. In addition, research by the E-skills National Training Organisation has shown that pupils' experiences of computing at school are a decisive factor in deciding whether to pursue a career in IT. The survey also raises concerns that 67% of schools are choosing to place IT in specialist laboratories, so limiting pupils' day-to-day access. Experts suggest that the UK should follow the example of Sweden, which integrates computers seamlessly into the classroom.

Despite the shortfalls, BESA's research shows that there have been dramatic increases in the usage of IT in the UK's primary and secondary schools over the past 12 months. The stock of computers has grown by 24% to an average of 34 desktop computers per school. By 2002 schools will have 1.1 million computers if current growth rates continue, and the number of laptops in schools is also increasing.

Computers in schools: the key facts

- The number of computers in schools increased by 24% during 2001 to 1 million.

- The number of schools with Internet connections rose to 75% in 2001.

- Only a small percentage of schools keep most of their PCs in the classroom.

- The number of schools with at least one laptop rose from 62% in 2000 to 87% in 2001.

- The Government's target of one PC per six pupils will not be reached until 2005.

(Source: Bill Goodwin, Computer Weekly, 9 November 2001)

Questions:

1 What would be the benefits and drawbacks of access to a computer for each lesson in all subjects?

2 Do you feel that having specialist ICT classrooms is the best use of resources? Would it be better to have the same number of computers spread throughout all classrooms in a school?

3 How do you think your experience of using ICT at school will affect your choice of career?

Computer-aided learning

Not very long ago many people thought that the day was not too far away when teachers would be superfluous. Students would be able to learn everything sitting at a computer. The computer would explain a topic, then set questions and mark them. Depending on how well the student did, the topic would be explained again or a new topic covered.

There are thousands of CDs available which promise 'Interactive Learning'. However, teachers still seem to be around!

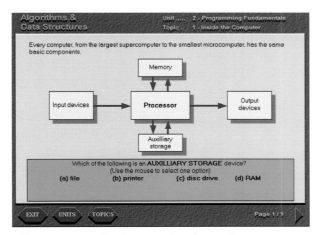

Figure 36.2: An Interactive Learning program

It may be possible in the near future to learn almost any subject on the school curriculum, online. The Government is developing Curriculum Online for this purpose. The BBC and dozens of other companies already have massive amounts of online material.

Figure 36.3: Online learning materials

Discussion

Have you used any computer-aided learning materials? What do you think are the advantages and disadvantages of computer-aided learning, as opposed to teacher-led classes?

CASE STUDY

Paul Eric

Paul Eric is a geography teacher who is keen to use ICT in the classroom, both to develop his students' skills in using equipment and to enhance their understanding of geography. The work that is set for this term is all about weather in the area of the school and about changing climates e.g. temperature, windspeed, rainfall, cloud formations. The students also have to compare the area with another region elsewhere in the world. Mr Eric explains that he enjoyed a similar project to this very much when he did it at school 15 years ago.

Questions:

1. What different pieces of ICT equipment could Mr Eric's class use to carry out their weather surveys?

2. What software applications could the students use to collect, analyse and present their results?

3. How could the students use the Internet to help them complete their projects?

4. How does this approach to the project differ from when Mr Eric was at school?

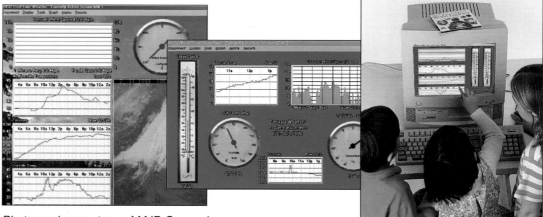

Photographs courtesy of MJP Geopacks

Classroom resources

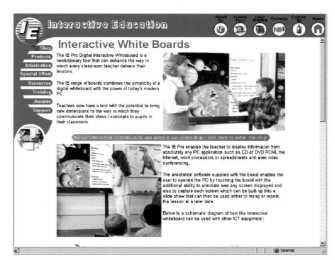

As well as the computers themselves, other computer-related equipment is being used in classrooms all over the country for many different subjects. The interactive whiteboard is an example of a device which enables the teacher to display the contents of a 14" screen to the whole class and to 'write' on the screen with a special pen.

Discussion

What other hardware and software can be used for presentations?

Lifelong learning opportunities

Most people, however long they continue their full-time education, need to learn new skills at some time in their lives. Maybe they regret never having gone to University, and decide to go back to education after raising a family. Maybe they have been made redundant and need to learn a new skill. Maybe they have retired and are looking for a new interest. There are hundreds of reasons why the concept of 'lifelong learning' is such an important one in today's society.

Courses for adults are available at all colleges, and Community Education facilities are widely available. The Open University enables people of all ages and from all walks of life to study for a degree.

Chapter 36: Education and Lifelong Learning

Thirty years ago, PCs did not exist and computers were used by only a few specialists. Computers have been widely used in schools for only the past decade or so. This means that anyone over the age of thirty is quite likely to feel nervous about using a computer. Many courses and qualifications such as ECDL (European Computer Driving Licence) exist for people who want to brush up on their existing computer skills or learn new ones.

Figure 36.4: The European Computer Driving Licence is a popular qualification

Scenario Jeanette Johnson

Jeanette is thinking of returning to work, having spent the last 8 years at home bringing up her family. She worked as a secretary in a factory before leaving shortly after getting married and having a baby. She has little experience of using IT, however, and does not feel confident in her ability to get to grips with using a computer.

Questions:

1. What new skills needs that Jeanette will probably need when she returns to work?

2. What advice would you give to Jeanette to help her achieve success in obtaining a job?

3. What problems will Jeanette have if she cannot overcome her fears of using a computer?

4. Who could help Jeanette overcome some of her fears of using a computer, and how?

Con men in training

Thousands of people are believed to have become the victims of a massive scam carried out by fake training organisations. The scam, which is being investigated by the Government, involves bogus organisations conning people out of their training entitlements under the Individual Learning Accounts programme.

A Trading Standards Officer said "We have identified several practices we are concerned about, including blank ILA forms being offered at car boot sales and 'sales people' knocking on doors urging the public to sign up for free courses.

The signed blank forms are then sent away and the 'training organisation' has accessed these people's ILA accounts. In return they have been offered material such as photocopies of the Word for Windows guide. These are not real qualifications or certificates."

ILAs were set up by the government in 1999 as an incentive for people to improve current skills or learn new ones. They provide up to 80% of the cost of a course up to a maximum of £200.

(Source: Computer Active 1-14 November 2001)

Fraudsters exploit lax security

Sloppy security allowed fraudulent training companies to siphon off millions of pounds of taxpayers' money. The ILA scheme was suspended last November, £60m over budget and facing allegations of fraud.

The system was embarrassingly easy to abuse. Training providers were able to access £200 funding via a website by entering a candidate's 10-digit PIN number. Fraudsters quickly worked out that the numbers were not randomly generated but ran in sequence. If the last two digits on each person's PIN were 10, you could obtain further payment by entering 11, 12, 13 and so on. Because 60% of the funds available for the scheme were unused, it was easy to find an account and take the money. There was no extra level of security, requiring a user name, for example. It was easy pickings for the conman.

Police are investigating allegations of theft and fraud.

(Source: Computing 24 January 2002)

Questions:

1 Two scams are described in the above case studies. What measures could have made these scams harder to carry out?

2 How do these scams affect legitimate training organisations, and people seeking training?

3 Who ultimately has to swallow the cost of this fraud?

Exercises

1. Describe what use you make of ICT in your schoolwork. In your answer, consider the following questions: Do you use computers for other subjects apart from ICT? Do you make use of the Internet? Do you use e-mail at all? Do you use reference CDs? Collect together some examples of work you have done where you have successfully used ICT.

2. Describe some advantages and some disadvantages of learning about a subject by using a computer-aided learning package, both for yourself and for someone going to College for an evening class, who has not used a computer before.

3. Is computer technology used in other ways in your school – for example, for pupil registration, recording library loans, buying meals or drinks, for access to certain rooms? Find out more about these and similar applications. (Some of the sites mentioned below may be useful.)

4. Look up some of these sites to see what educational software and resources are available. Notice that some of the applications described are used for teaching and learning, and others are used for school administration. Choose two applications from these sites or other ones that you find, and write about them.

    www.englishonline.co.uk   www.mathsonline.co.uk

    www.historyonline.co.uk   www.geographyonline.co.uk

    www.schoolmaster.net   www.edutrack.co.uk

    www.headstrong.demon.co.uk   www.interactive-education.co.uk

    www.weatherview32.com   www.taglearning.com

Chapter 37: Working Styles and Opportunities

The widespread use of ICT has led to massive changes in working patterns, bringing hardship to some and new opportunities to others. Almost every single person who has been in work for more than say, 20 years, will have seen a major change in the way they do their jobs, or the type of employment they are in. Much of this change is a direct result of the introduction of computers.

Discussion

Read through the list of statements below and decide whether the statements are true or not:

Over the past decade, the widespread use of computers has:

1. **put many people out of work**
2. **changed the nature of many people's work**
3. **resulted in a de-skilling of some jobs**
4. **made some people's jobs more interesting**
5. **resulted in an increase in the total number of unemployed people**
6. **enabled some organisations to operate more efficiently**
7. **resulted in an increase in the number of bankruptcies**
8. **created many new job opportunities**
9. **made some people's work environment more pleasant**
10. **forced people to learn new skills**

In the 1950s and 60s when computerisation was just beginning, computers were largely used to replace clerical or routine manual tasks. In the bank, for example, counter staff counted out cash for customers making withdrawals, clerical staff manually prepared customers' bank statements, and payroll clerks prepared payslips for thousands of employees. In the 1990s thousands of bank and Building Society employees lost their jobs, with many branches disappearing and being replaced by cash machines at

supermarkets and shopping centres, as well as online banking and postal accounts.

In the 70s and 80s, huge job losses occurred in industry, with factories making everything from cars to biscuits finding it cost-effective to automate production rather than to hire manual workers.

When computers first started to become widespread in industry and commerce in the 1970s, some people thought that they would take over from human workers and in 1979 one writer suggested that "Employment as we know it will be down to 10% in 30 years' time".

Chapter 37: Working Styles and Opportunities

New ways of working

The way that millions of people do their jobs, from garage mechanics, secretaries, and cabinet makers to pilots, architects and headteachers, has radically changed since the advent of computers. What different technologies are used by these different employees? Garage mechanics, for example, have computerised equipment to test emissions, balance wheels and perform dozens of tests and adjustments. Secretaries and managers use computers for word processing and other office applications.

Some of the changes to working practices are described below.

- Employees use e-mail to communicate with one another, even though they may be in the same building.

- People can be contacted anywhere at anytime by mobile phone.

- Employees can take work home with them and work remotely, e.g. on trains and in hotels, using their portable computers.

- Employees who work in an office now expect to have a desktop computer to carry out their day-to-day work. They therefore need to be able to use software and hardware.

- Manny people's jobs have changed – for example, a designer or architect who used to use a pencil and paper on a drawing board now uses a CAD system.

Discussion

What specialised computer technologies are used by people in different types of employment? Have their old skills become redundant?

Creation of new jobs

Although computers have undoubtedly replaced many manual workers, they have also created thousands of jobs that previously did not exist. New job opportunities exist for systems analysts, programmers, website developers, network managers, computer technicians, graphic designers, desktop publishers, and workers assembling PCs, mobile phones and other computerised equipment.

Discussion

Think of some other jobs that have been created because of computers.

Hundreds of new small businesses are being set up in the technology sector. Many of these companies grow with astonishing speed, making huge profits. A look at the website www.fasttrack100.co.uk will give you an insight into the type of new career opportunities available for entrepreneurs wanting to set up a business. Here is one example taken from the website:

CASE STUDY

Software 2000

The worldwide boom in computer printer sales has been good news for Oxford-based Software 2000, founded in 1989 by John Guy, Dick Hodge and Tony Harris.

The company develops printer drivers - the software that enables computers to communicate with printers - and licences them to major printer manufacturers around the world, such as Hewlett-Packard and Konica. Software 2000 has become the world's leading provider of third-party printer software. The company

receives a set royalty for every printer sold, benefiting greatly from a massive increase in printer sales and insulating it from price falls. Sales increased 48% a year from £7m in 1998 to £15.4m in 2000, when the company employed 73 staff.

Software 2000 now has offices in the US, Japan and Canada. In 2001 the company acquired CAI, a US-based Macintosh developer, to add the MAC operating system to Software 2000's technology portfolio.

Teleworking

This term means replacing the journey to work that many people make each day with the use of telecommunications and computers. When teleworking first became acceptable business practice, it was often programmers who had no daily face-to-face contact with other people who became teleworkers. Now, more and more organisations, particularly large ones, are allowing employees to spend time out of the office working from home, for some or all of their weekly hours. The number of teleworkers in Europe is expected to grow from 10 million in 2000 to more than 28.8 million in 2005, according to researcher IDC.

The benefits to employees of teleworking include:

- reduced cost of travelling
- long commuting journeys avoided
- opportunity to work in the comfort of their own home environment
- increased productivity
- easier childcare arrangements

The drawbacks include:

- lack of personal contact with fellow workers
- lack of teamwork and participation with shared projects
- home distractions may interfere with work
- lack of benefits given to other employees who attend the office, e.g. medical plans, pensions and bonuses

Discussion

What are the benefits and drawbacks to the employer of having teleworkers? What are the benefits, if any, to society?

CASE STUDY

Ageism still rife in IT

Almost a quarter of IT professionals (23%) say they have been denied career opportunities because they are considered too old, according to an exclusive Computing survey. The research shows that age discrimination is widespread, with contractors and the self-employed feeling particularly victimised.

The survey confirms that the IT industry is among the most ageist in the UK, claims Sam Mercer, campaign director of the Employers' Forum on Age.

"In the IT industry, 'older worker' is still defined as someone over the age of 35", she said, adding that the image is based more on myths about the supposed inability of experienced staff to learn new skills, than on reality.

Contrastingly, seven per cent of IT professionals feel they are overlooked for jobs because they are too young.

(Source: Rachel Fielding, Computing, 18 October 2001)

Questions:

1. Why do you think some employers are less keen to employ workers over a certain age?

2. Do you think this is a reasonable policy?

3. What benefits are employers overlooking in not employing older workers?

It's a young man's game

Blitz Games is an example of the type of teen techno business thrown up by the computer games revolution. Twins Philip and Andrew Oliver began writing computer games in their bedroom at the age of 13 and went on to found Blitz Games in 1990.

With customers including Microsoft, MGM and Disney, sales grew 66% a year, from £1.4m in 1998 to £3.8m in 2000. The Leamington Spa-based

company, whose hits include Chicken Run, inspired by the film, and The Mummy Returns for Microsoft's new X-Box, employs 105 staff with an average age of 23.

Blitz does not expect growth to slow for some time. In America last year, sales of video games exceeded those of books.

"Like it or loathe it, the video games market is the biggest entertainment market in the world," says Philip

Oliver. "It's great for us.

We would do this job even if there was no money in it."

IT must put gender on the agenda

It's time for IT to put gender on the agenda – that's the message from industry bodies and executives. Speaking at a conference to tackle the women in IT issue, secretary of state for Trade and Industry Patricia Hewitt called for greater cooperation between industry, government and education. "It is pathetic that fewer women are entering the IT industry than 20 years ago. The opportunities for industry and the economy in general are huge."

Ian Watmore, managing director of Accenture in the UK, said equal representation of females was essential. "It's not just a moral and ethical argument, it just makes

common business sense," he explained. "By 2010 I will represent a minority – white, able-bodied males. Eighty per cent of the growth market of the future will be women."

The number of IT jobs in the UK has more than doubled in the last five years. But while women represent over half the potential workforce in the UK, they form only 22 per cent of the IT workforce, compared with

29 per cent as recently as 1994, according to government figures.

(Source: Rachel Fielding, Computing, 24 January 2002)

Questions:

1 What should employers be doing to improve the image of the industry and thereby encourage more women to enter into ICT professions?

2 What more could be done in schools to prevent this gender imbalance earlier?

3 Why do you believe the industry has a problem in retaining females?

Working too hard?

In spite of predictions that only 10% of people would be fully employed by the turn of the 20th century, it appears that in fact many people are working harder than ever.

Employees working in IT in the UK are more likely to work longer hours than anywhere else in the European Union, according to a report by the Organisation for Economic Cooperation and Development. The culture of working long hours has serious health implications.

- More than 5,000 people die prematurely in the UK each year because of long working hours.

- 20% of IT professionals do not take their full holiday entitlement, largely because of the pressure of too much work.

- 75% of IT heads work more than 48 hours per week,

- 46% of IT Directors and Heads of IT say they are not happy with their work/life balance.

- Only 5% of employers offer all four of the most common forms of family-friendly provision: additional maternity leave, paternity leave, childcare provisions and flexible or non-standard working arrangements.

(Source: Rachel Fielding and Peter Skyte, Computing18 October 2001 and 12 December 2001)

Exercises

1. Investigate the way that computers are used in the workplace of three employees known to you. What skills or qualifications do they need? Has training been provided? What hardware and software do they use for their job? Find out whether their jobs have changed since the introduction of computers and how.

2. Find some advertisements for jobs that appeal to you. What skills and qualifications are required? What salary is being offered? Would you be required to have a knowledge of ICT for this job?

3. Describe a number of ways in which an adult known to you uses ICT in their professional, personal, social, home and work use. How well does ICT meet their needs in each of these categories?

Chapter 38: ICT Legislation

Personal privacy

The **right to privacy** is a fundamental human right and one that we take for granted. Most of us, for instance, would not want our medical records freely circulated, and many people are sensitive about revealing their age, religious beliefs, family circumstances or academic qualifications. In the UK even the use of name and address files for mail shots is often felt to be an invasion of privacy.

With the advent of large computerised databases it became quite feasible for sensitive personal information to be stored without the individual's knowledge and accessed by, say, a prospective employer, credit card company or insurance company to assess somebody's suitability for employment, credit or insurance.

CASE STUDY

James Wiggins – a true story

In the US, James Russell Wiggins applied for and got a $70,000 post with a company in Washington. A routine pre-employment background check, however, revealed that he had been convicted of possessing cocaine, and he was fired the next day, not only because he had a criminal record but because he had concealed this fact when applying for the job. Wiggins was shocked – he had never had a criminal record, and it turned out that the credit bureau hired to make the investigation had retrieved the record for a James Ray Wiggins by mistake, even though they had different birthdates, addresses, middle names and social security numbers. Even after this was discovered, however, Wiggins didn't get his job back.

If the pre-employment check had been made before Wiggins was offered the job, he would not have been offered it and no reason would have been given. The information would have remained on his file, virtually ensuring that he would never get a decent job – without ever knowing the reason why.

Questions:

1. Do you think your name and personal details are held on databases by different organisations?

2. Do you think it is a good thing that checks can be carried out by a 'credit bureau' to determine whether a prospective employee has a criminal record?

The Data Protection Act

The Data Protection Act 1984 grew out of public concern about personal privacy in the face of rapidly developing computer technology. It provides rights for individuals and demands good information-handling practice.

The Act covers 'personal data' which are 'automatically processed'. It works in two ways, giving individuals certain rights whilst requiring those who record and use personal information on computer to be open about that use and to follow proper practices.

The Data Protection Act 1998 was brought into force in March 2000. Some manual records fall within the scope of the Act and there will also be extended rights for data subjects.

The Data Protection principles

Once registered, data users must comply with the eight Data Protection principles of good practice contained in the Act. These principles can be looked up on the website www.dataprotection.gov.uk.

Personal data covers:
1. facts and opinions about the individual
2. information regarding the intentions of the data controller towards the individual
3. the processing of data including: 'obtaining', holding' and 'disclosing'

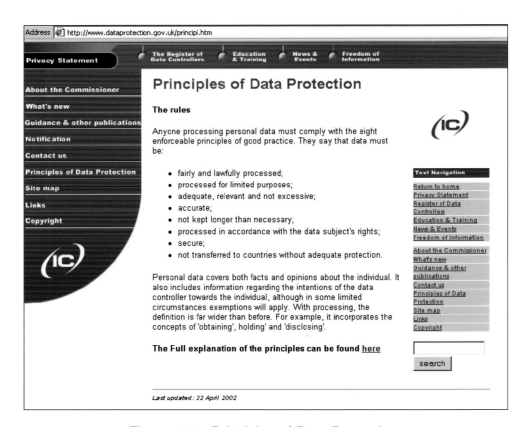

Figure 38.1: Principles of Data Protection

The Data Protection Act: March 2002 Compliance

The eight principles of the Act are now a virtually watertight regime. 'Data subjects' (the people about whom data is being held) are protected now more than ever before, and that presents a problem for businesses.

- Personal data must be processed fairly and lawfully. The data subject has to know who the data controller is, and why the data is being collected and must give their consent for use of their details.

- Personal data can be obtained only for specified purposes. If databases allow other employees to 'dip in' to data then that company may be in breach of the Act. This task will be particularly difficult for the 58% of UK companies that use more than one database, with some having more than 40 databases.

- Personal data should be adequate and relevant and not excessive. The Act now covers electronic and paper records. For example, many websites may be in breach if they insist on an excessive registration page with 'comments' fields.

- Personal data must be accurate and up-to-date or a business may risk having to pay a fine. This applies whether or not the company collected the data – it is equally liable for data from trading partners.

- Information should not be kept for longer than is necessary. Data must be processed in accordance with the rights of the subjects. Individuals have a right to see any data held on them, in a user-friendly format, within 40 days. The law also applies to CCTV images.

- Appropriate technological measures must be taken to keep the information safe from hackers. It must also be secured from other employees who don't have rights to it.

- Personal data cannot be transferred to countries outside the European Union unless the country provides an adequate level of protection. Personal data cannot be exported without the subject's consent.

Store admits to being in breach of DPA for 15 years

A leading high street retailing giant has been forced to tighten its procedures for dealing with its charge card holders after learning it had been acting in breach of the Data Protection Act for almost 15 years. The company will now make sure that they only disclose information about charge card accounts to the main account holder, who is legally liable for paying the bill, and not to other card holders on the account as they have been doing previously. In the past, these card holders were allowed to alter personal details, such as mailing addresses.

This is a breach of the eighth data protection principle, which calls for organisations to take steps to prevent unauthorised access to personal data.

The company denied they had received a warning from the Data Protection Registrar. They also made it clear in a statement that other companies might be breaking the law in the same way and the company was pleased to keep abreast of what's happening legally.

Questions:

1. Why would an organisation like the one mentioned in the extract be very concerned about any risk that they may be breaking Data Protection rules?

2. Do you think that sticking to the letter of the law will inconvenience and annoy their customers?

3. What other organisations may have made this same mistake?

Computer Misuse Act (1990)

In the early 1980s in the UK, hacking was not illegal. Some universities stipulated that hacking, especially where damage was done to data files, was a disciplinary offence, but there was no law under which a criminal prosecution could be brought. This situation was rectified by the Computer Misuse Act of 1990 which defined three specific criminal offences to deal with the problems of hacking, viruses and other nuisances. The offences are:

- unauthorised access to computer programs or data

- unauthorised access with a further criminal intent

- unauthorised modification of computer material (i.e. programs or data)

To date there have been relatively few prosecutions under this law – probably because most organisations are reluctant to admit that their system security procedures have been breached, which might lead to a loss of confidence on the part of their clients.

CASE STUDY

Hacker "Curador" escapes jail

 Teenager hacker and self-styled 'saint of e-commerce' (because his role was exposing security holes in websites), Raphael Gray, also known as "Curador", managed to escape jail when sentenced at Swansea Crown Court this week. Instead he faces three years of community probation and a course of psychiatric treatment. Nineteen-year-old Gray was apprehended by the FBI back in March after a month-long manhunt leading back to a tiny hamlet in Wales.

He was initially charged with illegally obtaining 23,000 credit card numbers and obtaining services by deception. He admitted illegally accessing eight online companies' customer databases, and his antics even included sending a shipment of Viagra to Bill Gates after obtaining the Microsoft boss's credit card details. He maintains that he was acting to draw attention to the necessity of security online and wanted to prove a point.

Yet one of the companies he hit folded, another stopped trading and Visa is said to have incurred costs of £250,000 as a result of his actions. The presiding judge had earlier said he had strongly considered a custodial sentence. There was, however, insufficient evidence to mount a credible case against Gray and prosecute him under the Computer Misuse Act.

In its current guise, the Act makes it an offence for someone to access, modify or delete computer data unless they have authorisation. Gray claimed that he was able to carry out many of his attacks without using hacking tools, and without having to bypass password screens. It was not clear from the Act whether or not his method of entry would constitute unauthorised access.

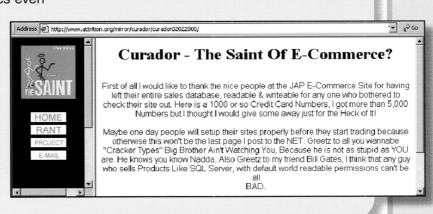

Address http://www.attrition.org/mirror/curador/curador02022000/

Curador - The Saint Of E-Commerce?

HOME
RANT
PROJECT
E-MAIL

First of all I would like to thank the nice people at the JAP E-Commerce Site for having left their entire sales database, readable & writeable for any one who bothered to check their site out. Here is a 1000 or so Credit Card Numbers, I got more than 5,000 Numbers but I thought I would give some away just for the Heck of It!

Maybe one day people will setup their sites properly before they start trading because otherwise this won't be the last page I post to the NET. Greetz to all you wannabe "Cracker Types" Big Brother Ain't Watching You, Because he is not as stupid as YOU are. He knows you know Nadda. Also Greetz to my friend Bill Gates, I think that any guy who sells Products Like SQL Server, with default world readable permissions can't be all BAD.

Questions:

1 What was the motivation behind Gray's actions?

2 Do you feel that his action was acceptable in light of your answer?

3 Do you feel that the punishment Gray has received is appropriate?

Software copyright laws

Computer software is now covered by the Copyright Designs and Patents Act of 1988, which covers a wide range of intellectual property such as music, literature and software. Provisions of the Act make it illegal to:

- copy software;

- run pirated software;

- transmit software over a telecommunications line, thereby creating a copy.

Software can easily be copied and bootlegged (sold illegally). In addition, the programming ideas and methods can be stolen by a competitor. Microsoft was sued (unsuccessfully) many years ago by Apple Computers for copying the 'look and feel' of their graphical user interface. It is possible for an expert programmer to 'reverse engineer' machine code to establish the specific algorithms used, so that they can be copied. Some software manufacturers put 'fingerprints' into the code – little oddities which do not affect the way the program runs – so that if the same code is found in a competitor's program, they can prove that it was illegally copied.

CASE STUDY

Pirates ahoy!

Bill Gates's empire is being jeopardised by Russian software pirates. Microsoft Office '97 is being sold for £3 on the Russian black market, a minute fraction of the normal retail price of £315. In 1996, 91% of software programs being used in Russia were pirate copies.

Gates recently travelled to Moscow in an attempt to persuade those trading in pirated copies of software programs to refrain from doing so. The overall cost of this illegal activity to the software industry is around £300 million each year. However, it is unlikely that this personal appeal will succeed while fines for being caught in possession of pirated materials are insignificant in comparison with the revenue generated from the pirate industry itself, set at over £500,000 per month. As one stallholder reportedly said: "Mr Gates has gone home and we are trading happily – he makes about £18 million a month, so we do not feel too bad about selling these copies to people who cannot afford to buy it."

(Source: Computer Consultant October 1997)

Questions:

1 Who are the stakeholders (the people affected) in this story?

2 Who are the victims?

3 Is the stallholder acting ethically?

Scenario The market stall enterprise

Joe Mills runs a successful market stall. He has always been really interested in computers and likes to keep up-to-date with all the changes in the industry. He is extremely busy all weekend selling bootleg CDs and DVDs. He sells a wide range of disks from computer games to branded software and even computer textbooks saved in browser format. He usually buys one title over the Internet from America and copies it himself on his home computer. This way he often has titles for sale that haven't been released in the UK yet.

Joe generally sells upwards of 1000 titles in one weekend. During the week he spends all his time copying disks. He usually uses his brother's computer as well and has two PCs copying at once. Joe is so busy, he is even thinking of expanding his mini-enterprise to another town. His family are really proud of him as he is running his own business. He lost his old job in a computer company for spending too much time developing his ICT skills and not answering the phone on the Help Desk.

Questions:

1 To what extent is Joe's business holding back technological development?

2 What is the long-term effect of these practices if they are widespread?

3 Advise Joe on a better strategy for either a successful business or career.

Health and Safety at Work Act (1974)

This law imposes a responsibility on the employer to ensure safety at work for all their employees.

- Employers have to take reasonable steps to ensure the health, safety and welfare of their employees at work.

- Failure to do so could result in a criminal prosecution in the Magistrates Court or a Crown Court.

- Failure to ensure safe working practices could also lead to an employee suing for personal injury or in some cases the employer being prosecuted for corporate manslaughter.

The employer also has an implied responsibility to:

- take reasonable steps as far as they are able to ensure the health and safety of their employees is not put at risk

- provide safe plant and machinery and safe premises

- provide a safe system of work and competent, trained and supervised staff

- care for and supervise employees; particularly disabled workers, pregnant workers, illiterate workers etc.

- consult with employees on health and safety matters

- provide a safe environment for customers or visitors who use the work place

- have a written code of conduct, rules regarding training and supervision, and rules on safety procedures

- give information on basic health and safety requirements via leaflets and posters, giving warnings of hazards

Figure 38.2: Note the Health and Safety poster behind this contented worker!

There are special regulations within this under the title of **Health and Safety (Display Screen Equipment) Regulations (1992)**.

These regulations affect employed workers who habitually use VDUs for a significant part of their normal work. Measures were introduced to prevent repetitive strain injury, fatigue and eye problems in the use of technological equipment.

Employers have to:

- analyse workstations of employees covered by the Regulations and assess and reduce risks

- look at the hardware, the environment, and factors specific to the individuals using the equipment. Where risks are identified, the employer must take steps to reduce them

- ensure workstations meet minimum requirements

- ensure there are good features in employees' workstations. For example, the screen should normally have adjustable brightness and contrast controls. This allows individuals to find a comfortable level for their eyes, helping to avoid the problems of tired eyes and eyestrain

- plan work so there are breaks or changes of activity, ideally short, frequent breaks are better than longer, less frequent ones, and ideally the individual should have some discretion over when they are taken

- arrange and pay for eye and eyesight tests, and provide employees with spectacles. Employers are responsible for providing further eye tests at regular intervals

- provide health and safety training so employees can use all aspects of their workstation equipment safely and know how to make best use of it to avoid health problems, for example by adjusting the chair

Employees also have a responsibility to:

- use workstations and equipment correctly, in accordance with training provided by employers

- bring problems to the attention of their employer immediately and co-operate in the correction of these problems

Scenario Pop-in printers

Pop-in Printers is a small printing firm located on a busy High Street in the Midlands. It prints mainly stationery, business cards, invitations and posters. It also offers photocopying, binding and image-scanning services. There are around 8 employees working in the small shop gathered closely together around a cluster of PCs. Some of the employees work back-to-back so they often 'bang chairs' when getting up to serve a customer. The photocopiers are located at the side of the office area and customers have to walk past some of the office equipment to use them.

Melanie James runs the business and has done so for the past few years. She is very proud of the way the business has grown and expanded into new projects. However, in recent weeks she seems to have been inundated with complaints by members of staff and customers about the shop and some of the Health and Safety risks posed by the way the shop is organised. She feels she is providing good service to the customers at all times and is therefore strongly hurt by some of the comments which have been made. She feels that as they cannot afford to move to new premises, people must make do with the current arrangements.

The complaints from staff have been about the amount of room at the cluster of PCs, the lack of correct seating and the customers walking past them and causing a hazard. Complaints from customers have been about tripping over trailing wires en route to the photocopiers and the lack of office organisation.

Questions:

1. What Health and Safety advice would you give to Melanie to ensure she is not contravening the Health and Safety At Work Act principles?

2. Describe how the workers' seating should be organised to ensure they do not suffer unnecessary strains and health risks.

3. What are the risks of non-compliance for Melanie?

4. Do you feel Melanie is adopting the right attitude to the complaints that have been made?

Regulation of Investigatory Powers Act (2000)

This act is about defining the powers the government has with regard to access to information and the security of that information. It gives the government the right to carry out intelligence surveillance and to spy on electronic communications and data.

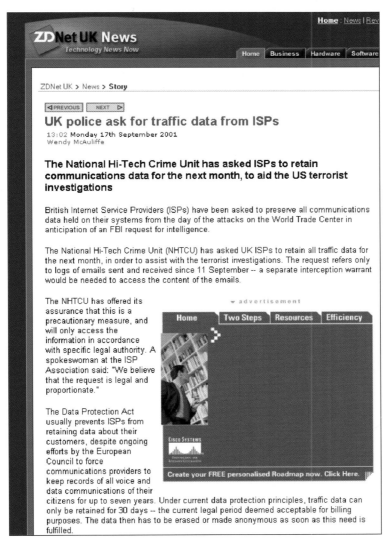

Figure 38.3: Story on http://news.zdnet.co.uk

Questions:

1 Do you think that the government should have such powers in the interests of national security and fighting technological crimes?

2 Do you think the government should have the legal power to monitor all electronic communications that the public make?

Internet Code of Practice (ICOP)

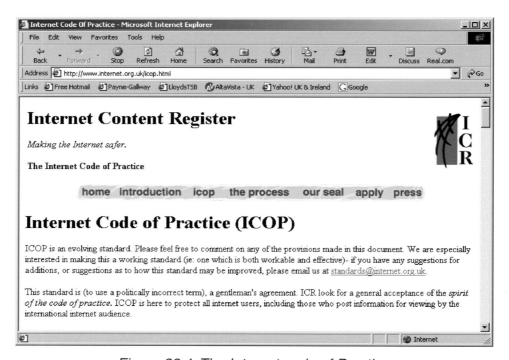

Figure 38.4: The Internet code of Practice

This Code of Practice is not law, but is an agreement which exists to protect Internet users. Website owners can apply to be registered for a small fee and, once registered, have the right to display the ICR **seal** to show that the site conforms to the code of practice.

A summary of the code is given below.

- **Audience**: Information must be suitable for viewing by its target audience, i.e. not of indecent material. Offensive material should have a security mechanism to prevent accidental access. Links to external sites should be checked for offensive material and commercial information must be clearly identified as such.

- **Advertising**: Unsolicited e-mail and SPAM should not be used as an advertising method. Advertisements should be legal, decent, honest, truthful and not misleading. Prices and delivery-date information should be clear. All advertisements should show the identity of the advertiser and the full contact postal address.

- **Contracts**: Any standard terms and conditions used must be clearly drawn to the attention of the customer. Goods must be of 'satisfactory quality' at the time of delivery to the customer.

- **Copyright and information ownership**: The international rights to all site contents must be secured or owned by the publisher prior to its release on the Internet. Copyright must be obtained in all countries concerned as the Internet transcends national boundaries. Links to other pages must have the permission of the target-link site. All trade and similar marks must be clearly displayed and identified.

- **Information**: Images, audio and video clips should be compressed to keep download times and bandwidth requirements to a minimum. Private data (such as e-mail, network and postal addresses, telephone numbers, payment card details etc.) should not be disclosed to third parties without permission of the data subject. Information should not incite or promote illegal acts.

- **Applets, browser scripts and CGI usage**: No program should consume system resources or network bandwidth unnecessarily. No program should destroy or damage any data held on the viewer's computer or network. No program should attempt to access information about the viewer or the viewer's computer system covertly.

- **Mail and news**: When sending e-mail to more than one person, e-mail is certainly cheaper than using conventional mail, however both parties pay for the communications systems used during upload and download. Sending advertising mail through the post merely costs the sender. Furthermore any kind of unsolicited communication is often considered by the recipient to be unwelcome. Therefore, ICR members agree not to send, encourage, or contribute to chain letters, hoaxers or SPAM.

Exercises

1. Look up the website www.hse.gov.uk and find out what health problems are associated with VDUs, and how these can be minimised.

2. Look up http://news.zdnet.co.uk to find some news stories relating to technology.

Chapter 39: The Downside of ICT

As well as bringing unimagined benefits to millions of people, the widespread use of ICT has inevitably brought a number of new problems with it. Many of these problems are caused by people motivated by greed or malice. Others are brought about by inequalities in our society.

Viruses

A major problem that has emerged with the increased use and reliance on technology is that of computer viruses. The risk of a computer virus attack is growing by 15% a year. Over the past five years the number of virus infections reported by businesses has increased from 21 a month for every 1000 PCs to 103 a month (Source: ICSA).

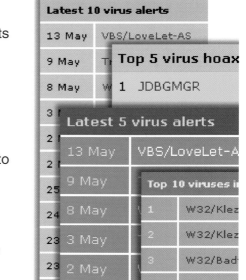

A virus is a computer program which usually acts to sabotage files or programs. A virus may:

- be passed onto your computer via the Internet e.g. downloading an e-mail attachment and saving it to your hard disk

- be passed onto your computer via the sharing of floppy disks from one computer to another

- destroy data, information, files and even hardware permanently

- be embedded in html code and not need to be hidden in e-mail attachments

The term 'virus' may lead us into thinking that a computer virus is just a bit of naturally occurring bad luck, like the common cold. It is not. Each and every virus is programmed and distributed by someone intent on doing damage. Some of the most damaging viruses of recent years have been hidden in seemingly innocent e-mail attachments, but designed in such a way that ensures recipients will open them (this practice is known as 'Social Engineering'). Some examples are:

- "Click here to receive a picture of Anna Kornicova"

- "I Love You" (known as 'The Love Bug')

- Christmas cards, jokes and screensavers

Look at **www.sophos.com** for information on viruses

Other severe forms of virus, such as the 'Melissa' virus, can use software weaknesses in order to carry out their actions. This virus used security weaknesses in Microsoft Outlook e-mail software to spread itself to every person in each user's address book and caused millions of pounds worth of damage. This virus evaded anti-virus protection

Position	Virus	Percentage of reports
1	W32/Nimda	27.2%
2	W32/Sircam-A	20.3%
3	W32/Magistr	12.0%
4	W32/Hybris	6.2%
5	W32/Apology	3.8%
6	VBS/VBSWG-X	3.6%
7	VBS/Kakworm	3.1%
8	VBS/SST-A	2.0%
9	W32/Badtrans	1.8%
10	W32/Navidad	1.8%
Others		18.2%

Top ten viruses reported to Sophos in 2001

CASE STUDY

Nimda worm costs firms dear

The Nimda virus, which caused havoc around the world last week, will cost businesses more to clean up than any virus attack so far. Although Nimda has spread more slowly than the Love Bug and Homepage viruses, it is causing far more damage to the organisations it strikes. It has hit businesses in at least 15 countries, and has been particularly active in the UK, the US and Hong Kong.

Some large City firms put their IT teams up in hotels while staff worked around the clock to repair their IT infrastructure. Other businesses had to close down their computer systems completely.

The virus, the most sophisticated to date, targets Microsoft systems and leaves a trail of infected computer files in its wake. Analysts are advising companies to restore damaged files from back-ups, rather than attempting to repair them using anti-virus software.

Nimda e-mails itself to all of the addresses in a user's address book and searches caches to find further addresses. It is quite ferocious in its attack.

Nimda's global victims:

- The Australian Parliament was forced to shut down its Website and internal e-mail system.

- In London, thousands of employees of GlaxoSmithKline could not use their PCs until the problem was fixed.

- In Thailand, the virus brought down networks at the national bank and the science ministry.

- The Italian town of Bari blamed the virus for altering its monthly inflation statistics.

(Source: Bill Goodwin and Karl Cushing, Computer Weekly 27 September 2001)

Questions:

1 Why would someone send a virus across the Internet?

2 What must individuals and firms always do to be prepared for the threat of viruses?

Data theft/fraud

The increasing dependence on the use of computers in business has meant that sensitive information is now often available to more employees than is wise. Information can often be very valuable and can be resold to rival companies. This kind of information could include customer databases and mailing lists, designs for new products, or simply new ideas.

Web scams

The Internet can be a hostile place and when using it you can be at risk of being defrauded. The most complained-about web scams are:

- being sold something via an Internet auction and then goods not arriving or not being as described;

- being charged huge amounts on your phone bill by modems being re-connected to an expensive international phone number so you can download 'adult' material;

- receiving e-mails asking for charitable contributions or access to your bank details for 'get rich quick' schemes, which inevitably have the opposite effect;

- selling of hundreds of 'miracle cures', from dieting pills and vitamins to baldness cures;

- most famously, the newsworthy adoption scams of the last few years where babies have been literally auctioned off on a website.

CASE STUDY

Teenager's web scam nets $1m

A high school student used his home computer to operate an Internet scam that conned an estimated $1 million out of investors, according to investigators in the United States

The Californian teenager called his website scheme "The Christmas Miracle" and offered investors returns of up to 2,500 per cent through sports betting.

The Securities and Exchanges Commission, which governs and controls financial investments, said over 1,000 US investors had joined the scheme which was run from the boy's home, and had parted with as much as $20,000 each. The boy, a budding baseball player, has now agreed to hand back $900,000.

Charity virus scam warning

A leading charity has warned web users to beware of a computer virus that steals credit card information from donors to the organisation's September 11th Fund. The virus acts as a Trojan horse, arriving as an e-mail attachment, and when opened displays a window looking like the genuine charity donation page.

When users enter their credit card and personal details, they are uploaded to a different website.

Distribution of the virus so far has been low, but the charity has warned legitimate donors could be caught out. It has sent an e-mail to 30,000 previous donors including a link to the official website.

Discussion

How does online fraud undermine the excellent potential uses of the Internet?

Chat rooms

A chatroom is an online venue for typed chat between different users. When computer users go online to chat, they are essentially in a public place where all kinds of people may also be present, some of them highly undesirable or dangerous. Chatrooms are seen as one of the largest risks areas to young people and their use of Internet.

- The FBI in the US has statistics showing that the number of children who have been lured away from home by people they have met online has risen from 113 in 1996 to 1498 in 1999, and rising. Only 60% of those children made it home safely.

- There are specially trained anonymous teenagers called 'Teenangels' who help protect youngsters using chat rooms, advising them on staying safe on the web.

- Police now use specialist Web-monitoring software to try to ensure the Internet does not become any more unpoliceable. They use software tools to track and trace illegal and threatening activity in Internet chat rooms, making it extremely difficult for those who use the Internet illegally to remain anonymous.

Scenario Caroline enters the society of chat

Caroline is a teenager who lives in a remote part of Scotland. Just like any other teenager she likes music and going out, finding out about the latest fashions and making friends. The Internet is a lifeline for her in that she can make contact with the outside world she rarely gets to see more than a few times a year.

Caroline is keen to make more friends on the mainland and would like to perhaps visit them later on when she gets to know them. She has heard of chatrooms and would like to try to use one as a way to get to know new people. A friend told her that you can access chatrooms that are specific to your interests. Caroline likes garage music and also is a keen photographer and seal spotter. She would like to make friends who share these interests.

Questions:

1. What advice would you give anyone about using a chatroom to make new friends?

2. Why is Caroline particularly at risk and how should she take extra precautions in using a chatroom's facilities?

3. Give further advice to Caroline about how she could use the Internet to make friends without relying on a chatroom.

The Internet: good or bad influence?

No matter what your opinion of the Internet, its existence has quite likely had some impact upon the way you live your life. Examine these extracts and discuss some of the negative aspects the Internet seems to have brought to people's lives. Is the Net ultimately responsible?

CASE STUDY

Internet Addict left her husband for a computer

A Kent woman today filed for divorce, rather than be separated from her computer. The woman met new people on the Internet and the conversations made her feel "interesting and attractive". Her husband told her to choose between him and her PC when she stopped cooking and cleaning and playing golf with him to spend up to 12 hours per day surfing the Internet.

Internet A case of going bug-eyed

A young boy has been diagnosed with IAD (Internet Addiction Disorder). He has been clinically identified as having a psychological dependency on the Net. These judgements were made on criteria normally used to assess addiction to chemicals or gambling. The boy was spending over 40 hours per week surfing the web either in chat rooms, looking up information about his interests or playing games. He admitted he would spend hours at a time going from one site to another randomly finding out information. Doctors admitted that the Net was not the cause of his problems; he was simply using the Net to avoid facing his problems of loneliness.

Internet Manners are lost on the Internet

A recent survey has found that there are shocking lapses of etiquette in the e-mail messages sent by people under 25. Many people do not use the correct spelling, punctuation and grammar. In addition many "Americanisms" were seen creeping in, blurring the distinction between English and American-English. At least two thirds of 18-24 year olds when questioned admitted they used casual language and grammar and didn't worry about over-familiarity in e-mail messages, signing their messages with love and kisses to their boss. The survey also found that 10 per cent of women have dumped their boyfriend via e-mail and now up to half of you think that an electronic note or birthday greeting is as acceptable as a paper one.

Can the Spam!

An I.T. graduate who was looking for work via online recruitment sites was using his home e-mail account to register with lots of job sites. When he used his e-mail editor to "send and receive", he ended up with a massive amount of e-mails to download and then a huge bill from his telephone supplier. Literally hundreds of different organisations were sending him "spam" junk e-mails and he had no choice but to download them as he was searching for those relevant e-mails containing potential job offers. When he tried to e-mail the companies to unsubscribe him and stop sending the messages, more ended up arriving from other sites as he had unintentionally confirmed his e-mail address this way and his details had been passed on.

Birth defect warning on PC waste

Companies that dump their old computers in landfill sites rather than recycling them risk damaging public health, industry experts have warned. The warning follows a government-sponsored survey which found that babies born near landfill sites are slightly more likely to be born with health defects.

Despite the host of toxins contained in PCs, only 25% of computer waste is recycled, according to Jon Godfrey, director of business development at technology recycling company Technical Asset Management. Godfrey said that many companies opt for the lower-cost option of dumping old hardware. "People don't associate the technology with hazardous waste but if you slash a computer up and stash it underground sooner or later the toxins will leach out," he said.

Godfrey called on IT directors to set a good example and construct an environmentally sound disposal policy for IT equipment. Current environmental protection legislation does not have a specific category for PC recycling and makes computer users, rather than producers, responsible for disposal of waste.

(Nick Huber, www.cw360.com 30 August 2001)

Questions:

1 Do you think that computer manufacturers should take responsibility for the safe disposal of old computers? Why?

2 How could users be encouraged to help in the safe disposal of computer waste?

3 Why does an increase in technology lead to increased environmental problems?

4 What can the government do to prevent this problem getting worse?

Exercises

1. Is there any law to stop people writing and spreading computer viruses? To what extent can legislation protect people from virus attacks?

2. Is there any law to stop people spreading pornography on the Internet? How can such people be caught? How can parents protect their children from being targeted by pornographers?

3. Access an online chat room and find out what security practices are advised.

4. "Those who do not have access to ICT may be disadvantaged by its widespread use." How far do you think this is true? Give some examples.

Chapter 40: ICT in the Community

The changes that ICT brings to community groups in society mirrors changes that the industry brings to other user groups, such as schools and colleges, rural groups, and official agencies. ICT has profoundly affected our lives within communities in many ways.

Public access to the Internet

Public access to the internet is becoming more important than ever before. People are familiar with its benefits and have a greater need than ever before to have access to online information services from wherever they are at any one time. Examples of these types of public access are given here.

- Public libraries: for all internet services, for research and access to public records. Libraries usually now have all their books and resources linked to an online catalogue, which often covers the whole of the county. Members can request any title from any library in the county by accessing the online catalogue and have it delivered to their local branch. In addition, members can access an online record of their account, renew books, pay fines and make further reservations.

- High speed Internet/Telephone kiosk points located in many train/tube/bus stations/hotel lobbies: to gain access to web-services, check and send e-mail.

 This is an example of a BT internet kiosk at Tower Hill underground station in London. It can be used by inserting a phonecard or coins and can be used for access to the internet or sending and receiving e-mail. There are now many of these located at railway stations all over the UK. It can also be used to make calls at the same time which may be useful for business people.

- Information/multimedia terminals: for advertising purposes, used at concerts and festivals to get information on line-ups and events

- Electronic bulletin board terminals located in courthouses to get up-to-date status information on court hearings

- Shopping Centre Information Points: for information about shopping and visitors' services and to link to individual stores' websites for special offers, product availability etc.

Cyber cafés

Cyber cafés are becoming part of our everyday culture and they are now in hundreds of small towns and in cities all over the UK. They are often ideal as they offer Internet access at relatively cheap rates without the need to invest in your own hardware. PCs can be used for a wide variety of ICT functions. Training courses are often available and they are useful to those away from home or without a computer. They usually offer:

- Internet access at a fast bandwidth

- controlled chat rooms

- commercial e-mail or address-searching software which would be too expensive to buy for a home user

- use of commercial software for college or business use

- online games; either alone or with friends who could be at terminals anywhere

- interactive CD-ROMs

- electronic book libraries; often web-based computer literature which would otherwise be very expensive to buy

- training courses; for example typical topics would be: Introduction to the Internet, Getting Online, Web Design, Marketing on the Internet, Internet Research and Putting your Business on the Web

- and of course; usually a wide range of coffees, teas, Danish pastries and deliciously-filled baguettes to munch whilst you surf!

Discussion

Have you ever visited a Cyber café?
What facilities were on offer?

Interest and pressure groups

Many organisations in the UK seek to provide an 'online' presence as an extremely important interface for communication. This is particularly the case with interest and pressure groups and helps communications, contacts and growth within these groups on both a local and national level. This communication may be in the form of:

- How to become a member, donate funds or become a volunteer

- Online discussion between interested group members, observing a specialist guest speaker and being able to ask questions

- Keeping members up-to-date with legal changes which affect their interest

- General information about an interest; e.g. demonstrating against fox-hunting; establishing a community village statement, about a newly developing pop group, transport groups, social groups, political parties

CASE STUDY

Dorsai

Dorsai is a community service which began life online as a community service group website where young people could chat. It has gone a step beyond just community service and has now expanded to developing youth programs for at-risk youth in New York and is proud to claim to be taking children off the street, offering them new direction and providing them with essential resources to attain their goals. With the adult guidance of Dorsai's volunteer staff, young men and women learn valuable computer skills and become adept in the ways of the Internet.

On Tuesday evenings, Dorsai becomes an open house, accepting hardware donations and restoring them as a team effort. The computers are given away to offer a presence on the Internet to those who would not ordinarily have one. Members can learn how to make best use of the Internet through hands-on training in a classroom environment.

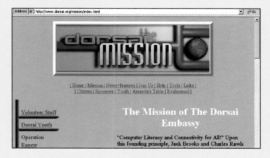

The Internet is an open community where its citizens are not judged by their appearance, age, or physical limitations. This gives the physically-challenged members of Dorsai the ability to go out into the virtual world and exist as true equals.

Sleepy PCs can be hard at work

ICT can now help in the field of collaborative research. It is possible to download a small program, such as a screensaver or similar, which will allow your PC to donate inactive time for number crunching/processing. See what you can find out about one of these two very famous projects or something similar:

- Intel-United Devices Cancer Research Project

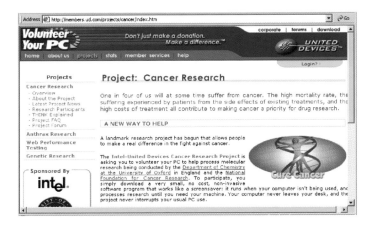

- SETI (a collaborative search for alien life)

copyright (c) 2002 SETI@home project

Discussion

The Internet is used by charities such as the Red Cross for tracing family members who have become separated after disasters such as earthquakes and volcanic eruptions. In what other ways is ICT useful to charitable organisations?

Government to test e-voting on councils

The Government has invited English councils to test electronic voting at the local elections in May 2002. Local government minister Nick Raynsford said, "Soundly-based ideas for modernising elections will be welcomed, and we are particularly interested in supporting pilots of electronic voting at polling stations, electronic counting, online voting and postal or telephone voting."

Raynsford has invited all councils in England to apply to participate in the pilot scheme, which will be used to analyse alternative voting methods. Councils have until the end of the year to apply, and successful applicants will be named in January. The Government recently unveiled a seven-month research project, led by De Montfort University, to explore the possibilities for remote electronic voting via the telephone, television and the Internet.

Online voting is already popular in the US.

(Source: James Rogers, www.cw360.com 11 October 2001)

Public transport and travel information

Web-sites are now available which cover all aspects of your travel needs. These include:

- rail information
- National Express Bus information
- plane bookings
- Underground connections
- water taxi
- cross-channel ferry crossings
- Eurostar train travel

Task 40.1: Plan a journey

Plan a journey from your house to two fixed points in the UK or abroad and home again. Choose specific times to travel and calculate journey times and costs. If you are curious, try accessing some of this information via another source to see how much longer it takes you. Compare the accuracy of the data from different sources.

CASE STUDY

In-Car Telematics

In Britain today there are around 30 million cars and that number appears to be growing. Traffic jams are becoming more and more common and therefore the technology of in-car telematics is being developed as a response to demands from the consumer and in turn the car industry.

In-car telematics are basically the use of GPS (Global Positioning Systems) technology with a smart satellite navigation system to feed back traffic-avoidance information to a computer located in the dashboard of your car. The computer in turn makes suggestions to avoid congested roads and gives alternative routes from a database of information, in order to avoid traffic pile-ups.

Some motor manufacturers offer real-time voice readouts of routes and directions sent via a hand-free mobile phone. This technology makes squinting at the map placed precariously on the steering wheel a redundant driving hazard of the past. Other features are readouts of local hotel, petrol station or tourist information activated by voice recognition technology. This information is brought by effectively having a second mobile phone installed in your car. It doesn't come cheap, as the information lines run at premium rates. Some in-car telematics software systems are now offering voice-activated and voice-response e-mail checking and composing, accessing of news headlines and weather information.

Questions:

1 Use the internet and find out about some of the latest developments in in-car telematics as this technology is changing all the time.

2 Do you think this technology is really helpful to a driver when he/she should be concentrating on the road?

3 What are the consequences of losing our map-reading skills in a future world where we are consistently advised by a computer where to go and what to do?

Global Positioning Systems (GPS)

GPS is a worldwide system of satellites and their ground stations which are used for identifying earth locations. They are owned and controlled by the United States Department of Defence. By triangulation of signals from three of the satellites, a receiving unit can pinpoint its current location anywhere on earth to within a few metres. GPS receivers have now been miniaturised to just a few integrated circuits and so are becoming very economical. That is making the technology more accessible and it is being included in more equipment than ever before.

GPS is to be found:

- in cars – in-car telematics makes use of GPS technology in order to pinpoint the location and assist the driver with directions

- in boats – in order prevent any sea vessel being lost, either at sea or through theft. It can help to accurately avoid storms and to expertly maintain a course in all weather conditions. It can help with coastal navigation and reduce the number of lives lost through shipwrecks. It assists in canal and river navigation, which reduces bank erosion and collisions

- in planes – aircraft which have lost contact with the control tower can be accurately and remotely guided. In addition, it helps with the complex technology of air traffic control

- in construction equipment and farm machinery – GPS can keep track of expensive equipment and can be used by companies to optimise its use at different locations

- in surveying – GPS technology can be used in the creation of more accurate maps and records of the planet and the oceans. This is invaluable to organisations and individuals such as wildlife and marine conservationists, engineers, oil companies, explorers and travellers

- in movie-making equipment – this is very expensive and GPS can be used to track equipment lost either through theft or carelessness after a large location shoot

- in laptop computers, cellular phones and hand-held devices – for access to location technologies e.g. maps and route-finding software, and for security purposes

Exercises

1. One effect of the widespread use of computers has been to replace cash with other forms of payment. Weekly and monthly pay packets are paid straight into the employees' bank accounts. Bills are paid by direct debit. Goods and services are paid for using a credit or debit card. What effect has this had on individuals and local communities? Do you think cash will disappear completely?

2. Walk along the High Street and consider the different ways in which the various organisations (shops, library, bank, travel agent, newsagent etc) use ICT. All of these technologies will be relevant to one of the reports you need to write on how ICT systems affect everyday life.

Edexcel Coursework Assessment Criteria

Assessment Criteria

ASSESSMENT EVIDENCE: UNIT 2 ICT IN ORGANISATIONS

You need to produce an investigation of an organisation (or a department in a large organisation) and compile a portfolio that includes a report on:

(a) the different purposes for which the organisation / department uses ICT

(b) the ICT system used in the organisation / department, and how it meets the needs identified in (a)

You also need to design and implement an ICT system. You must add to your portfolio:

(c) a design specification for the system including information sources, input, process and output requirements, and the types of application software needed

(d) evidence that you successfully implemented, tested and evaluated the system, together with guidance for the user.

Please note: You are expected to make full use of ICT in the production of your portfolio. Work that is entirely hand-written will not gain any marks.

ASSESSOR'S MARKING GRID

	Mark Band 1 At this level work must show:	Mark Range	Mark Band 2 At this level work must show:	Mark Range	Mark Band 3 At this level work must show:	Mark Range	Mark Awarded
(a) AO1, 3,4 10 marks	produce a report into the chosen organisation/ department that identifies some purposes for which it uses ICT	1-4	produce a report into the chosen organisation/ department that details a range of purposes for which it uses ICT	5-7	produce a report into the chosen organisation/ department that gives full details of a wide range of purposes for which it uses ICT	8-10	
(b) AO1, 3,4 14 marks	produce a report which describes the main hardware components used, together with some of the main applications software; give an indication of their purpose	1-6	produce a report which describes clearly the main hardware components used, together with the main applications software. Each should be linked to specific purposes	7-10	produce a report which describes fully the main hardware components used, together with the necessary applications software, and some evaluation of how the system as a whole satisfies the purposes identified in (a)	11-14	

	Mark Band 1 At this level work must show:	Mark Range	Mark Band 2 At this level work must show:	Mark Range	Mark Band 3 At this level work must show:	Mark Range	Mark Awarded
(c) **AO1,2** **17 marks**	work with support and guidance to produce a basic design specification showing a basic understanding of some of the input, process and output requirements; provide details of hardware and software needed	1-7	work with limited guidance to produce a design specification with some detail showing a clear understanding of the main input, process and output requirements; provide details of hardware and software needed	8-12	work independently to produce a detailed design specification which must show a creative and comprehensive understanding of input, process and output requirements; provide details of hardware and software needed	13-17	
(d) **AO1,2** **17 marks**	work with support and guidance to produce evidence of successful implementation; results of some basic testing and evaluation; some basic user documentation for the system	1-7	work with limited guidance to produce evidence of successful implementation; results of effective testing and evaluation; clear user documentation for the system	8-12	work independently to produce evidence of successful implementation; results of detailed testing and evaluation; detailed user documentation for the system	13-17	
				Total Unit Mark		58	
				Student Unit Mark			

Assessment Criteria

ASSESSMENT EVIDENCE: UNIT 3 ICT IN SOCIETY

You need to produce an investigation of how ICT systems affect everyday life. You must compile a portfolio with reports on the impact of ICT on:

(a) the way you do things at home and at school / college

(b) an adult in employment, including the way it has had an effect on his/her working style

(c) a person with special/particular needs

(d) your local community

When investigating each of these different aspects of ICT use, you should consider

(e) the legislation that protects individuals and groups from the misuse of ICT.

Please note: You are expected to make full use of ICT in the production of your portfolio. Work that is entirely hand-written will not gain any marks.

ASSESSOR'S MARKING GRID

	Mark Band 1 At this level work must show:	Mark Range	Mark Band 2 At this level work must show:	Mark Range	Mark Band 3 At this level work must show:	Mark Range	Mark Awarded
(a) AO4, 11 marks	a description of some of the technologies used by the student at home and at school /college, with some indication of how these meet their needs	1-5	a description of a range of technologies used by the student at home and at school / college, with an explanation of how these meet their needs	6-8	a description of a wide range of technologies used by the student at home and at school / college, with an evaluation of the extent to which these meet their needs	9-11	
(b) AO1,2, 3, 14 marks	a description of some of the technologies used by an adult in employment, with some indication of how these meet their needs and have affected working styles	1-6	a description of a range of technologies used by an adult in employment, with an explanation of how these meet their needs and have affected working styles	7-10	a description of a wide range of technologies used by an adult in employment, with an evaluation of the extent to which these meet their needs and have affected working styles	11-14	

	Mark Band 1 At this level work must show:	Mark Range	Mark Band 2 At this level work must show:	Mark Range	Mark Band 3 At this level work must show:	Mark Range	Mark Awarded
(c) AO1,2 3 11 marks	a description of some of the technologies used by a person with special or particular needs, with some indication of how these meet their needs	**1-5**	a description of a range of technologies used by a person with special or particular needs, with an explanation of how these meet their needs	**6-8**	a description of a wide range of technologies used by a person with special or particular needs, with an evaluation of the extent to which these meet their needs	**9-11**	
(d) AO1,2, 3 11 marks	a description of some of the technologies used in the local community, with some indication of how these meet local needs	**1-5**	a description of a range of technologies used in the local community, with an explanation of how these meet local needs	**6-8**	a description of a wide range of technologies used in the local community, with an evaluation of the extent to which these meet local needs	**9-11**	
(e) AO3,4, 3 11 marks	an indication of some of the relevant legislation and how it protects people and groups from the misuse of ICT	**1-5**	a description of the most relevant legislation, why it was introduced and how it protects people and groups from the misuse of ICT	**6-8**	a description of all relevant legislation and why it was introduced, and an evaluation of the extent to which it protects people and groups from the misuse of ICT	**9-11**	
					Total Unit Mark	**58**	
					Student Unit Mark		

Index

Index

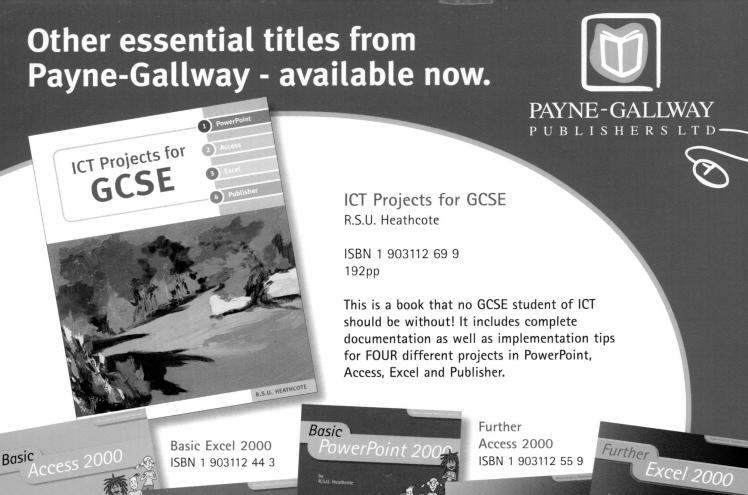